More Praise for the Elementary/Middle School Counselor's Survival Guide, 3rd Edition

"This *Survival Guide* is filled with realistic situations that we as counselors face daily. Dr. Schmidt has presented strategies and tools needed to develop a comprehensive counseling program. The book provides sample forms for needs assessments, surveys, and checklists that are essential to all counselors working in schools."

—**Pattic Amundsen**, school counselor, president, Association for Professional Counseling in Schools, Winston-Salem, NC

"As a counselor educator, I've invariably found Jack Schmidt's books on school counseling to be 'top drawer' and [this new edition] is no exception! The book is comprehensive, embraces standards for best practice, and provides hands-on examples for elementary-middle grade levels—even pre-K! I plan to recommend it to all of my school counseling grad students."

—**Dr. Salene Cowher**, professor/program head, Graduate Programs in Counseling, Edinboro University, Edinboro, PA

"If school counseling reform is going to be successful, books and other resources must depict a relatively accurate picture of the preparation and practice of school counselors in school settings. Dr. Schmidt's book affirms the profession and offers an accurate assessment of the work that counselors do in schools."

—**Dr. Delila Owens**, assistant professor, Wayne State University, Detroit, MI

Jossey-Bass Teacher

Jossey-Bass Teacher provides educators with practical knowledge and tools to create a positive and lifelong impact on student learning. We offer classroom-tested and research-based teaching resources for a variety of grade levels and subject areas. Whether you are an aspiring, new, or veteran teacher, we want to help you make every teaching day your best.

From ready-to-use classroom activities to the latest teaching framework, our value-packed books provide insightful, practical, and comprehensive materials on the topics that matter most to K–12 teachers. We hope to become your trusted source for the best ideas from the most experienced and respected experts in the field.

Titles in the Jossey-Bass Teacher Survival Guide Series

MATH TEACHER'S SURVIVAL GUIDE: PRACTICAL STRATEGIES, MANAGEMENT TECHNIQUES, AND REPRODUCIBLES FOR NEW AND EXPERIENCED TEACHERS, GRADES 5–12
Judith A. Muschla, Gary Robert Muschla, and Erin Muschla   ISBN 978-0-470-40764-6

A SURVIVAL KIT FOR THE ELEMENTARY SCHOOL PRINCIPAL: WITH REPRODUCIBLE FORMS, CHECKLISTS & LETTERS
Abby Barry Bergman   ISBN 978-0-7879-6639-3

THE READING TEACHER'S SURVIVAL KIT: READY-TO-USE CHECKLISTS, ACTIVITIES, AND MATERIALS TO HELP ALL STUDENTS BECOME SUCCESSFUL READERS
Wilma H. Miller, Ed.D.   ISBN 978-0-13-042593-5

BIOLOGY TEACHER'S SURVIVAL GUIDE: TIPS, TECHNIQUES & MATERIALS FOR SUCCESS IN THE CLASSROOM
Michael F. Fleming   ISBN 978-0-13-045051-7

THE ELEMENTARY/MIDDLE SCHOOL COUNSELOR'S SURVIVAL GUIDE, Third Edition
John J. Schmidt, Ed.D.   978-0-470-56085-3

THE SUBSTITUTE TEACHING SURVIVAL GUIDE, GRADES K–5: EMERGENCY LESSON PLANS AND ESSENTIAL ADVICE
John Dellinger   ISBN 978-0-7879-7410-7

THE SUBSTITUTE TEACHING SURVIVAL GUIDE, GRADES 6–12: EMERGENCY LESSON PLANS AND ESSENTIAL ADVICE
John Dellinger   ISBN 978-0-7879-7411-4

THIRD EDITION

The ELEMENTARY/ MIDDLE SCHOOL COUNSELOR'S SURVIVAL GUIDE

John J. Schmidt

JOSSEY-BASS
A Wiley Imprint
www.josseybass.com

Published by Jossey-Bass
A Wiley Imprint
989 Market Street, San Francisco, CA 94103-1741—www.josseybass.com

Jossey-Bass books and products are available through most bookstores. To contact Jossey-Bass directly call our Customer Care Department within the U.S. at 800-956-7739, outside the U.S. at 317-572-3986, or fax 317-572-4002.

Jossey-Bass also publishes its books in a variety of electronic formats. Some content that appears in print may not be available in electronic books.

Originally published as *A Survival Guide for the Elementary/Middle School Counselor*, First and Second Editions

Library of Congress Cataloging-in-Publication Data

Schmidt, John J., 1946-
  The elementary/middle school counselor's survival guide / John J. Schmidt, Ed.D.—3rd ed.
    p. cm.
  Rev. ed. of: Survival guide for the elementary/middle school counselor.
  Includes bibliographical references and index.
  ISBN 978-0-470-56085-3 (pbk.)
    1. Counseling in elementary education—United States. 2. Counseling in middle school education—United States. 3. Student counselors—United States. I. Schmidt, John J., 1946- Survival guide for the elementary/middle school counselor. II. Title.

LB1027.5.S259 2010
372.14—dc22   2010011066

Printed in the United States of America.
THIRD EDITION
PB Printing   10 9 8 7 6 5 4 3 2 1

About This Book

The *Elementary/Middle School Counselor's Survival Guide, 3rd Edition,* continues the philosophy of the original publication and expands its practical application. This book encourages you to develop a comprehensive school counseling program comprising services for students, parents, and teachers, with the ultimate goal of helping all students succeed both academically and in their personal relationships and begin exploring career information and interests.

This edition is expanded to thirteen chapters, each beginning with a scenario relevant to that chapter's topic. These vignettes offer opportunities for practical application of the information presented throughout the guide. All chapters also include worksheets and exhibits you can use or adapt in your own practice.

This edition of the *Survival Guide* will help you

- Plan, deliver, and evaluate a comprehensive program of services for elementary or middle school students, parents, and teachers
- Integrate your counseling program with the overall mission of the school
- Select and assess the effectiveness of appropriate counseling, consulting, and coordinating services to address developmental and critical concerns of your students
- Perform within the ethical and legal parameters of the counseling profession
- Take care of yourself personally and professionally as a school counselor

By focusing on these professional behaviors and competencies, this *Survival Guide* will become an essential resource as you strive to perform at an optimal level.

About the Author

John J. (Jack) Schmidt, Ed.D., is professor emeritus of counselor education at East Carolina University in Greenville, North Carolina. During his career, Dr. Schmidt has been a social studies teacher; elementary, middle, and high school counselor; school district supervisor of counseling and testing services; state coordinator of school counseling programs; licensed professional counselor; and university professor and department chair. From 2006 through 2009, he was executive director of the International Alliance for Invitational Education® (www.invitationaleducation.net).

An active writer and presenter, Dr. Schmidt has published over fifty articles, book reviews, and manuals, and more than a dozen books. His books include *Counseling in Schools: Comprehensive Programs of Responsive Services for All Students; Social and Cultural Foundations of Counseling and Human Services; Intentional Helping: A Philosophy for Proficient Caring Relationships; Making and Keeping Friends: Ready-to-Use Lessons, Stories, and Activities for Building Relationships; Living Intentionally and Making Life Happen; Invitational Counseling: A Self-Concept Approach to Professional Practice,* with Dr. William W. Purkey; and *From Conflict to Conciliation: How to Defuse Difficult Situations,* with Dr. Purkey and Dr. John M. Novak.

Dr. Schmidt is a former president of the North Carolina Counseling Association and the North Carolina Association for Counselor Education and Supervision. He has received recognition from professional associations and universities for his leadership, research, and publications, particularly in the field of school counseling. He was awarded the Elementary Counselor of the Year Award by the North Carolina School Counselor Association in 1978, is a two-time recipient of the Ella Stephens Barrett Leadership Award from the North Carolina Counseling Association (1997 and 2007), and received the Ruth C. McSwain Distinguished Professional Service Award from the North Carolina School Counselor Association in 2002. In 1999, the College of Education at East Carolina University named him a distinguished professor for his teaching, scholarship, and service to the university. In 2005, he received a Distinguished Career Award from the School of Education at the University of North Carolina-Greensboro.

Dr. Schmidt is a member of Chi Sigma Iota, the international counseling honor society, and has served on numerous boards, including the North Carolina Board of Licensed Professional Counselors (1997–2004) and the National Board of Certified Counselors (2005–2008). He lives in Roaring Gap, North Carolina, with his wife, Pat.

To my grandchildren,

Evelyn, Erica, Aidan, and Addyson

May their years in school and throughout life be enriching, empowering, and enjoyable

Acknowledgments

It is an honor to share this third edition of *The Elementary/Middle School Counselor's Survival Guide*. I thank Jossey-Bass for its continued support, and am particularly grateful to senior editor Marjorie McAneny and her assistant Julia Palmer for their superb guidance during this revision.

In addition, I appreciate the contributions of a group of elementary and middle school counselors from North Carolina who participated in discussions about surviving elementary and middle school counseling. They are: Patti Amundsen, Cynthia Clodfelter, Ken Dankwardt, Patti Durham, Michelle Gross, Debby Hendrix, Melanie Mills, Brett Pesce, Paulette Ream, Cheryl Tilley, Rinita Williams, Sharon White, and Jim Wuwert. Special thanks to my oldest granddaughter, Evelyn Bergquist, who advised me about kids and technology.

This book, as with all my others, would not have been possible without the support of my wife, partner, and best friend, Pat. Her patience and flexibility have allowed me to complete such projects and to enjoy my career in counseling so fully. I am deeply indebted to her.

Contents

11   INVOLVING SIGNIFICANT OTHERS   217

INTRODUCTION

Successful elementary and middle school counselors continuously search for useful information and ideas in order to deliver program services effectively. *The Elementary/ Middle School Counselor's Survival Guide* is a resource to help you identify who you are and what you do, become more capable and available, and account for your time and effectiveness in surviving and eventually flourishing as a school counselor. This third edition continues the focus of the original *Survival Guide* to help elementary and middle school counselors design comprehensive programs of responsive services to fit unique professional settings and address the needs of students, parents, and teachers.

As an elementary or middle school counselor, you might find the following exchange familiar. Two counselors were talking at a state counseling conference. One, a new elementary counselor, confessed, "I have so much to do and so little time to do it. I go from one crisis to the next or from one administrative task to another." The other, a middle school counselor, responded, "Me too! So many things take time away from students—coordinating the testing program and responsibility for exceptional children's referrals take up much of my time, not to mention application of Section 504 of the disabilities act! I need practical ideas and strategies to handle students' concerns and everything else that goes on in my school." This exchange reveals that the two counselors are struggling with their *identity*, questioning their *capability* to meet demands, and going in too many directions. They want to be *available* to students and are looking for ways to be *accountable* in their schools. For them and many other school counselors, the transition from learning about the art and science of counseling to being an artful and scientific practitioner is challenging.

Simply learning about art does not make you a masterful artist. Only with sufficient practice and personalization of the techniques learned can you approach an artistic level. Similarly, learning what the research says about a particular issue does not make you a scientific practitioner. Consistent application of such knowledge, evaluation of outcomes, and reflection on what you have done are mandatory for success.

Similar to an artist or a scientist, you seek practical and beneficial ways to apply your knowledge. In elementary and middle schools, where the counseling profession searches for clear, understandable roles, but where case loads often reach astronomical ratios, successful counselors establish a professional identity by emphasizing their capabilities, serving a wide audience, and accounting for the programs they establish and services they deliver. To be successful, these counselors structure comprehensive school counseling programs that permit optimal use of the time available.

This *Survival Guide* operates on the assumption that although the developmental needs of students in elementary and middle schools vary, counselors at these two levels have similar goals and objectives and facilitate comparable program services and activities. Although some specific activities and strategies in this guide are more suitable at one level than the other, this guide will, for the most part, be useful across elementary and middle schools.

HOW THE BOOK IS ORGANIZED

Chapters One through Four of this revision of the *Survival Guide* describe the general components and aspects of a comprehensive school counseling program. A comprehensive program includes a clear definition and description of your identity and role, input from those who use your services, and strategies to allow the most efficient use of time. An efficient use of time requires planning, coordination, and evaluation, as well as purposeful selection of responsive services.

Chapters Five through Nine present ideas and strategies to integrate your counseling program with the overall mission of your school. These include aligning your counseling program with the school curriculum, focusing on educational development for all students, reaching out to diverse populations, preparing for school and community crises, and helping with a broad range of student concerns that affect learning and development. The goals of these chapters are to enhance your capability as an elementary or middle school counselor and emphasize the importance of accountability in measuring your effectiveness.

Chapters Ten through Thirteen focus on relationships with colleagues, parents, and the community, and on you as a counselor. A counseling program is as strong as the staff that support and guide its development. Likewise, the strength of your assistance to students is contingent on parents' and guardians' involvement in the counseling process. In addition, your ability to function effectively is influenced by your own well-being—your personal and professional fitness. Professional fitness includes a practical knowledge of ethical codes, state and federal laws, professional competencies, and local school policies.

WHAT'S NEW IN THE THIRD EDITION

Among the additions to this revision are one or more scenarios in each of the chapters, which demonstrate practical applications of the ideas and suggestions given throughout this guide. Though fictitious, the scenarios are based on my years of school counseling practice, experience as a supervisor, and teaching in counselor preparation programs. In a workshop, practicing school counselors reviewed and tested the scenarios for practicality and realism.

A major change to this revision is a new Chapter Nine, "Responding to Critical Concerns," which focuses on more serious concerns of students. This edition also includes new material concerning the American School Counselor Association (ASCA) National Model, current and emerging communication and learning technologies, the relationship between your philosophy and effectiveness in counseling students, services after trauma and tragedy, cyberbullying, self-injurious students, the impact of poverty, school counselor competencies, and your responsibility to maintain ethical standards.

OVERALL PURPOSE AND FOCUS

The Elementary/Middle School Counselor's Survival Guide bridges the gap between theory and practice. Counseling theories help you understand human behavior and development and enable you to choose reliable approaches to professional helping. Practical strategies and materials, such as those in this guide, give you an opportunity to structure your theoretical stance around useful and effective helping behaviors. These practical suggestions encourage you to include many participants—teachers, parents, and students—in the process of designing and implementing comprehensive school counseling programs.

This book sets the stage for you to identify who you want to be as an elementary or middle school counselor. It shows you how to develop ways to make yourself available to a wider audience, expand your knowledge, improve your counseling skills, and measure your effectiveness as a professional counselor. In each chapter you will find ideas to move beyond survival toward flourishing as a counselor in an elementary or middle school. Whereas surviving conjures up an image of desperate endurance, flourishing conveys a notion of thriving and elicits a positive vision of what you can become. This book encourages you to look beyond basic survival skills to develop into a proactive counselor who provides a comprehensive program of responsive services for your school and community.

Throughout this book you will find lists of specific strategies, helpful guidelines, Web sites, and reproducible forms to use in a comprehensive school counseling program. Not all of these will be appropriate or feasible to apply in your school and program, however. Choose the ones that are, and feel free to adjust the others to create new and better strategies.

In an effort to make the *Survival Guide* a practical, readable resource for professional school counselors, I have used references and citations sparingly. You will find an extensive resource list of printed works and Web sites at the end of the book. Although I have made every effort to keep resources as current as possible, today's accelerated information age makes this a daunting task. My hope is that the resources provided will give you a head start on compiling your own list.

Thank you for allowing me to share my experience and suggestions with you. I wish you well in your career as a professional school counselor, and hope the strategies and tools in this guide are helpful as you move toward a higher level of artful counseling within a scientific framework.

chapter 1

WHAT, WHO, *and* HOW *of* YOUR SCHOOL COUNSELING PROGRAM

Scenario 1.1: Why Are Counselors in Schools?

Some parents were meeting, and one asked, "Why do we need counselors in schools?" Another followed with, "What is a counselor's primary purpose in providing services in the school?" These were not new questions. Educators, counselors, parents, policymakers, and others had asked similar questions countless times before. If you were listening to this conversation, how would you, as a school counselor, respond? Why are you working in a school, and what is your purpose?

One possible response to Scenario 1.1 is that you work in a school to help people become "more able" in their respective roles. As a school counselor, you help students become more able learners; assist parents in their nurturing roles; support teachers in providing beneficial instruction for all students; and, with administrators, help lead schools in becoming a more effective part of the community. In sum, everything you do as a school counselor—every program you plan and every service you deliver—aims at helping students, parents, teachers, and schools in the process of human development and learning.

If you agree with this conclusion—that you are in a school to help people become more able—you might also agree that to accomplish this goal, you too need to become more able in your professional knowledge and skills. To become more able as a professional counselor, you want to move beyond survival toward a confident stance that permits you to become identifiable, capable, available, and accountable—four characteristics of a successful school counselor. Being *identifiable* means knowing who you are and what you do in schools as a professional counselor. It also means letting others know about this identity. Being *capable* means practicing at a high level of skill while recognizing the limits of your competencies and professional role in schools. When you are *available,* you are accessible to the students, parents, and teachers you serve. *Accountability* brings together the first three abilities when you assess how you spend your time and measure the effectiveness of the programs you plan and the services you provide. Throughout this *Survival Guide* you will learn ways to accomplish these goals in becoming a successful school counselor. To begin, Chapter One explores the role and identity of counselors in schools.

Scenario 1.2: Role Identity

You are an elementary or middle school counselor. A new principal has arrived at the school to start the year, and you have asked to schedule a conference to talk about the counseling program. At the start of your meeting with the new principal, she begins, "I had a good guidance counselor at my previous school, but was never quite sure how he spent most of his time. He was good at helping out in the main office when we were short on staff, and he was quite sociable with the faculty. It was my first position as a principal, however, and I was uncertain how to direct his time and duties. My goal at this school is to take more of a leadership role in all special services, including guidance." How would you begin responding to the principal's statements? What key points would you make about the school counseling program, your leadership role, an advisory committee, program evaluation, and consultation with the principal?

Scenario 1.2 depicts a situation that many school counselors experience during their careers—explaining their roles in their schools and in their comprehensive counseling programs. This chapter will help you both answer the questions in the above scenario and establish your leadership role and identity as a school counselor.

Since its birth during the Industrial Revolution at the turn of the twentieth century, the school counseling profession has searched for an identity and role among the helping professions. Today such questions as Why are counselors in schools? and What are they supposed to do? are as prominent as they were over one hundred years ago. As a member of this profession, you now face the same questions: Why are you here? What are you supposed to do?

As an elementary or middle school counselor, you belong to an expanding profession that includes many areas of professional helping and service. The counseling profession of the twenty-first century has become an important member of mental health services, and school counselors are essential partners in this effort (Falls & Muro, 2009; Schmidt, 2008). Today's professional counselors work in settings that include mental health centers, family agencies, prisons, hospitals, funeral homes, crisis centers, employment agencies, colleges, and schools, to name a few.

In preparing to become a school counselor, you studied many areas of knowledge, including human development, psychology, career information and development, tests and measurement, and social and cultural foundations. In addition, you acquired skills in specific helping processes, such as individual and group counseling, consulting, and facilitative teaching. These skills and knowledge provide a framework within which you are able to establish and clarify your professional role and deliver specific services to students, parents, teachers, and others.

Unlike counseling programs in prisons, hospitals, and mental health centers that narrowly focus specific services for particular populations, your services span a broad program of activities to assist several populations. Your program includes preventive services, developmental activities, and remedial interventions for students, parents, teachers, administrators, and others. The challenge of offering such a wide range of responsive services to different populations renders you unique in your practice of elementary or middle school counseling. This notion of a *program of services* is a key element in school counseling, and your ability to define and describe your school's counseling program to students, parents, teachers, administrators, and community stakeholders is vital to your survival and ultimate success.

DESCRIBING THE PROGRAM

Although the range and diversity of the expectations placed on you illustrate the need for counselors in our schools, they can also threaten your effectiveness by pulling you in too many directions and spreading services across too broad an area. Among the most important steps you take each year, therefore, will be describing and defining the school's counseling program.

One element that influences how clearly you describe your program is the language you choose. Because school counseling is a relatively young profession, its practitioners sometimes struggle to articulate what it is and what it does. As a school counselor, you want to explain your program in language that is both consistent with your professional vision and understandable for students, parents, teachers, and others in the school community.

Choosing a Language

Over the profession's life span, such terms as *pupil personnel services, guidance program,* and *student services* have categorized and classified school counseling services. You, like many practitioners, probably identify yourself according to labels and language you learned in your graduate studies or encountered in your school system. What do you call yourself? How do you describe what you do? Why?

My preference is to call myself a *school counselor,* and the services I provide are part of a *school counseling program.* I belong to a *student services team,* which consists of other helping professionals, including the school nurse, school social worker, and school psychologist. For me, these terms accurately label the program of services I provide in schools. They are also consistent with the language of our profession, as used by the American School Counselor Association (ASCA) and its journal, *Professional School Counseling.* They are contemporary and more definitive than such older terms as *personnel services* and *guidance programs,* which are vague and often encompass conflicting roles and services for school counselors. For example, *personnel services* frequently imply and include record keeping, class scheduling, attendance monitoring, testing coordination, and other functions that detract from direct responsive services for students, parents, teachers, and others. Similarly, the term *guidance* is confusing and does not clearly indicate what counselors do in schools. Yet the word *guidance* has historical significance and remains prevalent in the school counseling profession.

Everything in schools relates in some way to the notion of "guiding students." Teachers guide students in daily instruction, as well as in their personal relationships with others—yet we do not call them "guidance teachers." Administrators guide students in regard to school policy, curriculum, discipline, and programs, but we do not refer to them as "guidance principals." Why then use the term "guidance counselor" instead of "school counselor"? Because guidance permeates every facet of the school, no single person or program has ownership of it.

In my view, a school counseling program encompasses a broad area of responsive services, including preventive services, developmental activities, and remedial assistance. The common ground for these three areas lies in counselors' prominent role in providing direct services to students, parents, teachers, and others. Some counselors believe that the term *school counseling program* is too restrictive because it limits services to remedial relationships. However, a more encompassing view is that counseling relationships are for everyone, not only for people who have problems, and they provide ways to help healthy, functioning people capitalize on their strengths and reach higher levels of achievement. In recent school counseling literature, this has been called "strengths-based counseling." For example, Galassi and Akos (2007) note that a strengths-based school counseling program allows counselors to design and deliver services that reach a larger percentage of students in their schools. It moves from a restricted emphasis on a few students' problems and deficits to a commitment to help all students identify their strengths and take positive steps to capitalize on those abilities. In this guide you will find suggestions for how to use counseling processes in preventive services, for developmental learning, and to remedy existing concerns.

Here are some helpful guidelines for selecting a language and vocabulary that describe accurately your role and function in the school:

1. *Understand the language.* The terms you choose—*counseling, guidance, personnel, strengths-based programs,* or whatever—should have meaning to you. You should be clear about the words you use to describe yourself professionally and be able to defend the language you choose.

2. *Educate the audience.* Once you choose the language of your program, teach it to the people you serve. Let students, parents, teachers, administrators, and others know what you mean by *counseling, group guidance, consulting,* and other terms. A language is useful only if the people with whom you communicate understand it, accept it, and use it.

3. *Use consistent language.* It is confusing to students and others when you use terms inconsistently. Consistency may be difficult at first, particularly if you have decided to change to new terms. Stick with it, and correct yourself when you confuse the language. Your audience will be as consistent as you are.

If you replaced another counselor who once served the school, the decision about language requires careful consideration. For example, if the previous counselor used terminology different from yours, you may need to adjust your thinking for a while. This is particularly true if your predecessor was at the school for many years and is well thought of by students and faculty. You may feel strongly about the terms you want to use to describe who you are and what you do, and these beliefs may be a healthy sign of your professionalism. Nevertheless, move slowly and explain your rationale as you introduce new terms. By being considerate and winning students, parents, teachers, and administrators' trust and confidence, you will be more likely to have your ideas and suggestions accepted.

Exhibit 1.1 presents a sample description for a school counseling program and the role of a counselor. You might use this description as part of a school brochure, student handbook, or faculty manual.

EXHIBIT 1.1

The School Counseling Program and the School Counselor

The counseling program in our school is available to help students, parents, and teachers develop positive learning experiences. The program consists of a variety of services and activities, including individual and group counseling, parent and teacher consultation, group guidance, information services, referral assistance to other agencies in the community, and student assessment.

The school counselor is responsible for developing, scheduling, and evaluating program services and is assisted by the counseling advisory committee and the school principal. Primary services of the school counselor provide direct assistance to students in the school. For this reason, a major portion of the counselor's day consists of responsive services that help students with their academic, personal, and social development. Parent and teacher consultations with the counselor usually occur in the early morning before classes or during after-school hours.

The counselor is a licensed professional with training in human development, learning theory, counseling and consulting, tests and measurement, career development, educational and related research, and other areas appropriate to the practice of counseling in a school. The counselor's office is located in the school, and appointments can be scheduled by calling (counselor's phone), e-mailing (counselor's e-mail address), or writing to (school address).

Leading the Charge

Regardless of the language you choose or how long it takes your school to adopt it, an important aspect of describing a program of services is the leadership role you take in the process. Remember that your leadership ability is paramount in helping the school build a successful program.

To survive and flourish as an elementary or middle school counselor, it is essential to identify and embrace the leadership role you have in the program and the larger school community. School counseling in the twenty-first century is not simply providing individual and group services to students. Rather, it is the orchestration of many services, some provided by you, the counselor, and some provided by other professionals. This orchestration, much like leading a major symphony, requires leadership characteristics and skills to develop working relationships, identify goals and objectives, and create appropriate action to demonstrate that everyone is playing the same tune and in the correct key (Baker & Gerler, 2008).

A first step in developing your leadership role is to assess your strengths in taking on this responsibility. What skills and knowledge do you already possess that will enable you to persuade people to create a comprehensive program of services and commit their involvement in carrying out its objectives? Next is to determine what additional knowledge you need to be a successful leader in your school. How can you obtain this knowledge—through workshops, professional associations, or more graduate training? A third step to consider is how to begin developing support for your ideas as a school leader. What will you need to do to win the confidence of your administration? Which teachers, support staff, and other school personnel are likely to support a comprehensive program, and how will you secure their support?

Throughout this chapter and book, you will learn how you, as a leader, can create a viable and valuable program for your school. Here are some starter tips for putting your plan into action:

- *Know what you want to do.* Plan the school counseling program around accepted counseling and related services and understand the literature and research to support your ideas.
- *Enlist help.* Identify school members—administration, teachers, parents, staff, and others—who will support you from the start. Recruit optimistic colleagues and administrators and tell them your plans.
- *Respect school traditions and culture.* Even though you might want to work toward changing old ways of doing things, understand the emotional ties that some people may have to historical aspects of the school.
- *Be inclusive.* Although you might identify people who give early support to your ideas, be careful not to exclude other people in the process. People who might disagree with initial plans could have constructive ideas that, when incorporated into the plan, will help make it better.

- *Listen, listen, listen!* As a counselor, one of your greatest strengths is your ability to listen fully to others without being judgmental. Use that skill in building support for the counseling program and for your leadership. This is particularly valuable when hearing the disagreements that people have with some of your ideas.
- *Maintain a consistent stance.* In an earlier book, William Purkey and I presented a professional counseling stance that consists of optimism, trust, respect, and intentionality (Purkey & Schmidt, 1996). Consider these characteristics and others that you believe will help you maintain a dependable leadership position in your school.

Focusing on a Comprehensive Program

By learning about yourself as a leader, gaining additional knowledge about the school counseling profession, and creating collaborative relationships in the school community, you place yourself in a stronger position to maintain a broad vision of what the program should be. This means focusing on the development of a comprehensive school counseling program.

All school counselors face the danger of feeling overwhelmed by the challenges that students, parents, teachers, and administrators bring. Sometimes, when you become overwhelmed, you might adopt a particular mode of operation because it is comfortable to do so. For example, a counselor who spends a major portion of her school day in a single activity, such as classroom guidance, individual counseling, or program administration, might do so because she feels comfortable and competent in this activity. Although such services are important, they do not, in and of themselves, establish a comprehensive school counseling program. As noted previously, a school counseling program ideally consists of a variety of activities and services, which aim at specific goals and objectives chosen as a result of careful examination and analysis of the needs of the school populations. You therefore want to move beyond routine reactions to situations and crises that emerge, and instead work according to a well-designed plan of counseling, consulting, and coordinating services.

All the suggestions and ideas in this guide relate to some aspect of a comprehensive counseling program. We can categorize these ideas under one or more of the four components of a comprehensive program—planning, organizing, implementing, and evaluating.

1. *Planning* is the process of assessing school and student needs, formulating a philosophy of school counseling that is consistent with the mission of the school, evaluating the current program (if there is one), and establishing and prioritizing future program goals.
2. *Organizing* entails the selection of specific objectives and program strategies. This selection process includes deciding who will provide which services. The selected goals and objectives assign specific responsibilities to counselors, teachers, and administrators, defining their roles in the school counseling program.

3. *Implementing* is the action phase of a comprehensive program. It involves the delivery of responsive services, such as counseling, consulting, coordinating, referring, and testing. Implementation of a comprehensive school counseling program also involves all the personnel who have responsibility for educating students in the school: teachers, counselors, media specialists, administrators, and others.
4. *Evaluating* is the phase of a program that determines success, examines weaknesses, and allows you to recommend changes for the future. In this edition of the *Survival Guide,* you will see that program evaluation is deemed essential to a comprehensive school counseling program. Effective programs are not guided merely by the intuitions, preferences, and desires of counselors and teachers. Rather, they are based on data that illustrate the needs of students and measure the outcomes of the services provided.

These four phases of a comprehensive school counseling program illustrate that to be successful you must move beyond traditional approaches to guidance and counseling programs. Exhibit 1.2 shows a few of the differences between traditional and comprehensive approaches. As you can see, the traditional guidance approach is counselor centered, informational in nature, and remedial in focus, whereas the comprehensive model focuses on serving broad populations with a wide spectrum of responsive services. The scale for program assessment in Worksheet 1.1, moreover, will help you evaluate how comprehensive or traditional your current program is. The scale emphasizes teacher input, group services, program planning, parental involvement, and other aspects of a comprehensive counseling program.

EXHIBIT 1.2

Comparison of Traditional and Comprehensive Programs

Traditional Program

· Predominantly one-on-one services
· Informational and administrative in nature
· Reactive to critical situations
· Clerically oriented
· Counselor dominated
· No data used for program planning
· Minimum use of group work
· Counselor's activities directed primarily by the school principal

Comprehensive Program

· Balanced program of responsive services
· Preventive, developmental, remedial in nature
· Proactive planning and goal setting
· Service oriented
· High level of teacher involvement
· Data used for planning and evaluation
· Extensive use of group services
· Counselor-led program development in consultation with principal and others

Program Assessment Scale

Directions: Underline your response to each question, and fill in the respective point values in the blank spaces. Total the points for all twelve questions to determine how traditional or comprehensive your school counseling program is.

1. Do you spend most of your time in individual counseling and consulting with students? Not most (3 points); Yes (1 point); No, I do not do any individual counseling or consulting (0 points) _____

2. Does your program emphasize a wide range of services, such as group counseling, teacher and parent consultation, parent education, individual counseling, student assessment, and classroom guidance? Yes (3 points); Somewhat (1 point); No (0 points) _____

3. Do you lead the development, implementation, and evaluation of a comprehensive program of services? Yes, I take a leadership role in the program (3 points); I have a program, but do not always lead its development (1 point); No, the principal directs my activities (0 points) _____

4. Are you involved with teachers in planning and presenting classroom guidance? Very much (3 points); Somewhat (2 points); Not at all (0 points) _____

5. Do you present all of the classroom guidance in your school? No, teachers also infuse guidance activities with their classes (3 points); Yes (1 point); We have no classroom guidance in the school (0 points) _____

6. Do you spend most of your time in crisis intervention and remedial services? Not most (3 points); No, but I but I still feel that I spend too much time on this (2 points); Yes, most of the time (1 point); No, I do not do any crisis intervention (0 points) _____

7. Do you have a written plan of goals and objectives that you revise annually? Yes, it guides program decisions (3 points); Yes, but the written goals and objectives are not actually implemented (1 point); No (0 points) _____

8. Do you have an advisory committee to help guide your school counseling program? Yes, an active committee (3 points); Yes, but not an active one (1 point); No (0 points) _____

9. Are you overburdened with paperwork? Not really (3 points); Somewhat (1 point); Yes, most of the time (0 points) _____

10. Do you use assessment procedures with students, parents, and teachers in addition to other school data to establish program goals and objectives? Yes (3 points); Occasionally (1 point); Never (0 points) _____

11. Are your teaching colleagues an important part of the school counseling program? Yes, their input is sought and they participate (3 points); Somewhat, a few teachers are involved (1 point); No, it is my program to develop and implement (0 points) _____

12. Does your principal understand and support the services of the program? Yes, always (3 points); Usually (2 points); Rarely (1 point); Never (0 points) _____

Scoring: The closer to 36 points you score, the more comprehensive your program. The closer to zero points you score, the less comprehensive your program of services.

An example of the differences between these two approaches lies in the area of career information and development. In a traditional guidance program, the counselor assumes full responsibility for disseminating career information to students. At the elementary level, for example, a counselor could offer classroom guidance by presenting information about "the world of work." In a middle school, individuals or groups of students might receive occupational information from the counselor without any involvement of teachers.

In comprehensive programs, career information and development go hand in hand and are the shared responsibility of the entire school staff. Ideally, elementary and middle school teachers accept responsibility for integrating career information into their daily instruction. This infusion of career awareness helps students see how they can apply the subject matter in the outside world. It also enables students to learn which subjects relate to their interests and to particular careers. You can assist with this integration by planning career guidance lessons and activities with teachers, locating appropriate resources, and presenting special topics in the classroom. Throughout the school year, you design and lead individual and group activities to focus on specific career development needs of all students. In addition, you work with teachers to plan schoolwide activities that focus on career information and development.

Adapting the ASCA National Model and Other Approaches

In 2003, ASCA introduced a new model for designing and delivering comprehensive school counseling programs. You can find out about the ASCA National Model from the association's Web site at www.schoolcounselor.org and through other resources listed at the back of this guide.

The ASCA National Model for school counseling programs is intended to help practicing counselors create data-driven and results-based programs. The hope is that a national model will help counselors across the fifty states design, implement, coordinate, manage, and evaluate responsive services that enable students to achieve success in school. The ASCA National Model provides a framework around which counselors can design and develop their programs (American School Counselor Association, 2005). Just because the profession now has a national model, however, does not mean that all school counseling programs will look and function the same. Each elementary and middle school is different, and the comprehensive counseling program that you design and implement in your school will reflect those differences.

The ASCA National Model is relatively young, and research about its efficacy has not yet been fully explored. In the past, authors and researchers have presented other models or structures for designing and implementing comprehensive programs. For example, Gysbers and Henderson (2000) are two notable authors and researchers who developed an approach to comprehensive program planning and evaluation. Likewise, VanZandt and Hayslip (2000) offered a systemic planning model and provided examples of other programmatic approaches from the literature. More research is needed to verify if any particular model or approach is better than others in delivering effective services.

Your responsibility is to find or create a programmatic structure that works in your school to serve students, parents, teachers, and others. An important part of your leadership role as an elementary or middle school counselor is to select an appropriate model or structure with which to build a comprehensive program of services. Such a structure may come from the ASCA National Model, another approach you find in the literature, or a program you have designed using your knowledge and experience as well as information about your particular school. The ultimate goal is to design a program that ensures appropriate services for all students.

Advocating for All Students

Elementary and middle schools reflect the populations and communities they serve. Typical schools consist of students who bring a range of hopes, challenges, and needs to class each day. Counselors and schools that design comprehensive programs of responsive services understand their role in advocating for all students, not only those who show promise but also those who struggle academically, personally, or socially.

The American Counseling Association (ACA) endorses advocacy competencies that include three levels of focus for school counselors: (1) the client/student, (2) the school/community, and (3) the public arena (Ratts, DeKruyf, & Chen-Hayes, 2007). A few examples of student-level competencies include

- Identifying students' strengths and resources
- Helping students develop self-advocacy plans
- Helping students identify barriers to their development
- Developing an initial plan of action to address identified barriers

Examples of school- and community-level competencies include

- Identifying environmental factors that influence student development
- Developing alliances with groups working for change
- Developing a plan for dealing with probable responses to change

Examples of public-arena-level competencies include

- Recognizing the impact of oppression and other barriers to healthy development
- Communicating information in ways that are ethical and appropriate for school populations
- Supporting existing alliances for change

The examples here are only a few of the extensive list of ACA advocacy competencies (see also Toporek, Lewis, & Crethar, 2009). It is important for you to gather and implement strategies that will support student development by eliminating barriers to learning and addressing social justice for all students. By doing so, you not only advocate for individual students but also encourage all students to empower themselves. For many students, their school failure relates to historic oppression and other barriers, which have to some degree contributed to the "achievement gap" in public education. Your advocacy on behalf of students, the school and community, and the public at large is important in addressing this issue.

One way that you can advocate for all students is by observing and listening to the culture of the school. At times, schools pass policies or develop programs that, though well intended, might discriminate against certain groups or individual students. When you see this happening in your school, it is imperative that you take action. Point out to the principal and teachers what you have observed or what you have heard, and help them understand the implications for all students in the school. For example, one elementary school started a program for students to bring their fathers for a turkey lunch before Thanksgiving. The counselor pointed out that some students did not have fathers, and others had fathers away in military service. After listening to the counselor, the principal and faculty decided to change the program to "Bring a Family Member to Lunch."

By advocating for all students, you demonstrate the democratic principles on which our educational and political systems were founded. Taking this professional stance is another way to win support from the principal, teachers, and parents. With their support, you are better able to describe and define the scope and limits of your role as a school counselor within a comprehensive program. For this reason, seeking input from administrators, teachers, and parents about the program and your role as counselor is essential.

SEEKING INPUT

A comprehensive school counseling program does not belong to one person and is not your sole responsibility as an elementary or middle school counselor. For this reason, the first step in establishing your program is to seek input and win cooperation from your teaching colleagues. When you make program decisions in isolation, out of reach of your teaching colleagues, services may tend to get out of touch with the needs of the school. As a result, the program may lose support from the faculty.

You may not win the total support of the faculty in the school, but you do want the majority of teachers to believe that the services you provide and the parts of the program for which they are responsible are important to meet the educational goals for all students. This is also true for your principal and the larger school community. If you succeed in convincing the school community of the counseling program's indispensability in meeting students' needs, you will win the support of a broad audience for the leadership you provide in designing an overall program of services. Winning the support of your colleagues and parents is the next step in the process of building a program.

Winning Support

The first person to include in the decision-making process for developing a comprehensive program is the school principal. If you have replaced a counselor, you want to assess how the principal viewed the program in the past. When starting a new counseling program, you should determine what expectations the principal has for this addition to the school. If you are a veteran counselor, you want to maintain a strong working relationship with the principal. In all cases, you should schedule a time at the beginning of the year to meet with your principal and gather insights and expectations about your role.

Before scheduling this meeting with the principal, it may be helpful to do some preparation. Whether you are replacing a counselor, beginning a new program, or revising an existing program, make a list of questions for your interview. You may want to memorize these questions so your interview is relaxed and spontaneous rather than stiff and structured (as it can be when reading from a prepared list). Although the following questions and explanations are designed to help you prepare to replace a counselor, you can adapt them to fit your own situation. If you are a veteran counselor, for example, an adaptation of these questions might help you and your principal examine where the program is and where it could be heading.

Questions to Ask the Principal

1. *What was the most beneficial service offered in the school counseling program last year?* The principal's answer to this question will help you assess his or her priorities for the program. This information enables you to compare your philosophy with the principal's expectations. By comparing your views with the principal's, you will know how much work you have to do to convince the principal of why a comprehensive school counseling program can benefit an elementary or middle school.

2. *Was there an annual plan for the school counseling program?* If there was a plan, you may have seen it during your interview for this counseling position. If you did not see one, ask about it. An annual plan will give you a clear idea of what the past program looked like. If the principal indicates that there was no written plan, this is an excellent opportunity to mention that you would like to create one to give the program a specific mission, goals, and direction during the year and an adequate evaluation at the end of the year.

3. *Do classroom teachers integrate or infuse guidance lessons in their daily instruction?* The principal's answer to this question will indicate how the school views guidance and who has responsibility for it. You might ask whether there is a guidance curriculum—learning goals and objectives that are part of the overall school curriculum. Some states and school systems have developed guidance curriculums for every grade level. If this is true in your school, do you know who has responsibility for implementing the curriculum? If you find that teachers are integrating guidance activities into their daily instruction, you will know that you have a strong foundation for a comprehensive school counseling program. However, if you find that the previous counselor had sole responsibility for classroom guidance, much work will need to be done to include the types of responsive services found in a comprehensive program.

4. *Are teachers involved in an advisement program?* This question is most relevant for middle schools, but can also pertain to elementary programs. By an advisement program, I mean procedures through which all students receive information about their academic progress, school programs that may assist them, and community services that could help in their development. If teachers are active in an advisement program, it is necessary to determine the school counselor's role. A comprehensive school counseling program often includes a type of advisement program that involves teachers, and for which the counselor might have coordinating responsibility. The counselor also provides staff development services for teachers to learn effective advising skills. A strong advisement program can be the heart of a school counselor's referral system.

5. *Is there an advisory committee for the school counseling program?* Building a successful comprehensive program that reflects the needs of the school and community requires the input of others. If in the past the counseling program had an advisory committee, encourage the principal to continue with one. If there is currently no committee, ask the principal to suggest names of teachers and parents who might serve. In middle schools, you also could recommend that students have representation. If your school has numerous committees, you may want to recommend that an existing committee serve as the advisory group for the counseling program—you will win favor with the teachers by combining your initiative with another committee's objectives.

Once established, the advisory committee will help you: (a) assess student needs, (b) design a comprehensive program, (c) inform the faculty and staff about program goals and their respective roles in reaching these objectives, and (d) evaluate services for the year. An advisory committee enables you to win support from the faculty for program decisions and changes. It also encourages the staff to accept responsibility for various aspects of the program.

6. *What about parental involvement in the school?* A comprehensive counseling program benefits from volunteers and parents who are involved in their children's education. A school that prides itself in strong parental involvement and volunteer programs is in good shape to establish a comprehensive counseling program.

How your principal answers this question may give you an indication of how welcomed parents are in the school. School climate, which has a bearing on student achievement and overall school effectiveness, is affected by parent attitudes. As the counselor, you can assist the principal in strengthening parents' relationships with the school, which would improve school climate and thereby improve student performance.

7. *Is the counseling center located in an ideal place, and is it adequately furnished?* If you have begun working as a school counselor, you have already assessed the facilities and made preliminary judgments. If your assessment is positive, you will not need to ask this question. If, however, there are some aspects of the counseling center that bother you, you may want the principal's perceptions.

The principal will be able to educate you about funding limitations, space restrictions, and other realities that have an impact on the placement and furnishings of a counseling center. If the principal is open to suggestions for changing the center, you may want to have a few ideas in mind. For example, suppose you are in an elementary building with three stories, and the counseling center is in the basement at the far end of a dark hall. You may want to emphasize that student access to the counselor is paramount to a successful program, and that kindergarten and first grade children would probably not be comfortable visiting the counselor under these conditions. You might ask whether any alternatives might be possible.

When focusing on facilities of the counseling center, it is wise to emphasize their impact on the program and on students, parents, and teachers. Avoid mentioning your own welfare, preferences, and tastes. The most important factor is how appropriate facilities contribute to a positive difference for clients the program intends to serve.

Is the furniture adequate? Are there adult-size chairs as well as student chairs? Is there a telephone for making confidential referrals and following up on cases? Is the center sufficiently private for confidential sessions with students, parents, teachers, and others? If some of the facilities are less than adequate, ask your principal how you can help improve the situation. Worksheet 1.2 provides a simple checklist to evaluate your facilities.

Because elementary and middle school counselors frequently work in old buildings designed and constructed before counseling programs existed, adequate facilities are sometimes unavailable. Take heart. Remember, just because the broom closet or boiler room is the only available space does not mean it has to look and function like a broom closet or basement. Use your imagination, ask teachers for ideas, and renovate!

Facility Checklist for a School Counseling Center

Directions: Check *Yes* or *No* for each of the items on the list.

Yes No

☐ ☐ The center has adequate space for small group sessions.

☐ ☐ The counselor's office has audio and visual privacy.

☐ ☐ A reception area exists for waiting and reviewing materials.

☐ ☐ The center has a display area for educational and career materials.

☐ ☐ The counselor has a telephone and desktop computer.

☐ ☐ There is storage area for equipment, toys, games, and materials.

☐ ☐ The center has appropriately sized furniture for students and adults.

☐ ☐ There is at least one table for group activities.

☐ ☐ The counselor has access to a conference room.

☐ ☐ There is a sink for washing hands and cleaning up paint, clay, and so forth.

☐ ☐ The center has a computer for student self-instruction and guidance programs.

☐ ☐ The counselor has access to a TV monitor for video, Internet, and closed circuit use.

☐ ☐ The school has a secure room elsewhere in the building in which records are stored and teachers can have access without disrupting services of the counseling program.

8. *What has been the most successful service offered in the counseling program?* If the principal has an answer, you may want to follow up by asking how he or she evaluated the service. In other words, on what basis does this principal believe this service was successful? The principal's response will give you insight into the kinds of accountability processes that have existed in the program. You will want to stress the importance of evaluating services so that the program can be altered each year to meet the needs of students, parents, and teachers.

9. *What service or activity, if any, would the principal prefer to discontinue?* Sometimes principals and counselors do not communicate sufficiently about the program. If your principal has allowed some services to continue, despite his or her feelings about them, you should know this up front. If the principal dislikes a service that you believe is important, you can examine what aspects of the service have been discomforting and negotiate changes to make it more palatable.

As a follow-up to this question, you might ask about activities that the principal wants you to handle, but that have no relationship to school counseling. As a member of the school staff, you will want to participate and accept your fair share of responsibilities to help the school run smoothly. Although you want to be involved, however, too many extra duties or administrative functions can detract from your primary counseling role, and might even defeat your purpose in the school.

The sample questions for principals in the previous paragraphs provide a starter list that you can tailor to suit your situation. Having an open, honest discussion with your principal sets the stage to win support for a comprehensive school counseling program. The questions for principals may also be adapted to help you survey your teaching colleagues to assess what teachers think will make a good program. Without knowing what they think you are less able to gain their support, which, along with that of the principal, is essential for the success of a school counseling program. Teachers' support is also important in helping you convince them of their role in assisting with student development.

Sharing Ownership

Winning support from your principal is the first step toward including your colleagues in planning and implementing a comprehensive program. As noted earlier, an advisory committee is an excellent vehicle through which to gain their cooperation. After discussing the idea of a committee with your principal, you will want to select members. This selection might come from the principal's recommendations or from parents and teachers who volunteer. The people selected for this committee should advocate a strong counseling program, believe that the program is the responsibility of all staff members, and be willing to attend committee meetings during the year.

If you and your principal decide to seek volunteers, you could make an announcement to the staff about the committee at a faculty meeting or through a memo to the teachers. You might consider following up your announcement with discussion at a faculty meeting. Exhibit 1.3 is one example of an announcement. The last part of Exhibit 1.3 includes a sample form that you could adapt for potential committee volunteers.

EXHIBIT 1.3

Advisory Committee Volunteers

Dear Teachers:

The principal, Mrs. Jones, has asked that we form an advisory committee for the school counseling program. This committee will consist of teachers, students, and parents, and will guide the counseling program during the year. The committee will

· Design a needs assessment procedure and make program decisions based on the results of this assessment
· Determine how classroom teachers will use the guidance curriculum during the year
· Assist the counselor with the design of a schedule of services
· Help the counselor determine topics for group counseling and group guidance
· Focus on school climate and recommend activities to improve the learning atmosphere
· Help the counselor design procedures to evaluate the program during the school year

The committee is to meet before the end of September, and will meet three more times during the year. The school counselor will chair the committee.

Mrs. Jones will select committee members next week. If you are interested or can recommend students and parents for the committee, please complete the form below and return it to the counselor's mailbox. Mrs. Jones will announce the committee members at our next faculty meeting.

Thank you for your assistance!

Advisory Committee Form

Name: _____

Please check the statements that reflect your wishes.

_____ I would like to serve on the School Counseling Advisory Committee.

_____ I nominate the following student for the committee: _____

_____

_____ I nominate the following parent for the committee: _____

_____

Home Phone: _____

Please return this form to the counselor's mailbox.

During the year, your advisory committee will help you and the teachers plan events and activities to focus on schoolwide guidance, parent involvement, student development, and school climate. As these activities are implemented, the involvement of students, parents, and teachers will be essential. This is another illustration of how the school counseling program belongs to everyone.

Letting everyone share ownership in the counseling program gives you support that is vital for functioning as a school counselor across a comprehensive program of services. Such support enables you to delineate clearly the expanded services of the program.

DEFINING WHAT YOU DO: A GLOSSARY OF RESPONSIVE SERVICES

As mentioned earlier in this chapter, school counseling is a broad professional practice that includes preventive services, developmental activities, and remedial interventions. As such, counseling in schools encompasses a wide variety of activities and services. The ASCA National Model adopted the term *responsive services* to describe many of the activities that school counselors perform to meet the needs of students. The term is appropriate because almost all of the services implemented by counselors in schools—such as counseling, consultation, group work, assessment, and coordination—are usually chosen in response to an identified need or situation.

An important characteristic of a successful school counseling program is the awareness people have about your role as a counselor. To be successful, you want to educate students, parents, and teachers about all the responsive services that you implement and how these services help students achieve academically, develop appropriate personal characteristics and self-worth, and learn valuable social and life skills.

One way to help others learn about your role as a school counselor is to list your functions, with a brief description of each, in a faculty manual, student handbook, PTA or PTO newsletter, or other resource. The first step is to identify what services and functions you believe are important to the program.

Identifying Responsive Services

The following sections will help identify and describe the services of a comprehensive school counseling program. Depending on your audience—students, parents, or teachers—you may need to adjust the language accordingly. You could use this description in a handout or on your school counselor's Web page.

Individual Counseling

Professional school counselors provide individual sessions for students to assist with a variety of educational, career, and personal concerns. The primary purpose of these sessions is to help students explore their concerns, make appropriate plans of action, and be successful in following through with their plans. Typically, the counseling provided is preventive and developmental in nature. Occasionally, school counselors provide counseling to help students remedy a problem, and these are usually short-term helping relationships. When more time is necessary for such counseling relationships, a school counselor will often encourage the family to use treatment opportunities in the community, such as private counselors, mental health centers, or other agencies. In instances in which other treatment opportunities are not available to families, an elementary or middle school counselor may decide to continue counseling a student as long as progress is apparent.

Individual Planning

Many contacts with individual students will not involve counseling relationships. Elementary and middle school students benefit from assistance in making decisions about school, academic subjects, extracurricular activities, career interests, and other matters related to their educational development. In such individual sessions a counselor's role is to provide information and other assistance in helping students make appropriate choices. These sessions may occur a single time, or may include ongoing sessions with particular students.

Group Counseling

In some instances, students help one another by working in groups with leadership from a counselor. Group counseling allows students to share ideas about specific issues, such as problem solving, career choices, educational planning, and peer relationships, as well as helping them use these ideas to resolve their concerns. Group sessions usually involve small groups of students led by a counselor and meet once or twice a week for a specific number of sessions. An advantage of group over individual counseling is that it can often be a more efficient use of the counselor's time. In addition, students gain personal confidence and social skills by learning to empathize with and help one another.

Group Guidance

School counselors often meet with groups of students to help them learn specific information about themselves (for example, testing results) and their development. Commonly referred to as group guidance, these instructional groups can be large, such as classroom size, or relatively small, such as three to five students. Ideally, teachers also lead these types of activities in their classrooms. Guidance groups usually focus on topics related to one or more goals and objectives in a guidance curriculum. As an example, a teacher might integrate activities about healthy peer relationships into a social studies unit.

Group guidance also can be part of a student-teacher advisement program. Whether led by a counselor or a teacher, guidance groups are instructional in nature and focus on such topics as self-concept development, study skills, friendship, health habits, career information, and good citizenship.

Guidance Curriculum

Some schools design learning goals and instructional strategies to assist students with personal, social, career, and educational development, and integrate these goals and strategies into the school curriculum. The intent is to have classroom teachers incorporate these goals and objectives into daily instruction. School counselors assist with this curriculum by planning its integration with teachers, providing resources and materials, and presenting some activities with teachers in the classroom. You will learn more about this service in Chapter Five.

Student Appraisal

Counselors help students, parents, and teachers by gathering information about student abilities, behaviors, and achievement in order to help make appropriate decisions about educational placement and instruction. In helping with these decisions, counselors use tests, inventories, observations, interviews, and other procedures to gather information.

Referrals

An important role for school counselors is to serve as referral agents when students and their families require assistance from other programs and services in the school system or from agencies outside the school. Counselors work closely with teachers and administrators in these referral processes. Key to being a successful referral agent is the counselor's knowledge and working relationship with other helping professionals in the school system and community.

Consultation

Schools help students develop to their fullest potential when everyone works together. For this reason, counselors consult with teachers and parents to plan appropriate services for every child. These consultations typically focus on the needs of the individual child, but sometimes counselors lead group consultations for teachers and parents to focus on specific issues and topics. For example, a counselor might present a workshop for teachers to learn about indicators of child depression, or might lead an education group for parents to discuss child-rearing techniques.

Coordination

A school counseling program includes a wide range of services and activities that require coordination for smooth administration, and for which the counselor assumes primary responsibility. The preceding paragraphs offer a sample of typical counselor functions and responsive services. Use them as a guide to develop a list that suits you and your school's counseling program. As you can see, responsibility for many activities is shared. Part of your role is to coordinate these many functions. Your next step in program development is to determine areas of shared responsibility: Who does what?

Communicating Your Role

As noted earlier, having a lexicon or description of your services is just the first step in defining what you do in your elementary or middle school. More important are the processes you use and actions you take to communicate your role to students, parents, teachers, administrators, and the community.

This *Survival Guide* devotes considerable attention to ideas and strategies that you can use to help people understand their roles in the school, so I will not devote much space to the topic here. However, there are three essential points that might help you create and communicate a role that is professionally satisfying and rewarding:

1. *Use existing avenues of communication.* For example, if you have regular faculty meetings, PTA or PTO meetings, assemblies, or other gatherings in the school, place yourself on the agenda each time and say something about what the counseling program is accomplishing. If your school puts out a newsletter periodically, write a "Counselor's Column" and share useful information for students, parents, and teachers.

2. *Commandeer a bulletin board.* Sometimes counselors shy away from being responsible for bulletin boards in the school, and this reluctance is understandable. Sometimes managing bulletin boards becomes a full-time job and takes counselors away from their primary responsibilities. Nevertheless, having control of at least one bulletin board can be an excellent way to communicate what you and the counseling program are doing in school. Be sure to include samples of students' drawings and other work if appropriate, because they will attract attention to your announcements.

3. *Launch your program into cyberspace.* In this rapidly changing world of advanced technology, it is essential that the counseling program be visible on all school communications, such as school newsletters, student handbooks, and the Internet. Ask for space or links on your school's Web site to feature the school counseling program.

These three ideas only scratch the surface of ways to communicate your role in a comprehensive school counseling program. What is most important, and stressed throughout this book, is the effort you make to communicate the role as you understand it in order to take professional command of who you are and what you do in the school.

In this chapter, you have learned about ways to describe and define a comprehensive school counseling program. This guide takes the position that planning, organizing, implementing, and evaluating a program of responsive services are key to your survival as a school counselor. To be successful in this endeavor, seek input from others and share ownership of the program. The next step is to determine the responsibilities that various players—administrators, teachers, and counselors—have in making a comprehensive program of services a reality. Chapter Two offers suggestions for determining these responsibilities, identifying your role, and learning to balance your time across the many services of a comprehensive eschool counseling program.

chapter 2

DEVELOPING YOUR ROLE *and* CREATING *an* IDENTITY

Scenario 2.1: Is There a Problem?

As the counselor in a school, you try to meet all the new students that enter during the year. A parent new to your school has called to ask why his daughter came to your office today. He inquires, "Is there a problem? My daughter said she visited with you today, but I did not give permission for her to see a counselor. What was your purpose in seeing my daughter? What do you do with students at the school?" What would you say to this father?

This chapter will help you frame a response to the parent in Scenario 2.1. Throughout each school year, you have countless opportunities to identify who you are and what you do in the school. It is important that you have not only a clear picture of that identity and role but also effective ways to communicate them to your audience.

Before considering various aspects of developing your role in a comprehensive school counseling program, remember that the ASCA National Model and other approaches to designing, implementing, and evaluating programs are available in the counseling literature, as discussed in Chapter One. You also want to be aware of any local or state initiatives that encourage you to design comprehensive programs according to particular guidelines. If you find that your school system or state has a plan for developing and implementing a comprehensive program of services, this *Survival Guide* will be a useful resource to complement that plan. If you do not find a local or state plan, this guide could be a primary source for developing a comprehensive counseling program for your school, as well as establishing your role and creating your identity as the school counselor.

Sometimes school administrators or committees of people other than counselors control the school counselor's job description. For this reason, it is imperative and ethical that you apply anything you learn about comprehensive programs in this *Survival Guide* or other useful resources within the context of the local school system and the state where you are licensed or certified and practice as a school counselor. Once you have checked to see whether any local or state initiatives exist to guide the development of school counseling programs and the counselor's role, you will be in a more knowledgeable position to use this guide. The first step after you have described the program for students, parents, teachers, and administrators is to determine who is responsible for particular services.

DETERMINING WHO DOES WHAT

A few key elements play an important part in helping counselors develop a clear role for themselves in a comprehensive program of services while also identifying assignments for teachers and other personnel. I introduced some of these elements in the first chapter, but it is helpful to repeat them here. First, it is vital that you work with an advisory committee to initiate some type of needs assessment. Through this process, you and the committee are then able to select program goals and objectives. Once you have identified the aims of the program, you can design services and activities to address broad goals and meet specific objectives. As you and the advisory committee identify appropriate services, you will be able to recommend assignments for administrators, teachers, yourself, and others to make sure that these services are delivered.

Details about performing needs assessments and setting program goals and objectives are presented in Chapter Three. By way of introduction to performing needs assessments determining program goals, Exhibit 2.1 illustrates ten key elements of implementing a comprehensive program. Throughout this and the remaining chapters of this *Survival Guide,* you will learn about the importance of these key elements.

EXHIBIT 2.1

Ten Keys to Implementing a Comprehensive Program

1. Design needs assessment instruments and processes for students, parents, and teachers. Include available school data, such as absentee rates, student achievement results, school climate assessments, and other information.
2. Interview the principal and other administrators to assess their perceptions of school needs.

---

3. Review the outcome of the needs assessment with the advisory committee.
4. Prioritize needs indicated by review of the assessment outcomes.
5. Select, design, and create activities, strategies, and services to address prioritized needs.
6. Assign responsibilities for particular services and activities.
7. Schedule activities and services.
8. Monitor activities and services to be certain all students are included in the program.
9. Evaluate ongoing activities and services throughout the year to measure outcomes.
10. Seek feedback from students, parents, teachers, and administrators to assess overall program satisfaction.

Results from needs assessments help drive decisions about the comprehensive program. For example, suppose the students' needs assessment indicates that many students want more friends but are unsure how to form friendships. To address this need, your school might decide to plan for a special schoolwide program that focuses on friendship, calling it "Friendship Week." For this program, students could make posters about different kinds of friendships; teachers could integrate friendship activities into language arts instruction; and parents and other volunteers could speak to classes about important friendships they have formed during their lives. You might lead group guidance sessions on how to make new friends. Each of these activities would contribute to Friendship Week, and each would allow different people to assume responsibility for making the program a success. Various assignments from the advisory committee would enable each person to accept responsibility for some aspect of this special event.

In managing special activities, it is helpful to have assignment sheets to specify everyone's responsibilities. Exhibit 2.2 gives an example based on the implementation of Friendship Week in a middle school. Use this exhibit as a prototype for other schoolwide activities you might plan.

EXHIBIT 2.2

Friendship Week Assignments

Monday: All teachers will plan a language arts lesson to focus on the importance of friendships. Stories, videos, and writing projects will be available for review in the media center to assist with lesson plans.

The counselor will visit all fifth grade classes during the day to make a twenty to thirty minute presentation on "Inviting New Friends." (For a friendship curriculum, see Schmidt, 1997.) Teachers should schedule time for the counselor to visit classes.

(Continued)

Tuesday: Teachers will plan art activities for students to make posters about friendship. All posters will be hung and placed around the school for the PTA meeting on Tuesday night. Volunteers will visit classes Tuesday afternoon to speak on "Friendships that Made a Difference." A schedule of volunteer visits will be sent to teachers the week before.

The counselor will visit all sixth grade classes to make a twenty to thirty minute presentation on "Ingredients of Positive Friendships." Teachers should schedule time for the counselor to visit classes.

Wednesday: Mrs. English's sixth grade class will present its original play, "My Best Friend," to all grades in the morning. The play will be repeated for parents at the PTA meeting. Teachers should plan follow-up guidance activities with their classes after the play.

The counselor will visit all seventh grade classes and present on "Friendships That Last." Teachers should schedule time for the counselor to visit classes.

Thursday: Mr. Pritchett from the community theater will present his one-man show, "Huck Finn and Friends." The media center has scheduled times on Thursday and Friday for each class to do follow-up activities. A schedule will be presented to teachers at the next faculty meeting. Peer helpers will be available Thursday and Friday afternoons to see students who want to talk about their friendships. The counselor will have more information about this activity at the next faculty meeting.

Friday: Teachers will meet with their student advisees during the regularly scheduled teacher advisement program meetings to ask students about the weeklong activities. Evaluation forms will be available at this time for students to complete. Each teacher will review the evaluations from their advisees and send a summary to the counselor.

A successful counseling program requires an understanding of who is responsible for what. If people do not clearly understand their assignments and responsibilities, the program becomes uncoordinated, some services are unnecessarily duplicated, and resentment might occur because "some people are not doing their job." The following example illustrates what can happen when you do not clearly define functions and have undetermined responsibilities.

A teacher in a middle school was advising a student about how to cope with the separation of his mother and father. At the same time, this student was in group counseling with other students who also were experiencing family changes. The counselor did not know of the teacher's relationship with the student and, as a result, there was no coordination of services. The student became confused because of contradictions between what the teacher advised and the direction of the group counseling sessions. This confusion could have been avoided if the teacher had known that students who need continued counseling should be referred to a school counselor. The counselor in this case had neglected to inform teachers adequately of their advisement and referral roles. Teacher advisement of students is an important part of a comprehensive program and can help to identify students who need assistance from a professional counselor. When counselors do not clearly communicate with teachers about their functions and relationships, confusion and misunderstanding can occur.

In another school, an elementary counselor realized the importance of determining and communicating roles when a new teacher asked, "When are you going to take my class for guidance?" The counselor inquired, "What do you have in mind?" The teacher replied, "The art teacher and music teacher have scheduled my class so I can get my lesson plans done. Will you be doing the same?" Apparently, this teacher mistakenly viewed counselors as special teachers, not as distinct helping professionals. Fortunately, this counselor had a strong advisory committee who supported the belief that classroom guidance is best accomplished when integrated by teachers into daily instruction. The counselor in this school assisted teachers in this process by helping them plan guidance activities, finding resources and materials for teachers to use, and presenting special guidance lessons with teachers in the classroom. At a faculty meeting, the advisory committee presented this idea of the counselor and teachers working together, which enabled the counselor to work out a suitable plan with this particular teacher. They planned guidance activities together and presented them with a team-teaching approach.

CREATING A COUNSELOR IDENTITY

Describing and defining your broad role as a counselor in the school provides a framework and the parameters for specific services you will offer. This framework is the structure within which to create an identity that encompasses who you are and what you do as the school counselor. Creating this identity is the next step in developing a successful program.

Once you have defined the program, you will want to develop ways to advertise it and promote yourself so people consistently understand and accept your role as counselor in the school. This is a continuous process because people and programs in schools are constantly changing. For example, in addition to the new students, parents, and teachers who come into your school each year, advisory committee members could change, or your school might find a new principal. Each change potentially influences the direction and definition of a school counseling program. Having methods in place to educate people about the program and about your role as a counselor is essential if you want to maintain continuity of services and leadership.

Advertising the Program

Plan ways to advertise your program. For example, design a school counseling brochure. Make it attractive, with the school logo on the front and your name, phone number, and e-mail address on the back. The contents of a brochure should describe the counseling program and your role as a school counselor. Be brief. Details are not necessary in this type of communication. Generally, it is best to highlight short descriptions and illustrate the overall program. Use Exhibit 2.3 as a guide in developing the content of your program brochure.

EXHIBIT 2.3

School Counseling Brochure

Hello, I am (counselor's name), the school counselor at (school name). I am available to help you and your child have a successful school year. As a school counselor I work with parents and students in different ways through a program of many services. Each service is aimed at helping students learn and develop to their highest potential. Some of the services in the school counseling program are

· Groups to help children learn how to study
· Individual sessions to help children adjust to school
· Classroom lessons to help children learn how to get along with others
· Groups for parents to share and learn ways to communicate with their children
· Conferences for parents to learn about their children's progress in school

These are a few of the services I offer you and your child. If you have questions or wish to see me about your child, please call me at school. The number is (counselor's telephone number). The best time to reach me is between 7:30 and 8:00 A.M. or after 3:00 P.M. Also, check out the School Counselor page on the school's Web site: http://www.schoolname/schoolcounseling.net.

Not everyone understands that counseling and therapy are helpful learning processes. Some people, including a few professionals, attribute similar meanings to counseling and therapy. These terms, though useful to professionals, raise unnecessary alarm among parents and move their focus away from the primary mission of your school counseling program: to help children learn. You will therefore want to convey this educational purpose to parents. Your goal as counselor is to help children achieve in school and in life.

In elementary and middle schools, therefore, it is wise to avoid the term *therapy* when promoting your services. Also, use the term *counseling* sparingly in brochures and handouts that describe to parents the responsive services of the school counseling program.

As noted earlier, additional media for advertising your program are the school Web site and newsletters. Ask your principal whether you can have a column in each issue of the school newspaper. You might use this column to announce upcoming, schoolwide activities planned by the advisory committee and the teachers, or to send home useful information to parents.

Local town and city newspapers are also sources for advertising school events. When you plan a special event, ask your principal whether it is permissible to call the local newspaper. An article in the local press will establish both an identity for you as the counselor in the school and an awareness in the community about the responsive services of the program. Local radio shows can serve the same purpose. Radio stations are often looking for material for public service announcements and other information—see whether there is a market in your area.

Parent coffee hours held during the day or evening are another opportunity to highlight services in your program. They are most successful when they include fun activities, icebreakers, and topics of interest for the parents who attend. For example, Tom Carr, an elementary counselor and a past president of the North Carolina School Counselor Association, has used an activity that allows parents to express their opinions about child behavior before they hear a presentation about discipline. The activity asks parents to use a scale of +3 to −3 to rate various statements about children and parenting. A plus rating indicates a positive feeling about the statement, and a minus rating indicates a negative feeling. Sample statements might include the following:

- Children should have a voice in purchasing large family items, such as automobiles.
- Allowances should be directly related to children's chores.
- Physical punishment is sometimes necessary.
- Television watching and Internet surfing should be restricted for children.
- In most instances, parents should ask permission or knock before entering a child's room.

The ratings (+3, +2, +1, 0, −1, −2, −3) are posted on the walls around the room. After the parents rate all the statements, the counselor reads each item and parents are asked to stand near the spots where their ratings are posted. As the counselor reads each item, parents move from one rating to another depending on how they scored the items, thereby learning how they responded compared to the rest of the group. They hold no discussion or debate about which rating is "correct," but parents see that there are different points of view in the group. It is a fun icebreaker and a good way to set the stage for a presentation on discipline at home or a similar topic.

Parent education programs, such as coffee hours, are excellent public relations activities for school counselors. Chapter Eleven discusses these types of activities in more detail. In addition to helping you advertise the school counseling program, they also promote you as a school counselor. Self-promotion is another way of creating an identity.

Promoting Yourself

Your success in creating a positive image for yourself as an elementary or middle school counselor is influenced by the methods you choose to advertise your program. For example, you can use newspaper articles, radio broadcasts, program brochures, and other methods not only to advertise the program and inform the public but also to contribute to your professional identity. Newspaper stories, a counselor's column in the school or town newspaper, PTA presentations, or workshops for community groups give you opportunities to highlight responsive services and accomplishments that you achieve as the school counselor. This process of promoting yourself is not egotistical but rather a means of focusing attention on the important contribution that counselors make in schools. Of course, you will want to be judicious about how you promote yourself, but the point is to let people know about the program and the many services you offer.

Volunteer services are another way to introduce yourself to groups outside the school. By assisting in a crisis center, serving on a community board, or participating in local youth organizations, you help community leaders and volunteers learn who you are and what you do in the school. Your professional identity is often most clearly defined not by what you say about who you are but by what you do in the community where you live and work. By being active and behaving in an exemplary manner, you paint a positive picture of both the counseling profession and yourself.

One method of promoting yourself is by introducing yourself to students in all the classes at the beginning of each school year. New students arrive every year. At the same time, students who were at the school last year may need a "refresher" to help them remember who you are and what you do. To help them, you should develop an introductory activity that tells students something about yourself and what you do as a school counselor.

As you think about this introduction, remember the developmental levels of the students to whom you are introducing yourself. This will influence the nature of your introductory activity, especially the media you choose to use. If you are a beginning counselor, you may want to confer with experienced elementary or middle school counselors to benefit from their advice.

Assess your talents and skills as possible vehicles with which to introduce yourself. If you play a musical instrument, use it in a sing-along activity with young children. Or, if you have a skill like juggling or performing magic, use it. You could entertain the students while relating an educational message. Juggling, for example, could be associated with the idea that some things seem very difficult, yet with a little training and practice we can accomplish these seemingly impossible tasks. In a similar way, magic tricks can show how we see things differently—sometimes what we see is not always the way things are, and counselors can help people see and understand things more clearly.

Puppets are a favorite medium of elementary children. Young students enjoy the animation and can easily relate to the counselor. Middle school students enjoy puppets, but only when the activities are appropriate to their age and developmental levels. If you choose to use puppets with middle school students, try them out in small groups with life-like puppets and a moderate level of puppetry skill. If you have no experience with puppets, or are uncertain about your skills, find out whether there are training programs or workshops available in the community. The local arts council and public library are two places to ask about these types of workshops.

Some counselors are creative in designing their introductory activities. Years ago, an elementary counselor used a simple, empty paper bag in an activity called, "The Counselor's Bag" (Bowman, 1986). This is how it works. Hold the bag at the top with the thumb and middle finger. As you explain what you do in the school, pretend to throw these "services" into the bag. While tossing in a service, snap the fingers that are holding the bag and make it sound as though something has dropped into the bag. Although this activity is a vintage, low-tech presentation, young children enjoy it while learning about who the counselor is and what the counselor does.

All of these activities—introducing yourself, being involved in your school, and participating in the community—will make demands on your time. You will find that time is a critical and elusive commodity, and that as you become successful and known in your school and community, people will request and expect more of you. To keep control of your personal and professional time while meeting these demands, you must decide how the time available will be balanced across all the services and activities offered in the school counseling program.

BALANCING TIME

Using time wisely and efficiently is like walking a tightrope—you need good balance. Balance does not occur by accident. We learn to balance ourselves by developing skills, accepting the support of others, and using appropriate and available resources. In learning to walk a tightrope, performers first learn basic skills and fundamental rules. They then accept the instruction and support of expert tightrope artists who offer encouragement and valuable experience. Finally, they use various apparatuses and equipment, such as a balancing pole, which increase the likelihood of their success.

Balancing time in a comprehensive school counseling program helps you be successful in delivering a range of services. You begin by designing a system to determine where time is most needed and to set priorities. Next, you establish a schedule of activities, recruit volunteers, and search for resources to assist in delivering these services.

Setting Priorities

As noted earlier, your advisory committee, other teachers, and administrators can assist in determining program priorities. By accepting their input and assistance, you will be able to decide which activities and services are important to the school and determine what will benefit students the most. You want to develop a process for allotting time to your program priorities. There is no precise way to do this, but if you design some type of process, you can justify to yourself and the school why you schedule activities in a particular way.

One way of allotting time is to list all your services according to priorities determined by your advisory committee with your guidance. After the list of priorities is complete, create a worksheet to determine the total amount of time you have to devote to the school counseling program. Typically, a normal work week is about forty hours. Begin allotting time to each of the activities and services listed. As you proceed, your worksheet may look eventually like the sample in Exhibit 2.4.

EXHIBIT 2.4

Sample Time-Balance Sheet

Individual counseling	10 hours
Group guidance	6 hours
Group counseling	6 hours
Program coordination	4 hours
Student appraisal	4 hours
Teacher consultation	2 hours
Parent consultation	2 hours
Peer helper program	2 hours
Referrals	2 hours
Parent education programs	1 hour
Student orientation	1 hour

Sometimes, as you can see from the list in Exhibit 2.4, the importance of an activity does not necessarily determine the amount of time allotted to it. For example, referral processes may be a very important service, but if few children or families in your school need referral assistance, you will allot less time to this activity. Usually, the most important services you deliver as a school counselor will be those that provide direct services to students: counseling and guidance.

Another fact about allotting time to your activities is that as the year progresses, some activities will change in their level of priority. For example, on the list in Exhibit 2.4, student orientation has only one hour of time devoted to it. This may be appropriate during the middle or end of the school year, but in the beginning of the year most counselors would allocate a greater amount of time to it.

Worksheet 2.1 helps set priorities and allot adequate time to each service. Begin by reviewing the services listed here, and modify as appropriate to include any other services you deliver as a counselor.

Establishing a Schedule

Counselors are different from teachers in that they do not have assigned students or a definite schedule of classes. Successful counselors, however, find that a schedule helps control their time and, if disseminated or posted in the school, can inform teachers and administrators about the activities and services of the counseling program. Some counselors post weekly schedules in the principal's office and the faculty lounge. This not only helps colleagues locate you in emergencies but also advertises the many services of the counseling program.

After you have allotted time for specific services of the school counseling program for which you have responsibility, you will want to design a schedule. This will not be a permanent schedule because, as noted above, your program priorities and responsibilities will change as the year progresses. You might find that a weekly schedule is best, or perhaps a monthly schedule will suffice. Whichever you decide, it is important to convey to administrators and teachers that a counselor's schedule is a guide that must remain flexible. Flexibility enables you to address and handle crises as they occur in the school. However, you should stay on schedule as much as possible once you announce it to the faculty. A posted schedule that is seldom followed is worse than no schedule at all. Most teachers are tolerant when crises interrupt their plans, but they appreciate dependability and respect a counselor who provides anticipated services reliably.

A sample schedule in Exhibit 2.5 uses most of the activities in Worksheet 2.1 above. You will want to design your own schedule based on the priorities and time allotments of your school counseling program. Worksheet 2.2 is a blank schedule that you can use in establishing a weekly schedule.

It might also be helpful to have a master schedule for the school counseling program. In the same way that you decide whether to use a weekly, monthly, or semester schedule for yourself as counselor, a master schedule could cover the same period. In the master schedule, you address major goals and activities planned across the school that are part of the school counseling program. Exhibit 2.6 provides a sample master schedule for a middle school counseling program at the beginning of the school year. Use it as a guide to construct a master schedule that is unique to your school program. When you have

Time-Balance Worksheet

Service	Priority	Time Available
Individual counseling	_____	_____
Group counseling	_____	_____
Small-group guidance	_____	_____
Classroom guidance	_____	_____
Program coordination	_____	_____
Student appraisal	_____	_____
Teacher consultation	_____	_____
Parent consultation	_____	_____
Peer helper training and supervision	_____	_____
Referrals to other services	_____	_____
Teacher in-service	_____	_____
Parent education programs	_____	_____
Student orientation services	_____	_____

developed schedules for the program, you are in a stronger position to examine and use various resources to implement the program.

EXHIBIT 2.5

Sample Schedule

Monday	Tuesday	Wednesday	Thursday	Friday	Time
Parent conferences	Individual sessions	Orientation sessions	Individual sessions	Individual sessions	8:00 A.M.
Group guidance	Individual sessions	Individual sessions	Individual sessions	Group counseling	9:00 A.M.
Group guidance	Group counseling	Group counseling	Group counseling	Group guidance	10:00 A.M.
Individual sessions	Testing	Observations	Observations	Parent group	11:00 A.M.
Peer helper	Teacher consultation	Peer helper	Group guidance	Group counseling	12:30 P.M.
Group guidance	Testing	Individual sessions	Individual sessions	Teacher consultation	1:30 P.M.
Program coordination	Group guidance	Group counseling	Individual sessions	Program coordination	2:30 P.M.

Using Resources

In addition to assigning and scheduling services for you and the school staff, you might want to recruit volunteers. Resourceful people can assist you in meeting the demands of a comprehensive school counseling program. The first step is to identify these people and the resources available, and to determine how to use them efficiently.

There are many ways to use volunteers in a comprehensive school counseling program. For example, as you saw in Exhibit 2.5, the counselor's sample schedule, a peer helper program is scheduled for two hours a week, during which time the counselor trains and supervises students. Student helpers can be tutors for their peers and younger students. They can be "buddies" and "welcome counselors" for new students who are entering the school. Older students can assist teachers and counselors with classroom guidance activities. Some students can learn basic listening and helping skills to assist their peers and make referrals to the school counselor.

Potential volunteers also include parents, grandparents, and retired citizens who can tutor or assist with special students in the classroom. To facilitate volunteer services, you can help the school administrators recruit and train these volunteers. Some volunteers can be buddies or older friends for students who need additional attention or have few adult role models in their families.

Schedule Worksheet

Monday	Tuesday	Wednesday	Thursday	Friday	Time
_____	_____	_____	_____	_____	7:30 A.M.
_____	_____	_____	_____	_____	8:00 A.M.
_____	_____	_____	_____	_____	8:30 A.M.
_____	_____	_____	_____	_____	9:00 A.M.
_____	_____	_____	_____	_____	9:30 A.M.
_____	_____	_____	_____	_____	10:00 A.M.
_____	_____	_____	_____	_____	10:30 A.M.
_____	_____	_____	_____	_____	11:00 A.M.
_____	_____	_____	_____	_____	11:30 A.M.
_____	_____	_____	_____	_____	Noon
_____	_____	_____	_____	_____	12:30 P.M.
_____	_____	_____	_____	_____	1:00 P.M.
_____	_____	_____	_____	_____	1:30 P.M.
_____	_____	_____	_____	_____	2:00 P.M.
_____	_____	_____	_____	_____	2:30 P.M.
_____	_____	_____	_____	_____	3:00 P.M.
_____	_____	_____	_____	_____	3:30 P.M.
_____	_____	_____	_____	_____	4:00 P.M.
_____	_____	_____	_____	_____	4:30 P.M.
_____	_____	_____	_____	_____	5:00 P.M.

EXHIBIT 2.6

Sample Master Schedule for a Middle School Counseling Program

Schedule for September

Beginning Date	Activity	Persons Responsible	Date Completed
September 1	Sixth grade student orientation	Counselors, sixth grade teachers, and peer helpers	September 20
September 1	Other new student orientation	Counselors and peer helpers	September 15
September 10	Schedule for individual counseling	Counselors	September 20
September 10	Screen students for October and November small groups	Counselors	September 20
September 15	Last year in review: successes and challenges	All teacher-advisor groups	September 30
September 15	"To Your Health" (sixth grade)	School nurse	October 30
September 20	First "Parents and Students in Transition" night (eighth grade)	Administrators, eighth grade teachers, and counselors	September 20
September 15	Career exploration classes (seventh grade)	Counselors and teachers	October 30

Recruiting school volunteers allows teachers and counselors to devote more time to their primary functions in the instructional and counseling programs. Coordination, training, and monitoring all these volunteer services is important, and your advisory committee can help you establish procedures and identify volunteer coordinators to assist with this effort. One caveat is that you do not want to create a program that, although intended to help you balance your time, becomes a drain on the limited time you have available. For example, you would not want to create a volunteer tutoring program that takes an inordinate amount of your time calling volunteers, scheduling students, and performing other tasks that take you away from other vital services. Program coordination is essential.

All the elements present in this chapter and in Chapter One set the stage for establishing a comprehensive program. You have learned how to describe and define a program, obtain input from teachers and administrators in your school, create a clear identity for yourself as a school counselor, and use time efficiently. Now that the school is ready for a comprehensive program, it is time to examine the script—how to plan and organize the activities and services you will perform and deliver.

chapter 3

SETTING SAIL *and* STAYING AFLOAT

Scenario 3.1: You've Got It Good!

A new teacher in your school laments, "I feel so much pressure to perform. With end-of-grade test results, my supervisor's classroom observations, and the principal's unannounced visits, it seems like I am constantly being evaluated. You have it good, don't you?" As a counselor, how would you demonstrate what you do, and how would you evaluate your effectiveness in helping students with their academic development?

Information in this chapter will assist you in responding to the new teacher in the above scenario and to others who ask about your role and effectiveness in the school. This chapter presents ideas for program planning, organization, and evaluation that may help you explain your role as a school counselor.

By describing and identifying a program of responsive services, you take the initial step toward getting ready to set sail. The next step is to plan and organize appropriate services to bring the program to life—to set full sail with your program and learn to stay afloat.

This chapter reviews aspects of program planning, including assessment procedures, organizational structures, and evaluation processes, and it suggests strategies for coordinating a comprehensive school counseling program. As discussed in the previous chapter, coordination is essential to the overall organization and success of a school counseling program. You demonstrate your coordination abilities by efficiently using a variety of skills, including scheduling, decision making, team building, program planning, and evaluating. Your use of these and other skills begins with planning, which is a critical function of effective elementary and middle school counselors.

PLANNING

Having a clear direction is important in your life and in planning a comprehensive school counseling program. You have probably heard the refrain, "If you do not know which direction you are heading, you will likely end up somewhere that you did not intend to be." If you are unsure of the direction and focus of your program, you will find it difficult to create effective, comprehensive services for students, parents, and teachers. In addition, two corollaries to the axiom above are

- If you do not know where you have been, you probably do not know where you are.
- If you do not know where you are, you probably do not know where you are going.

When planning a comprehensive counseling program, it is helpful to evaluate where the program has been in the past and what its present direction includes. Some services that were effective in the past may be retained in the present program; others might be eliminated or revised.

Assessing the Program

Chapter One presented some questions for interviewing your principal about a comprehensive program. Through such a process, you will gather information about past activities and services, current needs of the school's populations, and expectations for the future of the program. Information about these three areas reveals important aspects of your school and the counseling program, and will help you formulate assessment questions, such as the following:

- What responsive services and other activities are valued by the school community?
- What are the needs of students, parents, teachers, and others?
- What results are expected from the services and other activities of a school counseling program?

In the same way that you interview the principal, you could also design questions for teachers, parents, and students. Whether you are replacing a counselor or are continuing in a position, such surveys could gather information to help in planning a comprehensive program. What follows are some sample questions you might want to ask each of these groups if you are replacing a counselor who had served the school in past years.

Questions for Teachers

- What is the most valuable service delivered by the school counselor?
- Why is this service valuable?
- What service or activity would you want to increase this coming year?
- Are there additional services or activities you would like to have this coming year?

Questions for Parents

- What do you know about the school counseling program?
- Has your child benefited from any counseling service or activity at school?
- Have you participated in any activity of the counseling program?
- What are the most valuable services of the school counseling program?

Questions for Students

- Did you like anything that the counselor did in your school last year?
- What did the counselor do that you liked?
- Is there anything that the counselor did that you did not like?
- If a friend had a problem, would you encourage her or him to talk with the counselor?

You will need to design methods of assessing current needs of students, parents, teachers, and others. This could be done informally or formally. To collect this information in more formal processes, counselors often use questionnaires and surveys. An advisory committee can assist in designing some questionnaires. For students and parents, you may want to sample populations by choosing a certain percentage, say 10 to 20 percent, at each grade level. Such sample groups will give you data to evaluate needs across the entire school. With teachers, I recommend a survey of the entire staff, if possible. Here are a few hints for designing assessment questionnaires:

- Limit the number of questions and assess a few specific areas and services.
- Try out the survey with a "test group" to check for clarity of the items.
- Read the students' survey aloud to young children (primary grades) or students with reading difficulties.
- Word survey items in positive rather than negative language. Avoid "not," "don't," "doesn't," "won't," and other unenthusiastic terms.
- Design objective items that people can answer by checking a response rather than by writing lengthy answers.

Worksheets 3.1, 3.2, and 3.3 are sample questionnaires for students, parents, and teachers. The student form is for primary children and can be adapted for older students by rewording items and using the responses "Yes," "No," and "Sometimes" in place of the smiley faces.

Primary Student Needs Assessment

Name: _____ Date: _____

Instructions: Listen to the teacher or counselor as she or he reads each question to you. Circle the face that shows how you would answer the question.

1. I like coming to this school.

2. I am happy with my work.

3. I like my teacher.

4. I have many friends.

5. I like riding the bus to school.

6. I am happy in my family.

7. I like to look at books.

8. I like showing my parents my schoolwork.

9. My friends like me.

10. I am happy when I go home from school.

Middle School Parent Needs Assessment

Name: _____ Date: _____

Child's name: _____

Instructions: Please complete this questionnaire and return it to the counselor's office at the school. Thank you.

Circle your responses:

1.	My child needs to focus more on schoolwork.	Yes	No	Sometimes
2.	My child chooses responsible friends.	Yes	No	Sometimes
3.	My child enjoys school.	Yes	No	Sometimes
4.	I help my child with homework.	Yes	No	Sometimes
5.	My child does well in schoolwork.	Yes	No	Sometimes
6.	My child spends too much time alone.	Yes	No	Sometimes
7.	My child fights with other children too much.	Yes	No	Sometimes
8.	My child is very hard on himself or herself and occasionally self-injures.	Yes	No	Sometimes
9.	My child spends too much time on the computer, the cell phone, a listening device, or other technology.	Yes	No	Sometimes
10.	My child gets along with most teachers.	Yes	No	Sometimes
11.	I would like to be involved in parent programs at school to help me learn about my child.	Yes	No	Sometimes
12.	I am interested in volunteering in school.	Yes	No	Sometimes

Teacher Needs Assessment

Name: _____ Date: _____

Instructions: Please circle the responses that describe what you would like to see for students and yourself this year. Thank you.

1. Students need more opportunities for group counseling.   Yes   No   Unsure

2. More individual counseling is needed for students.   Yes   No   Unsure

3. Parent education programs are helpful.   Yes   No   Unsure

4. I would like to use peer helpers in my classroom.   Yes   No   Unsure

5. I want more conferences with the counselor.   Yes   No   Unsure

6. I need more information about students who receive services from the counselor.   Yes   No   Unsure

7. I want to do classroom guidance with the counselor.   Yes   No   Unsure

I suggest the following classroom guidance topics for this year: _____

_____

_____

I would like in-service on the following topics this year: _____

_____

_____

In addition to assessing the needs of students, parents, and teachers, you also want to evaluate the overall school climate. Research has shown that a school's learning atmosphere correlates with student achievement. Student success and progress are enhanced to the degree that your school establishes a positive, optimistic, and caring climate and invites all children to learn (Purkey & Novak, 2008). Conversely, schools with punitive and negative climates have the potential to become bastions of disruption, vandalism, low self-esteem, and poor performance.

Ask your advisory committee to design a process for assessing school climate. Do students, parents, and teachers feel welcome in their school? Are they comfortable in the school surroundings? Do they feel safe? Staff morale, student learning, and parental involvement are all influenced by "atmospheric conditions" in the school. When the places in which we learn and work demonstrate caring, respect, and value for our well-being, we are more likely to achieve our educational goals. The International Alliance for Invitational Education has developed a research-based survey, which your school can purchase or your committee could download a sample copy from the Alliance's Web site to use in designing its own survey (go to www.invitationaleducation.net for information).

To help your school focus on positive ways to improve the learning climate, design assessment processes to seek input from students, parents, and teachers. Worksheet 3.4 offers one example of a student survey. The results from such a questionnaire could help you and others in your school plan strategies to improve relationships, enhance the school's physical appearance, and create an optimal learning environment.

When you have completed an assessment of the school environment with students, parents, and teachers, summarize these findings and report them to the principal and faculty. These results will help you begin the next phase of planning—organizing a comprehensive counseling program.

Organizing the Program

Data from an accurate needs assessment enable you to

- Set priorities
- Identify program goals and objectives
- Select strategies and assign activities
- Design the counseling center
- Schedule your time

In consultation with your advisory committee and principal, identify the responsive services most needed in the counseling program. The most needed services are not determined simply by assessing the desires of the staff. Instead, choose them to reflect the needs of students and parents and to fit the realities of the resources and personnel available to deliver them effectively in the school. All these factors are important to consider as you set program priorities.

School Climate Survey

Instructions: Please read each of the following questions and circle your response to each question (*Yes* or *No*). Thank you.

1. Are you treated kindly in your school?   Yes   No

2. Is your school a friendly place?   Yes   No

3. Are you able to learn in your classroom?   Yes   No

4. Do the teachers listen to students?   Yes   No

5. Is your school neat and clean?   Yes   No

6. Are parents invited to your school?   Yes   No

7. Do parents and other people volunteer in your school?   Yes   No

8. Does the air smell fresh in your school?   Yes   No

9. Is the cafeteria a good place to eat lunch?   Yes   No

10. Is the playground safe and fun?   Yes   No

11. Do you have a school newspaper or newsletter?   Yes   No

12. Do people say nice things about your school?   Yes   No

13. Do teachers have enough materials for all students?   Yes   No

14. Is the counselor's room a good place to go?   Yes   No

15. Do students treat one another well?   Yes   No

16. Are girls and boys treated the same in your school?   Yes   No

17. Are you told about the rules in your school?   Yes   No

18. Are the rules in your school fair to everyone?   Yes   No

19. Is your media center a good place to find books and
    other resources?   Yes   No

20. Do you feel safe in your school?   Yes   No

Set Priorities, Identify Goals, and Select Strategies

Priorities set the stage for you to establish program goals and objectives. These goals are not restricted to what you will do specifically in your counseling role during the year. Rather, they are global goals for the entire school and for teachers and students alike. In this way, the activities and services you deliver as a counselor are supported and complemented by the activities of classroom teachers and other professionals in the school. In addition to teachers, you may want to include other student services professionals, such as the school social worker, nurse, and psychologist, to show how they contribute to the program. Worksheet 3.5 illustrates a format to use in designing your annual plan of goals and objectives. You can expand this form to include more goals and objectives. You might also create a timetable for meeting specific goals.

Your state or local school system may already have identified goals and objectives for student development, guidance, and counseling services. In addition, the ASCA National Model could be a helpful guide in this process (www.schoolcounselor.org). Generally, your advisory committee will develop goals across the following student development areas:

- Student educational planning
- Student learning and academic achievement
- Student career development
- Student personal and social development

After you set priorities and establish goals for the program, decide about specific activities and strategies to reach these objectives. Once you have chosen the strategies, assign responsibilities to ensure that these activities are implemented. As mentioned, a comprehensive school counseling program consists of a variety of responsive services and activities offered by counselors, teachers, parent volunteers, student helpers, and others. A well-organized program clearly delineates services and assigns responsibilities to appropriate parties. An advisory committee can be influential in helping you convince the school principal and faculty of the importance of these assignments, and you and your committee members can then advocate for wide participation and involvement of teachers in the counseling program.

Design a Counseling Center

The services and activities assigned to you help establish your daily schedule. They also have an influence on the counseling center that you design for your school. You want to design a counseling center that serves different populations of your school community efficiently. In some elementary and middle schools, the challenge of designing a functional counseling center seems an insurmountable task. Perhaps the space or room you are currently assigned looks nothing like an ideal counseling office. Yet the degree to which you are able to make your space organized, appealing, and functional is a measure of your ability to personalize your program and, in effect, survive as a counselor.

Annual Planning Sheet

Priority	Goals and Objectives	Teacher Activities	Counselor Activities
_____	Goal:		
	Objectives: _____	_____	_____
	_____	_____	_____
_____	Goal:		
	Objectives: _____	_____	_____
	_____	_____	_____
_____	Goal:		
	Objectives: _____	_____	_____
	_____	_____	_____

Many older elementary and middle schools were designed and constructed without counseling programs in mind. As a result, adequate facilities are sometimes unavailable. In my years of supervising school counselors, it was commonplace to find counseling centers established in broom closets, boiler rooms, off the stage, in a corner of the cafeteria, and other inadequate locations. Nevertheless, counselors worked in these spaces and attempted to meet the expectations of administrators to have comprehensive programs and deliver effective services. Perhaps you can identify with these types of facilities.

Whatever your situation, encourage yourself to "see the possibilities." Privacy, comfort, and function may have to be compromised to some degree, but if you are a survivor, you will be able to look at broom closets, boiler rooms, and classrooms and envision functional and productive counseling centers. Ask your teaching colleagues for their ideas. Teachers are a most resourceful group because they, too, often make do with inadequate space and facilities.

Choosing furniture for a counseling center can be challenging because of the different populations served. For example, in an elementary school that includes kindergarten through third grade, you want small tables and chairs that "fit" young children. Yet you will also be consulting with parents and teachers, for whom it is appropriate to have a few full-size chairs. Furthermore, some elementary schools include a wide range of grade levels, beginning with kindergarten and going as high as eighth grade. The furniture in a counseling center should reflect the age range of those served as much as possible.

The layout and arrangement of an elementary or middle school counseling center depend on the available facilities and the developmental needs of students. Figures 3.1

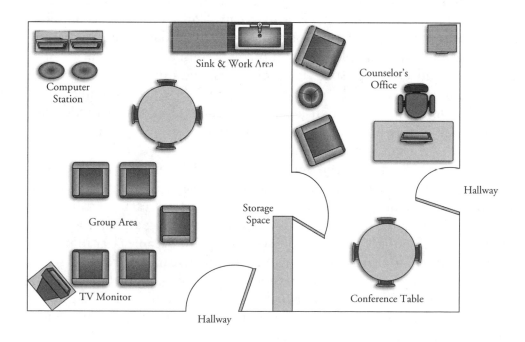

FIGURE 3.1

Elementary School Counseling Center

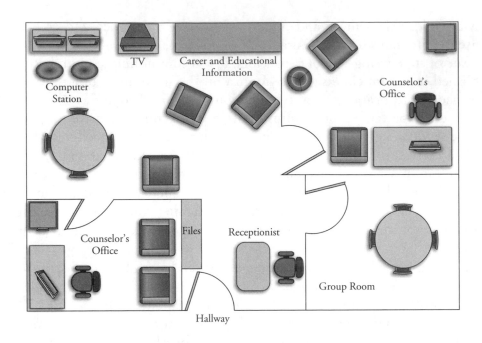

FIGURE 3.2

Middle School Counseling Center

and 3.2 illustrate two sample floor plans for elementary and middle school counseling centers, respectively. Figure 3.1 is a diagram of an elementary counseling center that includes space for individual sessions, small-group guidance and counseling, computer-assisted learning, video and PowerPoint presentations, and hands-on activities. The center has a private office; storage space for games, kits, and other materials; and a cleanup area with a counter and sink. The diagram in Figure 3.2 depicts a middle school counseling center that includes a reception area, offices for two counselors, and space for group guidance and counseling. In addition, this center has computers, a TV monitor, and displays for educational and career information.

Another important point about setting up and furnishing your counseling center is that it must be user friendly. As with all other spaces in a school, a counseling center encourages and invites patrons to enter and use the services and facilities available. Your comfort is important, too, but not at the expense of being available and accessible to the clients whom the program intends to serve. This point became clear to me when I revisited a school counseling center where I had been a few years before. The school had a new counselor, and my immediate impression upon walking into the counseling center was how open and friendly it was compared to what I remembered. The prior counselor had structured the center in a way that made it less inviting and accessible to students and others. She had valued privacy over function.

For counselors, students, and others, privacy is important at times, but if it dominates your vision for a counseling center, the need for privacy may become a barrier for everyone. As an illustration, Figures 3.3 and 3.4 show the same space designed differently. Figure 3.3

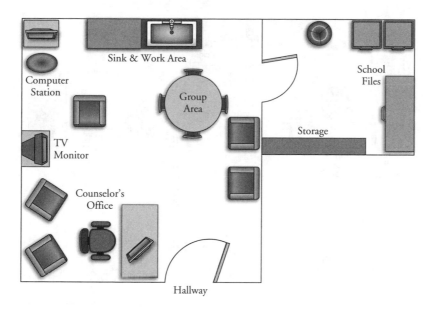

FIGURE 3.3

Inaccessible Counseling Center

shows a center that is limited in its openness and accessibility because the counselor's office dominates the available space. When the counselor is in a private session, the "In Conference" sign hangs on the outer door, discouraging people from entering. If teachers or other staff members need to get school files, they have to wait until the office is open to them. In contrast, the center shown in Figure 3.4 allows the counselor to use minimal space for private sessions, leaving the main room open for students and others to enter and wait to see the counselor, browse through materials, play with games and toys, or retrieve school records. (Files would be locked for security, and teachers and other staff would have access to keys.)

Schedule Your Time

In Chapter Two, you learned about how to efficiently schedule your time. The challenge of getting control of your time will come up again in the next chapter because of its importance in coordinating counseling services. A well-organized program and counseling center facilitate your ability to schedule events, set appointments, and generally manage how you provide leadership to the program while delivering responsive services each day. A graduate student once said, "You don't manage time, you schedule it. Time exists in the same amount and in exactly the same way for everyone." It is an interesting perspective. Although you cannot really manage time, you can use what time you have efficiently by scheduling things to do.

By organizing the program and counseling center efficiently, teachers will identify with the counseling program and understand their role in helping meet program goals and objectives. This understanding helps solidify teacher support and places you in a stronger position to evaluate services.

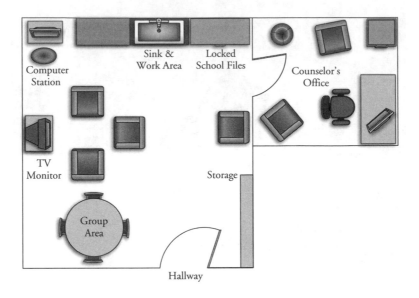

FIGURE 3.4

Accessible Counseling Center

Evaluating Services

To ensure that the responsive services you and the teachers provide hit the mark, you want to move on from scheduling time to the next stage of planning by evaluating program effectiveness. The credibility and acceptance of your counseling program depend on how others perceive its value and worth. Program evaluation is essential to your survival and career satisfaction as a school counselor. It helps you reassess and reorganize services such that they meet the future needs of students, parents, teachers, and others.

In implementing ongoing evaluation methods to assess the effectiveness and timeliness of services and activities, focus on two important aspects of your counseling services: the quantity and quality of service. Both aspects have importance in the assessment process.

Evaluating quantity means accounting for the time you spend in program activities and responsive services. By accounting for your time, you assess how the counseling schedule aligns with program priorities selected by you, an advisory committee, and the staff. If you are spending time in activities that are unrelated to these predetermined priorities, you should reexamine program goals and decide what adjustments to make in your schedule in order to meet the intended goals of the counseling program.

One way of accounting for your time is to keep weekly or monthly activity logs. Worksheet 3.6 is one example of a monthly report for a middle school counselor. You can adapt this form to design your own report. Some counselors gather this information to share with their administrators and teachers. You might do that or simply compile it for your own edification.

Middle School Counselor Monthly Report

Instructions: Record information on the appropriate blanks for each item. If an activity was not performed during the month, record *N/A*.

1. Number of individual counseling sessions _____

2. Number of group counseling sessions _____

3. Number of small-group guidance sessions _____

4. Number of teacher consultations (including group meetings) _____

5. Number of parent conferences _____

6. Number of classroom guidance sessions _____

7. Number of parent education group sessions

8. Number of observations (classrooms or elsewhere) _____

9. Number of individual student appraisals (testing, interest inventories, and so on) _____

10. Number of group assessment sessions (for example, group testing) _____

11. Number of extracurricular meetings (clubs, athletics) _____

12. Number of referrals to school system services and community agencies _____

13. Number of meetings attended _____

14. Number of teacher workshop presentations _____

Workshop topics: _____

_____

15. Number of other leadership activities or events coordinated during the month _____

Topics: _____

_____

Evaluating the quality of your services is more elusive than accounting for your time. Elementary and middle school counselors who are concerned about the effectiveness of their responsive services usually design methods to assess activities on an ongoing basis, as well as at the end of the school year. Methods of ongoing evaluation include

- Holding regular conferences with the principal and teachers
- Following up on teacher and parent consultations
- Receiving incidental feedback from administrators, students, parents, and teachers
- Receiving written evaluations from students, parents, and teachers

Develop ongoing evaluation processes and revise them throughout the year. By collecting formal evaluations from students, parents, and teachers about specific services, you will be able to share the results with the administration and faculty. Sharing results accomplishes two important goals: (1) it tells your principal and teachers that you value their opinions about your role and performance in the school, and (2) it lets them see the effects of your services and the counseling program. Your willingness to share this information contains some risk, but you will be rewarded in the long run.

Ongoing evaluation methods can also ask students to rate direct services they receive from you. Worksheet 3.7 presents a sample questionnaire for middle school students who have participated in a group counseling program. You can create forms to survey students about individual counseling; classroom guidance; and special events, such as Career Days, Friendship Week, or Drug Education Week. The opportunity for evaluation is limitless in a comprehensive program due to the wide range of activities and services offered.

One way to give teachers the opportunity to provide feedback about the effects of services is to ask them about behavior changes they have observed in students. For example, you can use Worksheet 3.8 to receive teacher input about students who have received individual counseling. Send these forms to teachers at different times during the year and summarize the results to let teachers and administrators know about the progress of particular students and about students receiving individual counseling in general. The summary should indicate how many students improved, how many stayed the same, how many regressed, and the average progress for the total group.

As you can see from the worksheets in this section, some of the forms you create might be primitive assessment tools. You should not intend these for scientific research (although with some additional effort, they could be). Nevertheless, such forms will demonstrate to you and your school whether or not students, parents, and teachers value the services of a comprehensive counseling program. Things that people value tend to last, and counselors who are valued tend to survive and flourish.

Another process in program evaluation is asking students, parents, and teachers to complete an annual survey about your counseling services. The results of these surveys often help in determining goals and objectives for the coming year. As with needs assessments, you do not have to survey every student and parent to evaluate your program. Sample groups of students and parents are sufficient. I do suggest, however, that you survey every teacher for your end-of-the-year evaluation.

Group Counseling Evaluation

Instructions: Circle your response to each question.

1. Did you ask to be in this group?   Yes   No   Maybe

2. Did you like being in the group?   Yes   No   Maybe

3. Did the group help you?   Yes   No   Maybe

4. Did you learn any new ways to behave?   Yes   No   Maybe

5. Were you able to help any members of the group?   Yes   No   Maybe

6. Would you want to be in future groups?   Yes   No   Maybe

7. Would you recommend groups like this one to your friends?   Yes   No   Maybe

Teacher Form for Individual Counseling Evaluation

In (month) of this year, you referred (student) for individual counseling because (identified concern). Please place a check on the line below to indicate your observations about the progress made with this student. When completed, return the form to the counselor's mailbox in a sealed envelope. Thank you for your assistance.

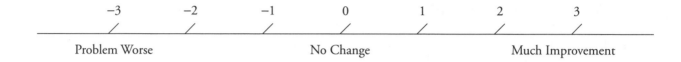

| −3 | −2 | −1 | 0 | 1 | 2 | 3 |

Problem Worse   No Change   Much Improvement

Tailor surveys to the sample groups you select. For example, if you want to survey parents who have actually used the services of the program, you would write questions specifically for that group of parents. Worksheets 3.9, 3.10, and 3.11 are examples of student, parent, and teacher evaluation questionnaires, respectively, to use as starters for designing your own instruments.

The three components of program planning presented here—assessing, organizing, and evaluating—will help you sail forth with the counseling program. Because you offer a variety of services, you also want to keep the program afloat. To do so, you establish efficient program coordination. This is a major challenge to your survival as an elementary or middle school counselor.

COORDINATING

By now it is probably apparent to you that all the activities and services of a comprehensive school counseling program require considerable coordination. Coordination consists of a wide range of behaviors and processes to ensure that each service, event, or project is planned, implemented, and evaluated satisfactorily. One study of elementary and middle school counselors identified about twenty activities that counselors orchestrated, representing a wide range of coordinating responsibilities. In practice, the actual list is probably longer because, as noted already, every service and activity included in a school counseling program requires some level of coordination. When coordinating the program, you want to organize information and services for students, parents, and teachers in a way that facilitates appropriate educational planning and adequate assistance yet avoids duplication of services.

This section looks at several activities related to program coordination. The examples are presented to assist you in "staying afloat" as you set sail with your elementary or middle school counseling program. Once the program is under way, you will discover and create further management strategies to be successful. The key to coordinating the wide range of services in your program is your ability to be organized. With today's technology, there are numerous software programs available to assist you with scheduling and time management. Here are a few tips on how to begin getting organized:

- *Keep a daily calendar.* The first thing each morning, review your schedule for the day. Scan the next two or three days to prepare for upcoming events.
- *Write a daily to-do list.* Put down the most important five to ten activities to accomplish that day and rank them in the order you will do them. Stick to your list!
- *Open a helper file.* Record names of students, parents, and teachers who are willing and able to assist with program activities.
- *Keep a reminder notebook or handheld electronic organizer.* As you remember tasks to do, jot them down. At the end the day, add any remaining items from the reminder notebook to your to-do list for tomorrow.
- *Break down major assignments into manageable tasks.* For example, if you are planning a parent education program for next month, you could list the following tasks: set a date, schedule the auditorium, ask the media specialist for a VCR or PowerPoint equipment.

Student Evaluation of a Middle School Counseling Program

Instructions: Please circle the response that best answers each question. Your answers will help us plan future counseling services and program activities. Write at the bottom of this questionnaire any comments or suggestions you may have for improving the counseling program.

1. Do you know who your school counselor is?	Yes	No	Unsure
2. When you began in this school, did you feel welcomed?	Yes	No	Unsure
3. Are you able to see the counselor when you want to?	Yes	No	Unsure
4. Has the counselor met alone with you this year?	Yes	No	Unsure
5. Has the counselor met with you in a group?	Yes	No	Unsure
6. Has your parent or guardian met with the counselor this year?	Yes	No	Unsure
7. Does the counselor come to your classroom and present information with your teacher?	Yes	No	Unsure
8. Does the school have a peer helper program?	Yes	No	Unsure
9. Has the counselor shared information about test results?	Yes	No	Unsure
10. Has the counselor shared information about jobs and careers with you?	Yes	No	Unsure
11. Has the counselor helped you solve any problems?	Yes	No	Unsure
12. Would you recommend the counselor to friends?	Yes	No	Unsure

Additional comments or suggestions: _____

_____

_____

Parent Evaluation Form

Name (optional): _____ Date: _____

Child's name (optional): _____

Instructions: Please complete this opinion form to help us plan future services for the school counseling program. Circle your responses for each question. Return the completed form to the school counseling office. Thank you for your help.

1.	Do you know the counselor at school?	Yes	No	Unsure
2.	Have you talked with your child's counselor?	Yes	No	Unsure
3.	Has the counselor helped you or your child?	Yes	No	Unsure
4.	Is the counselor available to all students?	Yes	No	Unsure
5.	Would you like more information about the counseling program?	Yes	No	Unsure
6.	Has your child been in a group with the counselor?	Yes	No	Unsure
7.	Does the counselor follow through on your requests?	Yes	No	Unsure
8.	Have you participated in programs for parents presented by the counselor?	Yes	No	Unsure
9.	Are programs presented by the counselor helpful?	Yes	No	Unsure
10.	Are school counseling services important?	Yes	No	Unsure
11.	Has the counselor shared test results or other information about your child?	Yes	No	Unsure
12.	Has the counselor met with you about your child's educational progress?	Yes	No	Unsure

Teacher Evaluation Form

Instructions: Please complete this form to help us assess the counseling program this year. Circle your responses to each question. You may write comments and suggestions for future program plans below or on the back of the form. Thank you for your assistance.

1. Does individual counseling help students?	Yes	No	Sometimes
2. Does group counseling help students?	Yes	No	Sometimes
3. Is the counselor available to all students?	Yes	No	Sometimes
4. Does the counselor provide meaningful feedback to you about student progress in counseling?	Yes	No	Sometimes
5. Does the counselor ask teachers for input concerning the counseling program?	Yes	No	Sometimes
6. Has the counselor been available to consult with you when necessary?	Yes	No	Sometimes
7. Does the counselor communicate effectively with students?	Yes	No	Sometimes
8. Does the counselor communicate effectively with parents?	Yes	No	Sometimes
9. Does the counselor follow through on referrals?	Yes	No	Sometimes
10. Has the counselor presented guidance activities in class with you this year?	Yes	No	Sometimes
11. Has the counselor provided material and resources for you to use in classroom guidance?	Yes	No	Sometimes
12. Has the counselor helped you plan ways to integrate guidance into your daily lessons?	Yes	No	Sometimes

Scheduling, organizing, and coordinating skills help you keep track of the goals and activities for your counseling program. These skills also help you manage and coordinate ongoing activities, such as receiving referrals; scheduling responsive services; keeping records; following up cases; organizing a peer helper program; using volunteers; orienting students, parents, and teachers; and coordinating teacher advisement programs. Let us now consider each of these activities.

Receiving Referrals

As an elementary or middle school counselor, you have primary responsibility for providing direct responsive services to students who are experiencing educational, personal, or social difficulties. Sometimes these students come to you because they realize there is a problem and hope that a counselor can help them. Other times, teachers and parents will ask you to see a child. In either case, you want to have a procedure in place to receive referrals in a timely manner.

The following are some suggestions for receiving referrals:

- *Place a secure mailbox outside your counseling center.* This way, when students, parents, and teachers stop by and you are temporarily unavailable, they can leave a note or referral slip. Check your box during the day so that immediate concerns do not go unnoticed.
- *Design a brochure for parents to receive at PTA or PTO meetings or for children to bring home.* The brochure can include information about how parents can reach you at school and the best times to contact you. List your counseling center Web site and phone number.
- *Ask your advisory committee to help you design a referral form for teachers to use.* Teachers can put these forms in your mailbox in the school office, or you can make a daily tour around the building so that teachers can give them to you personally. Worksheet 3.12 is one example of a referral form. Make it simple. Avoid asking the teachers to fill out lengthy questionnaires or write long explanations. Teachers' time is a valuable commodity.
- Use technology, such as e-mail, in place of paper-and-pencil referrals. Be sure to set up secure accounts to protect people's privacy.

Scheduling Services

As discussed earlier, because you are responsible for a wide range of services and activities, a schedule is essential to managing your time efficiently. It also helps you maintain a direction for the counseling program. With a schedule, you have reasonable control of what will happen and when it will happen.

Teacher Referral Form

To: (counselor's name)
From: (teacher's name)
Date:
Re: (student's name)

I am referring the above-named student for the reason(s) checked below:

_____ self-concept	_____ test grades	_____ friends
_____ fighting	_____ inattentiveness	_____ absences
_____ hyperactive	_____ class work	_____ homework
_____ family concerns	_____ withdrawn	_____ unhappy
_____ bullying	_____ anxious in class	_____ depressed
_____ always tired	_____ worried	_____ shyness

Other concerns: _____

_____

Comments: _____

_____

The best time for me to meet about this student is: _____

When setting your schedule, be sure to request input from teachers about the best time of day or best day of the week for particular services and events to occur. Teachers at different grade levels can let you know their instructional schedules so you can plan appropriate times to see students individually, schedule groups, hold parent meetings, and so forth. Because so much goes on in elementary and middle schools, it is impossible to avoid some scheduling conflicts. By asking for teacher input, however, you minimize the likelihood that counseling services and activities will interfere with the instructional program.

Keeping Records

A counselor's file, with the names of and information about students with whom you have contact, is an important part of your record keeping. This file is not part of the cumulative records. Rather, it is a confidential index of what you have done and what you need to do to assist children when you receive referrals.

One way to coordinate this information is to keep a file of index cards. As you follow each case, write brief notes about what you have done and what you plan to do next to help the student. Use caution when recording details of a case or confidential information revealed to you. You only need a file to recall what direction the relationship is going and for coordination purposes, so detailed accounts are unnecessary. A sample case card is provided in Exhibit 3.1.

EXHIBIT 3.1

Sample Case Card

Student: *Billy Jones*   Concern: *Peer relationships*

Date	Notes
9/10	First individual session. No one wants to be his friend.
10/12	Second session. Explored how to make friends; role-played.
10/30	Third session. Asked if he would like to form a group to work on friendships together. Made a list of potential group members.
11/3	Interviewed potential members of Billy's group.
11/10	First group session. Set ground rules and agreed on group goals. Billy said he liked being in the group.

Following Up

Most of the responsive services you provide are attempts to bring about some beneficial behavior change on the part of students, parents, or teachers. To ensure that these services are on target, you want to follow up with all the people involved. When you take on large caseloads, as do many elementary and middle school counselors, this process of following up may seem like an insurmountable task. One suggestion is to take time once a week to consult your counselor's file and identify a few cases that you will follow up.

It may be helpful to follow up on a specific number of cases each week. Depending on the cases' nature and who made the referrals, decide which follow-up activities to use. For example, if you are seeing Johnny in group counseling because his mother called about his lack of friends, you might call Johnny's mom and ask how things are going at home. You could also ask Johnny's teachers if they have noticed any changes in his peer relationships at school.

After you do a follow-up activity, record what you did on the case card in your file. This helps you keep track of what you have done and documents your follow-up activities. One rule of thumb to assist you with follow-up activities is for you to go back to the source of the referral within two weeks, and keep in touch at least once a month after that. Usually you can accomplish these contact activities with brief phone calls, e-mail messages, or personal conversations that let each party know what you have done and what progress you and others have observed.

Organizing a Peer Helper Program

In past years, professional literature has described and promoted peer helper programs as part of comprehensive school counseling programs. Although research about such programs is at best inconclusive, evidence exists that some schools and counselors across the nation are using them. While doing research for this edition of the *Survival Guide,* I received over 3,000 hits on an Internet search for "peer helper program." A few of these hits included individual school sites that explained peer helper programs and how they worked in particular schools. One site for information about peer helper programs is the National Association of Peer Program Professionals (NAPPP; formerly the National Peer Helpers Association) at www.peerprogramprofessionals.org. Among other services, NAPPP provides training and certification to individuals, programs, and consultants to help people and professionals establish and evaluate peer programs.

Elementary and middle school students are often available to help, and with some preparation can assist counselors with coordination of services. By establishing a peer helper program, you can recruit students to help new children become acquainted with the school, assist teachers with classroom guidance activities, work with the administration on improving school climate, tutor students in need of academic assistance, and provide other support throughout the school.

If you decide to establish a peer helper program, it will be necessary to design and plan ways to select and prepare your peer helpers. Teachers can help with this selection process, and there are several good resources for preparing students in peer helping. NAPPP publishes a journal, *Perspectives in Peer Programs,* and has made available past issues of its former publication, *The Peer Facilitator Quarterly.* It also publishes a newsletter. A series of books by Tindall (2008) and another by Varenhorst (2003) also provide useful information about preparing peer helpers.

Using Volunteers

Successful counselors are keenly aware of the demands on their time, and usually seek assistance from other people. In most communities, counselors find ample opportunities to tap volunteer groups willing to assist in schools. These volunteers include parents, retired citizens, and businesspeople, among others.

Parents and other adult volunteers can help counselors and teachers in a variety of ways. They can, for example, supervise in the cafeteria or on the playground to give teachers time to meet with the counselor and discuss program planning, student placement, or other issues. Volunteers can help the school secretary with clerical tasks and assist teachers by typing worksheets, designing instructional materials, and collecting school fees. They can also train to help with classroom guidance, supervise group testing, and greet children as receptionists in counseling centers.

Using volunteers in your school requires planning, coordination, and preparation. As the counselor, you can help with this effort. Let your advisory committee suggest ways that volunteers can help and ask committee members to assist in the planning and training of volunteers. Volunteer programs are discussed further in Chapter Eleven.

Orienting Students, Parents, and Teachers

Most schools admit new students, parents, and teachers each year. In today's mobile society, some schools admit new students every day. Another role for you, and for the student helpers and other volunteers who assist you, is to design ways to orient these new people to the school and to the counseling program. One idea is to compile a packet of materials for new elementary or middle school students that contains data about the school, including a building map; information about the town; and coupons and gifts, such as pencils, rulers, stickers, and other promotional goods supplied by local merchants. Orientation ideas similar to this one will help new students feel welcome, both at school and in the community.

Helping with School Transitions

Procedures to help students with transitions from one grade to another, from one school to another, and through many life-altering decisions are also important responsive services that you coordinate. These services are particularly helpful for elementary students who attend two or more schools before entering their middle school years. Begin early and plan transition activities with your teachers and administrators throughout the year. Contact the counselors at the feeder and receiving schools and make plans for a smooth transition.

A special issue of *Professional School Counseling* (Turner, 2007) provides an excellent resource on helping students at all school levels travel through various stages of schooling. It also has articles about using the ASCA National Model in helping students with transitions as well as articles that focus on working with inner-city youth, students with disabilities, rural adolescents, African American students, and Latino students, and on other concerns related to student development.

Coordinating a Teacher Advisement Program

In most elementary and middle schools, counselors have responsibility for many students. To help with advisement and follow-up for students, ask your principal about starting a teacher advisement program, also called a teacher advisory program (TAP). If your school already has one, be sure to get involved. If you are unfamiliar with TAPs, several schools have information about their programs on the Internet. A search of "teacher advisement programs" and "teacher advisory programs" yielded over 1,400 listings on the Web, many of which are the sites of individual schools. A classic resource on TAPs is the book *Nurturing a Teacher Advisory Program,* published by the National Middle School Association (Cole, 1992).

Teacher advisement programs assign each teacher in the school to a group of students, whom they assist with educational planning and academic progress. In some programs, teachers advise the same students throughout the years they attend the school. For example, in a middle school a teacher would be assigned a group of sixth graders one year and then be their advisor when they move to seventh and eighth grades the following years. This allows teachers and students to develop trustful relationships and helps teachers get to know the students well.

Teachers also provide developmental guidance for their advisees. In some middle schools, a specific time of the week is set aside for students to go as a group to their advisor's classroom for guidance activities. As the counselor, you can assist teachers by providing guidance topics, helping plan activities, locating resources, and copresenting these lessons with them.

Through individual advising and group guidance, teachers are able to assess student needs and refer students to counselors for additional or more intense services. This process of networking between you and the teachers contributes to the overall coordination of the school counseling program. As with other coordination activities, a teacher advisement program requires adequate preparation and training. Some teachers may need basic helping and facilitating skills to be effective as advisors, training that you can help plan and deliver.

Using Technology

The technology available today has many uses in schools and in comprehensive school counseling programs. Furthermore, you can expect that future technology will continue to help with information management; communication; student assessment; obtaining guidance information and instruction; and perhaps counseling and consulting with students, parents, and teachers. Here are samples of how emerging technology is influencing how schools and counselors do business today:

- *Web sites.* Almost every school has its own Web site today. Do you have a link on your school's site for the counseling program?

- *Chat rooms and e-mail discussion groups.* Advanced technology now allows voice and video formats for online communication. Chat rooms can take place in real time (synchronous) or at different times (asynchronous). Could this technology be useful in holding online parent discussions or after-school student groups in your program?
- *Listservs.* These are e-mail lists that students, parents, and others can join. Listservs are an economical way to contact a large number of people instantly, for example to notify people about upcoming school or program events. Is that a feature worth considering for your school or program?
- *Podcasts and webinars.* Both of these technologies provide ways to present instruction and information to individuals who are sitting at home or elsewhere and connected to the Internet. Do you see value in such technology to present parent education, peer helper training, or other information in an efficient manner?
- *Mass telephone messages.* This technology is in today's school systems. It is a way to send automated voice messages to students and families. If your school or system has this technology, what uses for it do you foresee in the school counseling program?

The above list shares only a fraction of the different types of technology that exist today in schools. Many more are available, and new ones are sure to emerge in the future (Bhat & Probasco, 2008). As with all new developments, you want to weigh the pros and cons when using advanced technology in a school counseling program. As you adopt and adapt technology to your program, here are some guidelines that might be helpful:

- *Be aware of ethical standards* developed by the American Counseling Association (ACA), the National Board of Certified Counselors (NBCC), and other organizations to help you use the Internet and other technologies appropriately.
- *Distance counseling,* the use of e-mail, chat rooms, and other technology to provide services and keep in contact with students and parents, may be a feature you want to have in the program. If so, obtain the proper license or other credential for doing so in your state or region. The NBCC's Web site is one resource for information: http://nbcc.org.
- *Stay abreast of professional trends and legal rulings* about using new technology for providing counseling services.
- *Maintain security* and encrypt conversations for confidential and privileged communications.
- *Screen assessment programs* and use those that demonstrate the same level of validity, reliability, and cultural sensitivity you expect from traditional assessment instruments.
- *Ensure that information* you post online and on your school's home page for the counseling program is up-to-date.
- *Be informed* about student and family access to the Internet and their basic computer knowledge.
- *Use traditional forms of communication* to contact students and families and disseminate information. This will ensure that students and families without ready access to computer technology remain informed about counseling services.

- *Help students, parents, and teachers learn* about the wealth of information on the Internet and how to discern the accuracy and usefulness of Web sites they enter.
- *Technology can assist* with the services you provide. It does not replace you, the essential human element, in helping students, parents, and teachers find and use information for educational, personal, and career development.

There are countless ideas and strategies beyond those mentioned here that can help you and your teachers plan and coordinate services and activities in the school counseling program. You may not use them all, but with input from teachers and administrators you should be able to choose ones that fit your program and school.

By planning and coordinating services and activities, you provide leadership for a comprehensive program. Your leadership is essential in helping distinguish among the various responsive services you offer and the purpose of each. Responsive services encompass an array of counseling, consulting, and appraising activities that enable you and teachers to react to and address the needs of students and parents. In Chapter Four, you will have the opportunity to review the responsive services of a typical school counseling program.

chapter 4

IDENTIFYING RESPONSIVE SERVICES

Scenario 4.1: School Anxiety

You are an elementary or middle school counselor. A father has called about his child or preadolescent daughter because she has suddenly become frightened about coming to school. According to the father, the advice, support, and encouragement that he and his wife have given the girl have not seemed to diminish her anxiety about school. She has missed several days of school as a result. He asks if you might see her to determine what to do to get her back to school on a regular basis. How would you handle this request? What additional information would you seek from the parents, teachers, and other sources? What responsive services might best help this student, and how would you proceed?

Within the structure of a comprehensive program, you provide specific functions and services that complement the overall educational program in your school. They are *responsive* services in the sense that you deliver them in response to some identified need or concern. These services—commonly categorized as counseling, consulting, and appraising services—identify the unique role of a professional school counselor, and distinguish you from other professionals in the school. Each of these three functions is important in a comprehensive school counseling program, and each consists of specific helping skills.

You have learned about theories and techniques of counseling, consultation, and student appraisal in your preparation as a school counselor. I will not repeat these important lessons here, but will explain how these three processes fit into a comprehensive school counseling program. No matter which of the helping approaches you choose and the counseling theories you embrace, you want to structure your theories and practices in a way that establishes a broad program of responsive services. Individual and group counseling; student, parent, and teacher consultations; and educational assessment each have a vital role in elementary and middle school programs. In this chapter, you will review each of these processes and their practical applications in elementary and middle schools. To begin, let us start with the namesake of our profession, the process of counseling.

COUNSELING

When I speak of *counseling*, I mean any helping relationship that includes the following qualities and characteristics:

- An individual or group process that focuses on specific personal, social, educational, or career objectives for the purpose of beneficial development or to remedy existing concerns.
- A process of helping a person or group move in positive directions toward specific goals.
- A confidential relationship. (You will learn more about the legal and ethical issues of confidentiality in Chapter Twelve.)
- A high level of professional skill, which allows a counselor to choose from a wide range of personal, behavioral, and therapeutic approaches to assist other people.
- An understanding of competencies necessary to deliver these responsive services and an appreciation of the limitations inherent in school environments and comprehensive programs for providing extensive counseling.

As you can see, these qualities and characteristics define counseling as a goal-directed helping process, requiring confidentiality and a high level of professional skill. In your elementary or middle school, you probably use counseling skills in three types of services: individual counseling with students, group counseling with students, and parent and teacher counseling. How you use each of these services and the amount of attention each one receives within the total program will define and describe in large part your role as a counselor in the school. Let us now consider each of these types of counseling services.

Individual Counseling

Many elementary and middle school students are assisted by counselors through individual relationships in a series of one-on-one sessions, typically twenty or more minutes in length depending on the age and maturity of the child, and usually scheduled once or twice a week. Most counseling with children in elementary and middle schools is developmental counseling, meaning that the focus is on normal developmental issues—peer relationships, feelings related to self-concept, relationships in the family, academic achievement, and career exploration among others. Sometimes, you will counsel students to remedy existing concerns or problems.

During these counseling sessions, you guide the child through the introduction, exploration, action, and closure stages of a helping relationship. Individual counseling relationships are most beneficial with elementary and middle school children when you consider the child's

- Language development
- Behavioral development
- Cognitive development
- Understanding of helping relationships

The above conditions are not unique to counseling with children. They also apply to individual helping relationships with older people. In most cases, and particularly with elementary and middle school students, these conditions have a significant impact on the success of individual counseling. Students who do not have adequate language development will benefit little from "talking" relationships. Similarly, children who cannot yet conceptualize their role and responsibility in forming relationships with others will struggle to accept the goals put forth in individual counseling. This is not to say that children with weak language and conceptual development cannot be helped through individual relationships, but in choosing individual approaches with these students you want to select carefully the activities and techniques to use.

Since the early years of elementary school counseling, experts in child counseling have debated whether individual counseling can help young children. In an early report, the American Personnel and Guidance Association (APGA; now the American Counseling Association) took the position that individual child counseling offered opportunities to

- Help children establish relationships to see themselves as worthwhile persons, learn about their development, and use this knowledge in setting goals for themselves
- Communicate with children by listening to what they have to say about themselves, others, and the world in which they live

The position of this early APGA report remains true for counseling children in schools today. Individual counseling is a beneficial service when you adequately assess the developmental level of each child and choose approaches accordingly. The content of the relationship and the techniques you choose are guided by the developmental level and needs of the individual child. With young children, for example, play activities often take the place of introductory verbal exchanges.

Once you decide to see a child for individual counseling, it is important to set clear goals. In their book *Counseling Children,* Thompson, Rudolph, and Henderson (2004) suggested that you first ask the following four questions:

1. What does the child identify as the primary problem?
2. How does the child feel about this problem?
3. How does the child rate the intensity of the problem on a scale of 1 (low) to 10 (high)?
4. What does the child expect to have happen about this problem in counseling?

By answering these questions during the introductory phase of the counseling relationship, you and the child will be able to set goals for the sessions, which will give the direction and structure that are essential to counseling in elementary and middle schools.

After you gather this information, you are ready to consider other developmental conditions, mentioned earlier, that enable you and the student to move the relationship in a beneficial direction. When counseling elementary and middle school students, this means deciding whether a strictly talking relationship is feasible, or whether other avenues of interaction are more appropriate. There are countless techniques and resources that counselors apply in individual helping relationships with children. They include role playing, bibliocounseling, drawing, listening to music, playing games, storytelling, and other methods of establishing relationships and communicating concerns. You can learn about these techniques by reading professional journals, attending conferences, visiting appropriate Web sites, and participating in workshops.

When counseling very young children, there are some practical factors to consider. Due to their egocentric perceptions, children have difficulty focusing in personal relationships, such as counseling. It is a challenge to help children focus on specific issues related to their own development and behavior. Their attention is short and children can frequently be distracted and wander off the subject. For this reason, it is appropriate to avoid wearing clothing, jewelry, and other accessories that distract a child's attention and to limit sessions to a reasonable length of approximately twenty to thirty minutes.

Sometimes children's perceptions inhibit their ability to focus on the issues raised by counselors, in that they may fail to see the identified concerns as problems. At these times, you can create exercises and adopt innovative techniques that deviate from the more popular talking approaches to counseling. For example, you might find therapeutic stories useful in working with reluctant and resistant children. Stories provide an entertaining avenue through which children can creatively deal with problems and concerns.

When starting a counseling relationship with a young child or preadolescent, a structured interview may help. In this interview, you will want to avoid too many closed questions, which often elicit limited, one-word responses, such as "Yes," "No," "Sometimes," and "Maybe." Use open-ended questions that encourage children and adolescents to elaborate on their answers. As noted earlier, a student's language development will influence your success in using a structured interview. Exhibit 4.1 presents a sample list of statements and questions to use in an initial interview with a child. Do not use all these statements and questions in a single interview, but rather be selective in the beginning. Invite the child to expand on them by following his or her responses with such phrases as "Tell me more about . . . ," "That sounds as though . . . ," and "You seem pleased to talk about . . ."

EXHIBIT 4.1

Interviewing Children

The following are sample questions to ask when beginning a counseling relationship with an elementary school student. Adjustments to these questions might be appropriate with middle school students.

1. Tell me about the people in your family. What are the names and ages of your brothers and sisters? Tell me what your brothers and sisters are like.
2. Talk about the home you live in. List some things you like and dislike about your home.
3. What about pets in your family? Who takes care of the pets?
4. If you could be an animal, what animal would you be?
5. Tell me about your favorite things—things you like most to do. What are the things you like least to do?
6. Tell me about sad things that have happened to you. How do you help yourself when you are sad?
7. Do some things scare you? What are they? What is it like to be scared?
8. Tell me what you think about school. Have you gone to other schools? Talk about those other schools.
9. What things do you like to learn about at school? What do you not like to learn about in school?
10. What are some ways that you help your family?
11. Tell me about your best friends. Why are they your friends?
12. If you could be a magician, what would you make disappear?
13. If you were a magician, what would you make appear? What would you do with this thing that appeared?
14. Of all the important things in your life, what one thing is the most important?
15. I have asked you many questions. Now you can ask me some. What would you like to know?

Another aspect of counseling with young children that differs from counseling with older clients is how you handle termination, or closure. You might make the decision to end a counseling relationship jointly, involving the child's parents and teachers. Prepare children for ending their counseling relationships with you by reviewing their thoughts and feelings about you as their counselor, reinforcing their successes and the progress they have made during the relationship, encouraging them to express their feelings about the sessions' coming to an end, and teaching them about other sources of support and assistance.

Before closing on the topic of individual counseling, a few points about middle school students are noteworthy. If you are a middle school counselor, you have observed that students at this level have higher verbal and conceptual skills than do younger children.

For this reason, individual counseling can include more verbal interaction between the counselor and student. Nevertheless, even though a preadolescent is more verbal, effective individual relationships will combine verbal counseling with other interactive techniques. Middle school students are action oriented, and the choices you incorporate into the counseling relationship are best if compatible with their development levels, just as with very young children. Artwork, role playing, stories, and other activities can facilitate helping relationships with preadolescents when they reflect the developmental needs and levels of these students.

Educational and other types of games are also appropriate for most middle school children and help to establish a relationship and move it toward verbal counseling. In this age of electronic advances, you might play games and activities with students on computers or through other interactive devices.

Middle school students differ from elementary children in their reliance on and interest in group activities. Preadolescents are much more aware of their peers and want to belong to the "group." Sometimes this desire to belong seems contradicted by the students' striving for independence and searching for individual identities. Added to these conflicts are the realities of students' changing bodies; the pressures they feel to excel in school, sports, and other ventures; and the uncertainty of interpersonal relationships, particularly those with the opposite sex.

Individual counseling with elementary and middle school students can address all the preceding concerns. Because school counselors typically have large caseloads and are responsible for many services in a comprehensive counseling program, many authorities advocate brief counseling approaches, to which we now turn (Murphy, 2008; Paterson, 2009; Schmidt, 2008; Sklare, 2005).

Brief Counseling

In recent years, many models of brief counseling have appeared in the literature and research, several aspects of which have merit for use in elementary and middle school counseling (Davis & Osborn, 2000; Murphy, 2008; Sklare, 2005). Brief counseling approaches limit the time spent in the relationship by attending to solutions to problems rather than dwelling on causes. These approaches are helpful in working with students to focus on immediate concerns and make appropriate educational and career plans. Although the explanation of brief counseling models may appear easy to understand, the implementation of such approaches is not necessarily so.

Brief approaches to counseling typically focus on specific concerns and behaviors that block students from making appropriate decisions. At the same time, they make the most of students' strengths and the successes they have had in handling other concerns. Most of these approaches are action oriented and use a sequence of steps in helping students explore their concerns, review what they have done to resolve the issue, and form action plans to move forward in a constructive manner. Such models of short-term counseling emphasize student independence, self-reliance, and self-responsibility, traits worthy of attention for all elementary and middle school students.

Exhibit 4.2 offers a list of generic steps, gleaned from several different models, that give an illustration of how you might use brief counseling in an elementary or middle school program. This generic model is only a sample, and you will need to visit the professional literature and research to become more familiar with tested models of brief counseling. As you examine and select (or develop) a model that suits your style and program, please keep this caveat in mind: brief counseling does not mean hasty help. Although efficiency is admirable with any counseling service, you always keep the best interests and well-being of students in the forefront of what you choose to do as a professional counselor. Brief counseling is not a call for unreasonable control, neglectful action, inappropriate manipulation, or any other behavior used simply to get things done faster. Brief counseling is practiced with all due attention to ethical standards of practice, as is any other service a school counselor provides to students, parents, and teachers.

EXHIBIT 4.2

Seven Steps to Brief Counseling

Models of brief counseling frequently use a series of questions to help students process information and make decisions to resolve issues and move forward. Here are sample questions compiled from various models of brief counseling.

1. How does the student describe the current problem or situation in observable terms? You might also ask the student to scale the level of concern about the situation from 1 (low) to 10 (high).
2. How would the student like this situation to change?
3. What has the student already tried to address or resolve this concern or situation?
4. Has the student thought of other behaviors or strategies that might help change this situation?
5. What will be different in the student's life if this problem or situation is resolved? You might ask the student to scale his or her response by choosing from 1 (not very different) to 10 (very much improved).
6. What immediate goal is the student willing to set to help create this difference?
7. What next step is the student willing to take to address this concern and reach this goal?

Brief counseling is an alternative to traditional forms of lecturing, punishing, analyzing situations, or explaining to students to help them make changes. It capitalizes on research findings indicating that change in counseling comes largely from the abilities and willingness that students bring to the counseling sessions (about 40 percent of factors that facilitate change). Another 30 percent comes from the relationships that counselors are able to establish with students; optimism and specific techniques (for example, relaxation, imagery, bibliocounseling, role play) combine to account for the remaining 30 percent

(Murphy, 2008). Brief counseling and other forms of individual counseling are vital to a comprehensive program. Equally important are group processes that allow you to help more students and can teach them to help each other.

Group Counseling

Although individual counseling is a useful strategy with most students, you eventually want to move toward a group process of helping them focus on developmental issues. Group counseling with both elementary and middle school children is an essential service of a comprehensive school counseling program.

One of the most important outcomes we can hope for in school counseling is to help children learn about helping others. Learning to help oneself is important, and learning to reach out and help others is an essential ingredient of a democratic society. Group counseling is a vital responsive service because it offers a setting in which you can assist several students, and in which the students, in turn, learn from and help one another.

There are two types of group formats: open and closed. An open group has members who come and go, and the sessions continue indefinitely. An example is an orientation group for new students, in which newly enrolled students come into the group while other students, now adjusted to the school, leave the group. In contrast, a closed group consists of a specific number of members who are screened and selected for that particular group and are expected to stay in the group through the final session. A closed group meets for a designated number of sessions and works through the phases of the helping relationship—introduction, exploration, action, and closure.

I recommend closed group counseling for most groups you establish with elementary and middle school students. Students at these levels function better when structure exists, such as a specific number of sessions, and relationships are clear. With open groups, members come and go, and there is little certainty about the interactions and relationships formed. A second reason for having closed groups is that schools are typically rigid organizations with precise schedules and traditional routines to follow. Counselors who attempt open group programs risk confrontations with teachers who want to know where their students are and with administrators who do not like having frustrated teachers. Choose a structure that is favorable to your staff so you have a fair chance of selling them on the usefulness of group counseling with students.

Selling Group Counseling

The current emphasis on accountability in education has put great pressure on teachers to ensure that all students achieve sufficiently in their academic development. For this reason, teachers are understandably reluctant to excuse students from class for such services as group counseling. Teachers believe that it is more important for students to remain in class and receive the necessary instruction. No one disputes this point. Indeed, your challenge as counselor is to demonstrate that counseling services can enhance student achievement by helping students improve perceptions, attitudes, and behaviors toward learning.

Your work as a counselor complements that of the teacher, in that self-awareness, coping skills, career decisions, and other developmental elements learned about through group counseling contribute to student achievement in academic areas. To persuade teachers of this, you first need to convince your administration of the value of group processes in the school counseling program. Once you are successful with some students in groups, teachers will be more inclined to allow other students to participate. Remember, although group counseling might focus on a variety of student concerns, your primary mission in helping students address these issues is to enable them to become more successful learners.

Your advisory committee can help you "sell" group counseling to your administrators and teachers. Ask members to help you design a survey for teachers to assess the types of concerns that are blocking student learning. Once you identify these concerns, establish groups to focus on these issues. For example, one focus with middle school students might be to have them learn to use their time better and improve their study skills. If group sessions help students with these types of teacher concerns, the overall outcome should improve learning in the classroom. Worksheet 4.1 shows a sample survey that you could use to begin acquainting teachers with group services. Results from this survey could also inform you and teachers of what types of groups are needed.

Teachers' concern about students' missing instruction is legitimate. Therefore, when students participate in group counseling, it is wise for you to design a schedule so they do not miss the same class period for all group sessions. For example, if you schedule a group to work on peer relationships, you might begin the group on a Monday at 9:00 A.M. The second session would be the following week on Tuesday at 10:00 A.M., the third on Wednesday at 11:00 A.M. of the next week, and so forth until the group ends. By staggering the days and times of the group meetings, students will miss different classroom activities, and no single subject area will be unduly affected.

Once you have a schedule and the teachers agree to let students participate in groups, you will need a system of keeping track of your groups and identifying which students belong in what groups. In an elementary school, it may be helpful to give teachers a copy of your group schedule each month. With very young children, you may need to go to classrooms and get group members (or use a peer helper who can escort the children to the counseling center). At the middle school level, you might use a pass system. Fill out the passes a day before the meetings and put them in teachers' mailboxes. Exhibit 4.3 shows a sample pass.

EXHIBIT 4.3

Group Pass to the Counselor's Office

For: _____ (student's name) _____ Day: _____ Time: _____

Teacher: Please give this pass to the student named above for the time shown. If the student is absent, please notify the counselor. When the group session is over, the student will return to class with this pass signed by the counselor.

Thank you!

Time the session ended: _____ Counselor: _____

Teacher Survey for Group Counseling

Teachers:

I would like to help with some of the children who are having difficulty learning and completing their assignments in your classes. Group counseling can be an effective way to help students focus on their behaviors and make appropriate changes.

Please take a minute to complete this survey if you have students who might benefit from counseling services. Check the items that describe students in your class. Your input will help us decide what types of groups are most needed in our school. Thank you!

Teacher's name: _____

I have students who

_____	Do not pay attention in class	_____	Disrupt the class
_____	Are underachievers	_____	Seem unmotivated
_____	Are uninterested	_____	Waste class time
_____	Do not cooperate with others	_____	Do not hand in their work
_____	Give up easily	_____	Do poorly on tests
_____	Talk out of turn	_____	Put others down
_____	Are perfectionists	_____	Have poor peer relationships
_____	Put themselves down		

Specific students I am concerned about are: _____

_____

Organizing Group Counseling

For group sessions, you need a room that is comfortable and private. Group counseling is a confidential relationship for all members, so the room or space you choose for these sessions should be appropriate for private, personal conversations. (Chapter Twelve will address the limits of confidentiality in groups.)

Some elementary counselors like to work in groups while sitting with young children on the floor. Others prefer to have chairs so children can have a special space in the group, and the chairs provide structure for that space. If chairs are not available, you might consider using pillows or marking a spot with tape on the floor for each group member. Without a specific spot or chair for each child, you may spend more time keeping the students in the group than you do counseling them. It is important for group management that each child has his or her own space.

The developmental issues discussed earlier for individual counseling also apply to groups. Select group members according to their developmental levels, areas of concern, willingness to commit to group goals, and ability to understand why they are in the group. This screening process is an essential procedure guided by ethical standards of the American Counseling Association (ACA), the American School Counselor Association (ASCA), and other professional associations. When choosing group members, you also must consider such factors as sex, age, cultural differences, intellectual ability, and socioeconomic background. When the diversity of any one of these factors is too wide, it may inhibit group communication and progress.

One vital point about forming groups is that you, the counselor, should be in control of which students are in which groups. Assessment and selection of potential group members involve a professional decision that can make or break the success of a group. Several factors must be considered: verbal skills, cognitive development, attitude toward being in a group, willingness to work on one's concerns, commitment to helping others, and severity of the individual students' problems.

Group counseling can be a strong part of a comprehensive school counseling program if you plan and schedule properly. Administrator and teacher input is vital in helping you be successful. By way of summarizing, the checklist in Exhibit 4.4 will help you stay on target with your group program. Exhibit 4.5 presents a sample list of ten ground rules for group counseling adapted from Greenberg's book on group counseling in schools (2003).

Parent and Teacher Counseling

On rare occasions, individual and group counseling services may also be useful with parents and teachers. Although there is not unanimous agreement among school counselors about their role in parent and teacher counseling, many counselors find that individual parents and teachers request their services. If you have not already dealt with this issue, you eventually may face the question of whether to provide this service as part of your program.

EXHIBIT 4.4

Counselor's Checklist for Group Counseling

_____ Introduce group counseling to your administration and faculty by explaining how groups will help children achieve academically in school.

_____ Ask your advisory committee to help you plan a schedule for group counseling.

_____ Introduce group counseling to students during your classroom visits at the beginning of the year and survey students' needs and concerns at the same time.

_____ Find an appropriate room in the school with adequate furnishings and privacy to lead groups.

_____ Establish specific ground rules for group members to follow (see Exhibit 4.5).

_____ Interview and screen prospective group members, and select members for appropriate groups.

_____ Design evaluation methods for each group.

EXHIBIT 4.5

Ten Ground Rules for Participating in Group Counseling

1. Be on time for each group session.
2. Attend every group session.
3. Keep everything said or that happens in the group confidential (private).
4. Be courteous and respectful to all group members and the group leader.
5. Avoid interrupting another group member or the group leader.
6. Actively participate in all group sessions.
7. Avoid talking about people who are not in the group (other students, teachers, parents, the principal, and so on).
8. Let other group members have a chance to speak.
9. Agree that group members who violate ground rules may be asked by the leaders to leave the group.
10. Agree that participating in a group does not relieve you of your responsibility to complete class assignments and homework.

In most cases, when parents and teachers approach you about helping them with personal concerns, you should establish initial relationships with them and direct them toward appropriate professional services outside the school. In doing so, your role is one of a referral agent. Although this is the best role for you to assume in most cases, there may be times when you need to provide direct services yourself. In some communities where there is not an abundance of helping professionals and agencies, the school counselor is one of the few trained helpers available. If this is true in your community, you have to decide how much counseling assistance you are able to offer parents and teachers. Can you provide these services without jeopardizing services to students? Do you have the competencies to provide appropriate assistance?

The question of providing counseling for teachers raises ethical issues because you are their professional colleague. If no reasonable avenue exists for referring teachers to agencies in the community, you may want to consult with another counselor in your school district who can assist you and the teacher by providing services. Another option is to check with your school system's personnel office to see whether an employee assistance program (EAP) is available. In any event, the initial counseling you provide teachers and parents should be guided by a few basic considerations:

- Are appropriate referral sources available in the community for this teacher or parent?
- Do you have the competencies to assist this person in short-term counseling?
- If you counsel this person, will students benefit from the outcome of this relationship?
- Is time available to provide counseling so it does not disrupt other services in the program?

If you can assist parents and teachers in your school with brief counseling, and if this service helps them make positive choices, the outcome can be beneficial to the children and adolescents who relate daily with these adults. By helping one parent or teacher, you might indirectly improve the learning situation for many students.

Your Philosophy and Effectiveness as a Counselor

Before leaving this section on counseling, it is worthwhile to consider the general effectiveness of counseling services in schools. At the same time, it is important for you to reflect on your counseling philosophy and skills and how they relate to your overall effectiveness as a professional counselor.

Over the past several years, some research has examined the effectiveness of counseling as a professional helping process. Research findings suggest that given the right conditions, a willing client, and a skilled counselor, counseling can result in productive relationships and beneficial behavioral change. However, a review by Eder and Whiston (2006) noted that although counseling has the potential to help children and adolescents, many students who might benefit from such services are not receiving them. One reason for this may be that school counselors are too busy performing other activities and, consequently, are not providing sufficient counseling services. Another possible reason is that some school counselors may not believe they are skilled enough to provide effective counseling services. In this regard, your responsibility is to determine what role counseling services will play in your school's comprehensive program and the skills you possess to deliver such services when needed.

Concerning the discussion about when and by whom counseling services should be delivered in schools, the ASCA National Model has stated a position on counseling services presented in a clinical and therapeutic mode. Clinical and therapeutic counseling involves helping relationships that over time help students assess personality traits, adjust perceptions, and alter behaviors to live healthier lives. The ASCA model promotes the view that such services by a school counselor are inappropriate (Reiner, Colbert, & Pérusse, 2009). Although some school counselors accept this perspective (Schneider, 2009), other counselors and counselor educators do not (Astramovich, Hoskins, & Markos, 2007).

In an apparent contradiction to the ASCA perspective, a study of high school teachers' perceptions about appropriate and inappropriate school counselor functions found that teachers believe therapeutic forms of counseling services are very appropriate (Reiner, Colbert, & Pérusse, 2009). If elementary and middle school teachers hold similar views, such findings may not only contradict the ASCA position but also confuse practicing counselors. For example, counselors who adhere to the ASCA perspective while their teachers think it is appropriate for them to offer clinical and therapeutic counseling services may be conflicted about which view to follow.

If you, your administration, and your colleagues view a school counselor's role as a first-line provider of mental health counseling services, then it seems therapeutic counseling would be an appropriate, albeit limited, part of the comprehensive counseling program. At the same time, you want to consider the ASCA's opinion that counselors in schools should "Provide responsive services including internal and external referral procedures, short-term counseling or crisis intervention focused on mental health or situational (e.g., grief, difficult transitions) concerns with the intent of helping the student return to the classroom and removing barriers on learning" (Schneider, 2009, p. 57).

Research suggests that between 10 and 20 percent of children and adolescents experience some form of mental stress or emotional disorder. The problems that some students bring to school are far ranging and, therefore, challenging to teachers in the classroom and to school administrators. It makes sense that a professionally prepared counselor who is on staff at the school would provide at least short-term intervention to help these students. Because your primary focus is to help all students achieve academically, helping to remove or remedy existing mental and emotional barriers to learning seems appropriate. At the same time, many communities do not have free or affordable mental health services for children and adolescents. This is another reason for counselors in schools to provide some type of therapeutic counseling when needed. In making a decision regarding whether or not to provide therapeutic counseling, you evaluate the scope of the problem, assess the appropriateness of delivering direct counseling services, and determine your readiness to be effective in providing such services. Exhibit 4.6 might help you in this decision-making process.

EXHIBIT 4.6

Questions About Your Counseling Services

When situations arise in your elementary or middle school indicating that a counseling intervention may be appropriate, these questions may help you decide if you should be the counselor to provide initial services to the student, parent, or teacher.

· Are you knowledgeable about the particular concern, issue, or disorder?
· Do you have access to resources about the concern, issue, or disorder and about effective treatment processes?
· Are you aware of and skilled in effective counseling techniques that are most likely to be successful in this situation?
· How much time does this situation require of you and how much time can you reasonably give to it?
· Is the student (or other person) who will receive your counseling services willing to work on the situation?
· What community resources, professionals, and agencies exist to address this situation?
· Is it feasible that the family will accept a referral to a community practitioner or agency, and will the family follow through on such a referral?
· Do your principal and teachers support this role for you as a school counselor?
· How will you assess progress with this situation if you provide services?
· If you are unsuccessful with this situation, what steps would you take to help the person?

In most situations in which you are assisting parents and teachers, the services you provide will be of a consulting rather than counseling nature. Sometimes when a parent or teacher approaches you for assistance it is difficult to determine whether you are counseling or consulting with this individual. Although many of the helping skills you use in both processes are similar, there are distinct differences between the two. Scenario 4.2 illustrates a case where you might consider some direct helping relationships to assist the student and explore consulting relationships to help the school address broader issues the scenario raises. In the next section, you will review the consulting relationships that are part of school counseling programs.

Scenario 4.2: Girls' Bathroom

A sixth grade student in your middle school confides that she never uses the girls' bathroom at school. She is afraid of being bullied by other girls. After getting beyond your amazement at this physiological feat, you wonder how you can help this student deal with her fear. Certainly, some responsive services covered in the preceding sections of this chapter might be helpful, but what about the larger issue — safety and comfort in the school? Some responsive services you might consider may not directly serve this student. Rather, they may involve consulting services to help administrators, teachers, students, and parents create a safe and welcoming environment in the school for all students.

CONSULTING

The counseling literature, and this *Survival Guide,* discuss a consulting role for school counselors (Dougherty, 2009; Parsons & Kahn, 2005; Schmidt, 2008). Typically, consulting is a process that

- Helps teachers learn about the needs of individual students, adjust instructional strategies to benefit classes of students, and identify resources to improve student learning
- Teams up counselors with teachers in an effort to examine the curriculum and make instructional plans to increase learning opportunities for all children
- Provides instruction for all students concerning developmental issues, personal growth, peer relationships, learning, and other topics
- Assists parents with information about their children and ways to support learning and development
- Collaborates with other school and community professionals to design strategies that enhance student development
- Offers information to students to help them with educational and career decisions

As you can see from the list above, consulting, like counseling, is used with several different populations. To understand how to use consulting skills effectively in your program, it is helpful to examine three basic forms of consulting processes, the first of which is situational consultation.

Consulting About Situations

When a student, parent, or teacher approaches you about a particular concern, you form a triangular helping relationship. In this triangle, you are the consultant; the student, parent, or teacher becomes the consultee; and the concern is the situation. In the eyes (and mind) of the consultee, the situation is the problem. For example, Figure 4.1 shows a consulting relationship between a counselor and teacher regarding poor behavior of a few students in class. The role of the consultant (counselor) in this process is to explore the situation

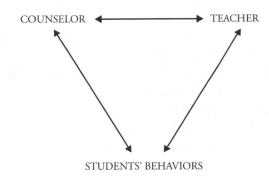

COUNSELOR ⟷ TEACHER

STUDENTS' BEHAVIORS

FIGURE 4.1

Counselor-Teacher Consulting Relationship

with the consultee (teacher), examine alternatives, facilitate decision making, and arrive at a strategy with which the consultee (teacher) can improve the situation.

You can find several models for situational consultation in the literature. I use a model based on the notion that an effective consultant is like a magician (Schmidt & Medl, 1983). The "Six Magic Steps" proposes that a successful consultation is the result of well-planned, carefully timed steps that allow solutions to be skillfully disclosed and accepted by all parties. The six steps are as follows:

1. *The big decision.* When you receive requests for consultation, you might respond by asking yourself, Why me? This initial, internal response is an anxious reaction to what appears to be a difficult situation. Recognizing the skill and ability you have to help others find reasonable solutions helps you readily answer this question and move on to the more important issue: Who needs what? When people ask for assistance, frequently the information they share indicates that perhaps both counseling and consulting services may be needed.

2. *The gathering.* After you answer the initial questions (Why me? Who needs what?), the next step is to gather information. This is a process of collecting information from the consultee and other sources, such as cumulative records, test results, observations, and interviews. This gathering of information is a nonjudgmental process; you accept all evidence as presented by the consultee. Acceptance does not necessarily mean you agree with the consultee's perspective about the evidence.

3. *Clarifying.* You and the consultee examine the information gathered in step 2, and identify and discuss the primary concern. During this step, the process must identify and clarify exactly what the problem is. Once you reach agreement on the problem, you clarify your role in the relationship. This clarification is essential, because at times consultees (students, parents, teachers) may look toward you, the consultant, to solve the problem. In a consulting relationship, the consultee actively chooses a strategy and moves toward a solution for the identified problem. You want to avoid becoming a "magician" who makes all problems disappear. Clarification of a problem is a critical step in determining each person's responsibility in resolving it.

4. *Exploring.* After clarifying the problem and agreeing on each person's role in the solution, you begin to explore possible strategies. This step includes brainstorming processes, listing strategies that have already been attempted, and seeking suggestions from other resources. The immediate goal is to generate as many reasonable solutions as possible and prioritize them according to the consultee's perceptions of what might work best. Which strategies are most likely to work, and which are most reasonable to implement?

5. *Decision time.* Once you make a list of possible solutions, the next step is to make a decision about which strategy to use. In addition, you will again clarify everyone's role and obtain agreement about who will do what to carry out the chosen strategy. Agreement and commitment are critical if a consultation is to be successful. If you do not achieve agreement, you must return to step 3 above.

6. *Making the rounds.* The consultee assumes major responsibility for carrying out the strategy, but you accept responsibility for monitoring progress and evaluating the outcome of the consultation. To ensure that services have been beneficial, you will want to follow up on the consultations you have with students, parents, and teachers. A visit to the classroom, a note to a student, an e-mail message, or a phone call home can quickly collect information that will tell you whether the consultee carried out his or her responsibilities, and what the outcomes were.

These "Six Magic Steps" offer one model to address situational consultations. In working with students, parents, and teachers and focusing on situational issues, you want to design an approach that best fits your style and the needs of your school community.

Providing Information

Sometimes when students, parents, and teachers ask for assistance, what they are seeking is essentially information. To make educational, career, and personal decisions, students need access to accurate and up-to-date information. In guiding their children, parents search for information about medical care, special education programs, child-rearing strategies, summer educational and recreational programs, and other resources that will help children develop to their fullest potential. Teachers request information about student learning styles, school system policies, community programs, test results, student behavior, and much more. Your school uses and disseminates a vast amount of information, and you are a vital part of that network.

Being a main source of information is a great responsibility because people will use the information you provide to make important life decisions about themselves and others. It is also a critical position because some of the information you process about people is, by nature, confidential. Frequently, school administrators, teachers, and parents are concerned about students and want information to help them look after students' best interests. When they request information, be sure you follow federal and state laws, local school policy, and your own professional code of ethics. Although ethical and legal issues are discussed in more detail in Chapter Twelve let us consider practical ideas about handling these information requests.

To handle requests efficiently and accurately, you will need up-to-date and accessible information. Design a computer file and storage system from which you can retrieve materials and resources easily. All your computer knowledge and capability, along with access to a current community resource guide, will come in handy. Sometimes community organizations, such as the United Way and the U.S. Chamber of Commerce, publish guides that are available for free or for a nominal cost. Today much of this information is on the Internet through Web sites of state and local agencies. If there is no such resource in your community, you may want to start one for your school system.

Keeping up-to-date files and disseminating information can become a time-consuming task. As one counselor, you cannot have access to all the information needed or know all there is to know about community resources. Parent and student volunteers can assist in maintaining resource files and other stored information so that services consist of current and accurate materials and listings. Relying on the input of others to create a comprehensive information file is the hallmark of an efficient and effective consultant.

To facilitate the handling of information requests, design a short form for students, parents, and teachers to fill out and return to your mailbox. These forms could also be links on your school's Web site or attachments that people can send you via e-mail. In either event, you can pass completed forms on to student or parent volunteers who "fill the order" if the information is readily available. Worksheet 4.2 is one sample of an information request.

Another type of informational consultation is any presentation to groups of students, parents, or teachers. The orientation you do at the beginning of each school year, going from classroom to classroom to introduce yourself and the counseling program to students, is one such example. Presenting test results to groups of parents or teachers is another.

Sometimes the activities counselors use to disseminate information have the look and flavor of teaching. When you design a group activity to teach students concepts and skills to enhance their development or to help parents and teachers learn skills to facilitate student growth and learning, you use a third type of consulting process, which I call *instructional consultation*. The next section provides information to help you in presenting different instructional services.

Delivering Instruction

If you plan to work with all the children in your school, large-group instructional presentations will be an important feature of your program. The ideal role for a school counselor in instructional consultation is to work closely with classroom teachers in identifying the developmental needs of students, planning appropriate classroom activities to address these needs, and presenting these instructional activities with the teachers. The most common term for these activities is classroom guidance, and the most effective delivery system incorporates guidance lessons into daily classroom instruction. Later in this section, you will learn more about classroom guidance. In addition, Chapter Five explores in more detail the integration of guidance into classroom instruction.

Instructional consultation also includes group presentations to parents and teachers. As part of your counseling program, you can take an active role in parent education programs and teacher workshops. You will find information about parent education programs in Chapter Eleven. For teacher in-service, start by seeking input from your colleagues.

Information Request

Name: _____ Date: _____

If you are a student, your teacher's name: _____

If you are a parent, your home phone or e-mail address: _____

Information you need: _____

_____

_____

Please return to the school counselor's mailbox or attach to an e-mail message. Thank you!

You might do this informally by asking teachers and administrators what types of information they want to receive during the year, or you might use a survey with the faculty. Worksheet 4.3 is a sample survey to help you gather information about topics that teachers might want covered in workshops.

A key element in being successful with group consultations, whether in classroom guidance, parent education programs, or teacher workshops, is your ability to plan, organize, and use effective group leadership skills. School counselors who have experience as classroom teachers are able to use that background in making a transition to classroom guidance activities. Counselors without classroom experience are often able to learn these skills during their counselor preparation programs and by collaborating with teachers in their schools. Research has found no difference in delivery of effective services between counselors with teaching experience and those without.

Instructional and informational approaches require certain skills and behaviors similar to teaching on your part as a consultant. An excellent resource on instructional skills and strategies is Good and Brophy's *Looking in Classrooms* (2008). For the purposes of this *Survival Guide,* I group their suggestions into four related processes and skills: preparation, presentation, feedback, and evaluation (Schmidt, 2008).

Preparation

To be successful with your instructional and informational sessions, you will want be adequately prepared. Your success with classroom guidance, teacher workshops, and parent education events will be in direct proportion to the time and planning you put into identifying instructional goals, selecting appropriate strategies and activities, and scheduling time wisely. If you are going to present a classroom guidance lesson, for example, you will want to choose activities that are developmentally appropriate for all the students in the class or group. This means choosing and using concepts and vocabulary that elementary or middle school students will understand. You should also provide sufficient time for the lesson—elementary and middle school students present a wide variance in regard to the lengths of time they can attend to new information and in the types of lessons that will maintain their interest.

Presentation

As noted earlier, the skills and processes you use in presenting instruction or information are similar to those used in classroom teaching. Research indicates that some of the behaviors related to effective instruction and learning are

- Letting students or other participants know what is expected of them and what they can expect to learn
- Providing regular feedback to participants and giving them task-oriented assignments
- Using a well-paced style of instruction or information sharing
- Asking high-level questions that require students or other participants to analyze, synthesize, and evaluate the information presented
- Having high expectations for all participants
- Managing groups with careful skill, encouragement, and attention to achieving the objectives of the lesson or session

Teacher In-Service Survey

Dear Teachers:

The advisory committee of the school counseling program seeks your suggestions for in-service programs this year. Please take a few minutes to complete the form below and return it to the school counselor's mailbox or attach as a file to an e-mail message by the end of the week. Thank you for your input!

In-service topics for the coming year:

_____ Classroom management strategies	_____ Strategies for resistant learners
_____ Classroom guidance ideas	_____ Conflict resolution strategies
_____ Enhancing self-concept	_____ Child abuse and the law
_____ Communication skills	_____ Parent conference skills
_____ Legal issues in school	_____ Volunteers in the classroom
_____ Sexual harassment in school	_____ Effective homework
_____ Using test results for instruction	_____ Controlling your time

Other topics of interest to you: _____

Please indicate what you prefer for in-service:

_____ After school, one-hour programs

_____ Evening programs

_____ Half- or full-day workshops

Do you want to receive continuing education credits for attending workshops?

Yes _____ No _____

Would you like to plan and present a workshop? If so, on what topic(s)?

_____

_____

The preceding list includes processes and skills that teachers use in their classrooms and are ways you will convey information or instruct students about a developmental task. When presenting instructional or informational types of activities, you might consider the list in Exhibit 4.7, which offers further guidance in giving presentations.

EXHIBIT 4.7

Ten Ideas for Leading Successful Presentations

1. Start your presentation promptly and use time efficiently.
2. State the purpose clearly and ask for understanding from the group.
3. Give clear instructions and directions.
4. Encourage all group members to be active participants.
5. Use your group leadership skills.
6. Facilitate each session by listening, questioning, reflecting, clarifying, and summarizing for the group.
7. Respect the individuality and diversity of group members.
8. Affirm group members' willingness to contribute to the session.
9. Give effective feedback concerning group members' comments and suggestions.
10. Evaluate the outcome of every presentation.

As a presenter, you are involved in every activity of the presentation, facilitate exchanges between you and your audience, encourage useful interaction among group members, maintain order without inhibiting participation, and briskly pace your presentations without moving so quickly that some group members get confused. Your success as a presenter will be determined, in part, on how well you monitor audience feedback during the session. By seeking feedback during and at the end of a presentation, you place yourself in position to strengthen future instructional and informational consultations.

Feedback

When creating environments and group relationships in which people receive information or attain skills, you want to seek ongoing feedback from all participants. By encouraging and accepting feedback, you invite a free exchange of ideas and opinions about the material presented. Classroom guidance often propounds character traits (for example, integrity, loyalty, helpfulness) and other values revered in U.S. society. Nevertheless, as a counselor you will want to remain open to different and sometimes opposing views. Such a stance encourages a healthy exchange, demonstrates acceptance, and upholds democratic principles. Ongoing feedback is also related to summative evaluation of your presentations. Following each presentation, you want to consider an evaluation from the audience to help you strengthen future sessions.

Evaluation

You want to measure the effectiveness of your presentations. The following are some questions to pose to participants:

- Was the information presented helpful to you?
- Were you satisfied with the presentation?
- What have you learned from this presentation?
- How will you use the information?

In addition, you want to ask about how efficiently you used time during the session, activities that were useful, and other aspects of the overall presentation. In Chapter Ten, you will find a workshop evaluation form in Worksheet 10.1 that you might adapt for presentations given to teachers and parents. Worksheet 4.4 is a sample evaluation form to use for an eighth grade presentation about the transition to high school. Use this form to create your own evaluations of classroom guidance. Periodic evaluation of your presentations will help you ascertain whether services are meeting the needs of students, parents, and teachers, and will allow you to adjust program goals and services accordingly. Before leaving this section about instructional and informational presentations, a few comments pertaining to the roles that you and teachers have may be appropriate.

Delivering Classroom Guidance

You may have surmised from the preceding paragraphs that I view classroom guidance as a special form of instructional and informational consultation. The professional literature has long promoted classroom guidance as an important function of school counselors. For example, the ASCA National Model considers it a significant part of a school counseling program and recommends that elementary and middle school counselors spend a certain portion of their time delivering this service. How the ASCA determined these percentages is unclear, but Gysbers and Henderson (2000) also recommend that counselors at different school levels spend a percentage of their time in classroom guidance.

This *Survival Guide* makes no recommendation about the percentage of time you should spend delivering classroom guidance. As a practical issue, the decision of where to spend your time in a comprehensive program stems from the unique needs of your school. This guide does take the position, however, that an appropriate way to deliver a guidance curriculum is by integrating or infusing guidance lessons into daily instruction. A partnership between classroom teachers and the counselor may be the best way to ensure that every student receives information and instruction concerning particular guidance objectives.

The school counseling profession has generated little research to demonstrate the effectiveness of classroom guidance in the student learning of values, character traits, or new behaviors (Akos, Cockman, & Strickland, 2007). Over the years, a few studies have indicated that classroom guidance demonstrated positive results in improving student learning, but the studies are few and far between (Schmidt, 2008). Much more research is needed to support the time and effort that the ASCA National Model and other authorities propose for the counselor's role in classroom guidance.

Sample Classroom Guidance Evaluation Form

Please complete this questionnaire about the classroom presentation, "Getting Ready for School." Circle your answers and return the form to your teacher, who will give it to the counselor. Thank you!

1. The presentation about going to high school was interesting and helpful.   Yes   No   Unsure

2. The counselor used all the time available.   Yes   No   Unsure

3. The counselor encouraged students to ask questions.   Yes   No   Unsure

4. I will be able to use this information in making plans for ninth grade.   Yes   No   Unsure

5. The counselor was able to answer our questions.   Yes   No   Unsure

6. The counselor listened to students' views.   Yes   No   Unsure

7. The counselor came prepared for the presentation.   Yes   No   Unsure

Additional comments: _____

If classroom guidance is a significant function in your program, the above ideas about preparation, presentation, feedback, and evaluation may be helpful to you in delivering useful instruction and information to students. In addition, Geltner and Clark (2005) provide several suggestions for middle school counselors, which could be adapted by elementary counselors, about how to engage students and manage the classroom environment. Here are some of their ideas:

- Begin each session with a few simply stated, positive rules.
- Move around the room as you present a guidance lesson.
- Be friendly, enthusiastic, and optimistic about the lesson.
- Integrate appropriate humor into the lesson and create a fun, motivating atmosphere.
- Engage students through active listening, open-ended questions, and other helping skills.
- When possible and appropriate, break the class into small groups to work on specific tasks or ideas.
- Help students connect with one another by noting similarities and common themes in their contributions.
- Be fair and direct in handling student misbehavior during the classroom guidance lesson.
- Speak to disruptive students privately to avoid public embarrassment.
- When you have exhausted your management strategies to help a student participate appropriately in classroom guidance, consult with the teacher and administrator about an alternative service for the student.

As a counselor you have knowledge and training in many areas of human development and learning. For this reason, you are able to make presentations on a number of different topics of interest to students, parents, and teachers. Being an instructional consultant, however, does not mean that you must always be the primary presenter. Sometimes the most effective consultation you can give is to coordinate in-service by locating presenters for different workshops.

As noted in Chapter Two, coordination demands an effective use of time and an accurate assessment of people's needs. Effective counseling and consulting have the same requirement. To be successful in counseling, consulting, and coordinating relationships, take time to assess and appraise the people and situations referred to you. This process of appraising, discussed in the next section, is the third responsive service in a comprehensive school counseling program.

APPRAISING

Students, parents, and teachers who make referrals to you do so because of a need or concern they have. To provide the most effective and efficient service, you first want to gather as much information as possible. The process of gathering information about students, families, and instructional approaches is termed *appraisal*. You use the information gathered in the appraisal process to decide who needs what services.

A common error made by beginning counselors is deciding what services to offer students, parents, and teachers before making a thorough appraisal of the situation. Usually when this happens the decision is to "counsel" the student. A more complete evaluation of the problem might lead to a different decision about what services are needed. For example, you may find that a teacher needs assistance with classroom management techniques, that you should invite the parents into the school for a consultation with the teacher, or perhaps that the child's instructional program needs adjustment. Although counseling processes help with many cases, they do not always provide the most effective or efficient service for elementary and middle school children.

A thorough appraisal helps you diagnose problems more accurately and prescribe appropriate strategies. Diagnosis and prescription are sometimes uncomfortable terms for school counselors because of their medical implications, but in practice, this is what effective counselors do. They collect data and other information, make professional judgments about what the data mean, and help different people choose appropriate actions to address the identified concerns. To make accurate appraisals of referrals made to you, rely on a few basic methods of data collection: testing, observing, interviewing, and reviewing records. Each method, when used skillfully, adds to the appraisal process and provides information with which to make appropriate decisions.

Testing

School counselors have knowledge of educational assessment and are competent in administering and interpreting standardized tests. You probably use these instruments to help students, parents, and teachers identify achievement levels or ability levels to make decisions about academic placement. Many schools use standardized tests to appraise the academic achievement of all students at the end of the year.

Some schools have testing coordinators. If your school does not, your administrator might ask you to coordinate the school testing program to ensure that the tests are administered according to published practices. Whether or not you coordinate the testing program, you will probably be involved with interpreting testing results to parents and teachers. At the middle school level, you also share the test results with students, so they understand the progress they are making and are more aware of their academic strengths and weaknesses.

You could also help your faculty review schoolwide test summaries. These reports show teachers the strengths and weaknesses in the instructional program. Comparisons of current test results with those of previous years, across grade levels, and for specific classes in successive years can reveal patterns of student achievement that may help evaluate present instructional goals and objectives. Test publishers often offer forms and suggest processes to make these comparisons. If your school does not have such a process in place, you might help create one. For example, individual classroom teachers could use a form similar to that illustrated in Worksheet 4.5 to identify the learning objectives for which performance was below the school standard. By identifying these objectives, teachers can give more emphasis to mastery of those skills. Using schoolwide test data in this way enables you to become involved with administrators and teachers in curriculum planning and instructional improvement for all students. To accept this role, you must have a high level of competency and knowledge in testing.

Learning Objectives Summary

Teacher: _____ Grade level: _____

Test: _____ Subtest area: _____ Year: _____

Instructions: List the learning objectives reported on the summary sheet you received about the most recent testing results and write the percentage of your students who mastered each objective under the heading ''Class %.'' Then write the percentage of students in the entire grade who mastered the objective under the heading ''School %.'' Subtract the two and write a (−) or (+) result under the ''Difference'' column. A (−) response means your class scored lower than the school percentage, and a (+) response means it scored higher. Rank all the objectives from the highest (+) difference to the highest (−) difference to show you the class's strengths and weaknesses.

Learning Objective	Class %	School %	Difference	Rank
_____	_____	_____	_____	_____
_____	_____	_____	_____	_____
_____	_____	_____	_____	_____
_____	_____	_____	_____	_____
_____	_____	_____	_____	_____

Individual and group inventories, such as self-concept scales and career questionnaires, can help you gather data about students. These instruments supplement the results gathered on individual or group tests. When using these instruments, be careful to note that each result is only one piece of the appraisal process and therefore should not be the sole guiding force in making decisions. One single ability test score, for example, is not a valid assessment with which to make educational placement decisions. Much more information is required. For this reason, counselors use other appraisal methods beyond testing, such as observing.

Observing

In most cases, the referrals you receive are a result of countless observations by students, parents, teachers, and administrators. Part of your appraisal process is to validate these perceptions, which you do by observing the situation yourself. For example, if a middle school teacher refers a student because of "daydreaming" in class, you verify this behavior by observing the student in the classroom at a time when the teacher says daydreaming is most likely to occur. In the same way, you might observe on the playground an elementary child who has been bullying other children during recess.

Effective observation is one skill that counselors typically do not learn in their counselor education programs. If you agree that classroom and other observations are a part of the appraisal process, you will want to be competent in this process so that your observations are productive. To begin, here are a few suggestions:

1. In your faculty orientation at the beginning of the year, let the teachers know that observations are an important part of your assessment process. Tell them that you need their help in identifying where and when to observe students they refer.

2. When you and a teacher have agreed to a classroom observation, be on time and go directly to the desk that the teacher has designated for you. Normally, it is best if you have a prearranged seat at a rear desk in a corner of the room. Ask the teacher to mention to the students before you arrive, "The counselor will be visiting our class today and has work to do. Please be courteous and try not to disturb the counselor."

3. Bring a record sheet to write down your observations. A legal pad with margins on both sides provides a simple format to use. In the left margin, record the time every two to three minutes. This will help you keep track of the times when events occurred. In the right-hand margin, record significant observations about which to ask the teacher or events you are unsure about. Record your observations objectively, without judgment. Judgments can come later when you and the teacher review your observations. Worksheet 4.6 illustrates a possible format for your notepad.

4. When you finish the observation (usually a class period of about forty-five to fifty minutes), leave the class quietly and thank the teacher on your way out. Later, at a time agreed on by the teacher, report your observations and give feedback to the teacher about what you saw. At the feedback conference with the teacher, you will want to ask, "Was the class I observed typical of how it usually goes? If not, what was different?" Often the student you observe is never quite as "good" or "bad" as reports have indicated. If the teacher says, "Oh, he didn't do anything like he usually does!" take a positive approach and support the teacher by responding, "He did seem to do quite well. Which tells us he can do it when he wants to, and that is good to know!"

Student Observation Notes

Student: _____ Classroom: _____ Date: _____

Time	Observations	Notes to Self
_____	_____	_____
_____	_____	_____
_____	_____	_____
_____	_____	_____
_____	_____	_____
_____	_____	_____
_____	_____	_____
_____	_____	_____
_____	_____	_____
_____	_____	_____
_____	_____	_____
_____	_____	_____
_____	_____	_____
_____	_____	_____
_____	_____	_____

Let the teacher know that you appreciated the opportunity to visit the class, and be sure to share positive observations about the class in general. Most teachers take pride in their students and classrooms. Tell the teacher that you would like to read your observations, exactly the way you saw them, and then let the teacher give reactions. When you read the observations, remember to report them back exactly as you saw them, without judgment on your part. Your report might sound like this:

At 9:00, the teacher said, "Open your books to page ten." Billy got up and went to the pencil sharpener. The teacher said, "Billy, what are you doing?" He replied loudly, "Sharpening my pencil, what does it look like?" The teacher answered, "Please hurry, we're about to begin the lesson." Mark giggled and Billy hit him on the head on his way back to the desk. At 9:03, the teacher continued with instructions to the class about the lesson.

Continue reporting to the teacher without judging what was good or bad about the class and lesson. If the teacher volunteers a judgment, accept it. The purpose of sharing this observation is to see whether you and the teacher can find clues that will guide you in making a decision about how to help the student.

Interviewing

Counselors also collect information by interviewing students, parents, teachers, and others who can shed light on identified problems. When you interview teachers, the information they provide often complements the findings you observed in the classroom. Parent interviews are valuable because they give you a glimpse of the total family and the child's position in that frame of reference. Depending on the counseling approaches you use, information about a student's birth order and family constellation may be valuable in making decisions.

Initial interviews with students allow you to gather yet another point of view for your appraisal. The listening, attending, questioning, clarifying, and other skills used in establishing counseling relationships are essential in these initial interviews. Data collected through these interviews help construct the various perceptions of the major players: students, parents, and teachers. This construction gives additional evidence to help you decide who needs what. In some instances, you might want to interview other key players, such as other students, siblings, and grandparents who might share significant recollections and observations to assist you in the appraisal process.

Reviewing Records

Some information revealed during interviews relates to past events and prior school years. One source to confirm what people have told you about past events is the student's school record. Cumulative records include report cards from previous years, medical histories, family data, and test results that may confirm or contradict current observations and findings of the appraisal process. Occasionally it is helpful to share this information with the student and teacher because they may be unaware of it. For example, a middle school student who self-deprecates because he is "stupid" or "dumb" might be helped by learning that his test results indicate that he is as academically capable as most students in his class. Sometimes information in cumulative folders can destroy negative myths perpetuated by students and others. Likewise, it may be helpful for a teacher to know that a student who is inattentive in class is not wearing glasses prescribed by the ophthalmologist.

All the procedures described above can help you design a complete appraisal system for evaluating each of the referrals you receive. You do not need to adopt all these procedures for every referral, but it is important to collect information from as many sources as possible. Testing, observing, interviewing, and reviewing records give you a sound framework to make reliable decisions about which services to provide in a comprehensive school counseling program. Sometimes the data you collect will lead you and the teachers to conclude that what is needed is instruction and guidance for all the students in the school, not simply counseling for a few children. Such a decision would move you, the counselor, beyond the delivery of individual and group services to the broader arena of orchestrating services across the school. The next chapter, therefore, focuses on the relationships among the school curriculum, the counseling program, and guidance.

chapter 5

INTEGRATING *a* SCHOOL COUNSELING PROGRAM *with the* CURRICULUM

Scenario 5.1: Classroom Behavior

A veteran teacher in your school asks you to plan and deliver guidance lessons on appropriate classroom behavior. She explains that several of the students are being disruptive and she is having difficulty controlling the class. The teacher thinks that if you presented a series of lessons it might be helpful. How would you respond to this teacher's request? What would you do first? What data would you collect and how would you collect it? What role boundaries do you perceive in this teacher's request? How would you try to help her, and whose support, if anyone's, would you solicit?

The integration of guidance objectives with your school's curriculum is a major goal of a comprehensive counseling program. This chapter offers philosophical concepts and practical ideas to help you answer such requests consistently within the scope of your role as a school counselor. It includes ideas and suggestions on planning guidance integration, locating resources, and presenting lessons, as well as discussions about character education, homework, and educational planning.

Scenario 5.1 gives one example of the type of requests that elementary and middle school teachers ask of counselors. It contains additional dimensions beyond a simple request by a teacher to receive guidance lessons in her classroom. This teacher's request includes a plea for assistance with classroom management, which is beyond the intent of guidance integration. For this reason, you would need to explore information in earlier chapters about consulting and collaborating relationships to assist this teacher fully. Nevertheless, information about guidance lessons and your role in classroom guidance may be helpful in formulating an initial response to her request.

More than a half-century ago, the Association for Supervision and Curriculum Development (ASCD, 1955) published *Guidance in the Curriculum* as its annual yearbook. In it the authors presented the view that guidance is not a separate, supplementary service to a school curriculum but rather an essential part of the curriculum, integrated into daily instruction by teachers and counselors. At the time, however, this was generally not the case because, as the authors noted, guidance was a separate entity from the curriculum in most schools and primarily viewed nationwide as the responsibility of guidance specialists.

During the years following the publication of the 1955 yearbook, the practice of guidance in schools remained relatively unchanged. Labels that identified guidance professionals and services effectively isolated them from the school's curriculum by giving ownership to a single professional group, namely school counselors. Many of these labels still exist today, not only in schools but also in the counseling literature. Such terms include *guidance counselor, guidance personnel, guidance program,* and *guidance office.* These names separate guidance from the curriculum because they neglect the role of teachers in providing guidance activities and fail to recognize the importance of guidance in daily instruction and student-teacher relationships.

In the 1960s, the counseling movement in elementary and middle schools began to emphasize cooperative relationships between counselors and teachers and the important role that classroom teachers and other school specialists have in providing guidance to all students. As a result, many states and numerous school systems wrote guidance curricula aimed at ensuring that schools exposed all students to appropriate developmental activities in their daily instruction. Today, advocates of developmental counseling programs promote the concept of teacher-counselor cooperation first put forth by the ASCD in 1955. For example, according to the ASCA National Model, the "guidance curriculum is infused throughout the school's overall curriculum and is presented systematically through K–12 classroom and group activities" (www.ascanationalmodel.org/content.asp?contentid=28).

As an elementary or middle school counselor, you can take advantage of this trend toward collaboration with teachers and give your program a clear identity by winning support from your teaching colleagues. Your first step is to introduce teachers to the idea of integrating and infusing guidance into their daily instruction and to persuade them that a partnership of teaching and guidance is the highest form of affective education, a values-based curriculum that encourages students to address and solve problems by changing some views about themselves and others. In addition, successful student learning will result to the degree that your school incorporates affective education into the instructional program.

AFFECTIVE EDUCATION: INTEGRATION AND INFUSION

Successful schools teach the *whole* child and teach *every* child. This is neither a simplistic notion nor an easy challenge. It requires the entire school staff to embrace a philosophy that every child can learn and that teaching in isolation, without relating subject matter to the overall development of students, is an ineffective approach to education. Because this is so, the teaching of math, science, language arts, and other subjects to elementary and middle school students includes knowledge of how particular subject matter relates to the acquisition of life skills. Teaching the whole child is, in essence, the incorporation of guidance into the school curriculum.

This *Survival Guide* promotes the perspective that guidance does not occur at 10 A.M. on a Tuesday morning when the teacher tells students, "Put your books away, the counselor is here for guidance." Rather, successful guidance occurs in concert with the teaching of all subjects, and when it relates its subject matter to everyday life situations. In this way, teachers integrate guidance goals and objectives with science, math, language, and other learning objectives of the day. They also infuse guidance into every aspect of their student-teacher relationships. I believe that the best teachers have done this since the dawn of education. It is not a new concept, but it is a challenging one to implement. Before continuing, you might consider how this concept of integration of guidance into the curriculum would influence your response to the teacher in Scenario 5.1. How would teaching appropriate classroom behaviors fit into a fully integrated curriculum?

Your role as a school counselor is to help teachers with this challenge of integrating guidance. To start, you may want to consider some of the points highlighted by the ASCD in its 1955 yearbook, as well as more contemporary perspectives from the ASCA National Model and other approaches to comprehensive school counseling programs. The ASCD's concepts remain applicable in the twenty-first century. They suggest that teachers who effectively integrate guidance with their classroom instruction do the following:

- *They realize that all children face an array of problems in the process of growing up, and for this reason all students will benefit from guidance.* As noted, excellent teachers have always taught the whole child and have incorporated guidance into their daily instruction. This was true for teachers in the single-room schoolhouses of the nineteenth century and will be true of effective teachers of the twenty-first century and beyond. How you convey this message to your faculty, showing them that guidance in the curriculum is not an additional burden for them but is simply effective teaching, is critical to your success as a counselor.

- *They know that children of the same age are often at different levels of readiness concerning specific learning experiences.* When schools treat all students "the same," without regard for individual uniqueness and differences, they fail to infuse guidance into the curriculum. Help your school understand that equity in education means equal opportunity, not uniformity of instruction. Sometimes, the passage and implementation of state and federal initiatives, such as No Child Left Behind, miss this important concept.

- *They are skilled in gathering and using information to determine student readiness.* Chapter Four describes the role counselors have in gathering data to help teachers make appropriate decisions for optimal student development. Your expertise in student appraisal can assist teachers so they, too, can assess, observe, interview, and relate with students to produce accurate information and make sound educational plans.

• *They know that school success correlates with student self-concept and the positive beliefs that students hold about themselves.* In his classic book *Self-Concept and School Achievement,* William Purkey (1970) made a clear case for self-perceptions as a guiding force in all human endeavors. Teachers who accept this view incorporate a guidance philosophy into all their relationships with students. They make every effort to support each student and instill confidence to succeed in school and life. (Also see Purkey and Novak's *Inviting School Success* [1996].)

• *They plan lessons with the whole child in mind.* Effective elementary and middle school teachers are concerned about helping students learn basic knowledge and skills while also helping them form healthy attitudes toward education and an appreciation for learning. You can assist when teachers identify students who are not responding to their guidance and instruction. At these times, students may benefit from individual and group counseling, or the teacher may profit from consultations with you and the parents.

• *They accept the diversity of students and recognize the social and cultural uniqueness each student brings to class.* Counselors can help teachers through in-service activities that explain cultural differences and by supporting them in working with an ever-expanding and challenging student population. Help your school community celebrate the cultural, ethnic, familial, and other differences among students.

Teaching is a challenging vocation, and it becomes more so every day. Your understanding of human development and helping relationships is essential to support the efforts of all teachers. Recognize the expertise they bring to the table and invite them to join a guidance-oriented approach to learning for all students.

GUIDANCE: EVERYONE'S RESPONSIBILITY

As the preceding concepts illustrate, guidance permeates an entire school program. There is a vital role for everyone. If teachers assume a central role in guidance by integrating affective education into daily instruction, what is your role as a school counselor? Everything we know about elementary and middle schools suggests that the best educational programs depend on cooperation among administrators, teachers, and specialists. As one of the specialists in your school you have an obligation and responsibility to assist teachers with their guidance efforts.

There are countless ways to provide this assistance, but for the purpose of "survival," I will discuss three major avenues for assisting the school with guidance activities: (1) helping teachers integrate guidance into the curriculum, (2) providing in-service for teachers, and (3) coordinating schoolwide guidance activities. You can help teachers plan the integration of guidance in classrooms and throughout the school, locate guidance resources and materials to use in the classroom, and copresent special guidance lessons and activities with teachers in their classes. Let us briefly consider each of these approaches.

Planning Guidance Integration

By working with teachers to plan specific guidance topics, you assist them in designing lessons to fit a variety of subject areas. In elementary schools, meeting with teachers from each grade level to talk about ways to incorporate affective education into language arts, reading, and other subjects could do this. Depending on how a middle school is organized, counselors can meet with grade-level, departmental, or unit teachers to determine how to reinforce specific guidance concepts across units of learning. Whatever means you try, the important point is that the integration of guidance with classroom instruction only occurs when someone intends it to happen.

In middle schools, the integration of guidance sometimes takes place as part of the teacher advisement program (TAP), as discussed briefly in Chapter Three's section on coordinating a TAP. You can help teachers design guidance units for a TAP based around topics that they present sequentially according to the school's guidance curriculum and in conjunction with important school events during the year. The following list includes sample topics for developmental guidance units appropriate for classroom guidance and teacher advisement programs:

- Getting to know your fellow students
- Getting to know yourself, particularly the strengths you have
- Learning to communicate so that others understand you
- Improving your study skills and managing your time
- Making decisions about school, career, and life
- Building friendships and increasing your interest in the diversity of others
- Understanding what motivates you
- Resolving conflicts and reaching conciliation
- Managing, measuring, and monitoring your health and wellness
- Planning an educational route to get where you want to go in life
- Serving your community

Encourage teachers to select a few major topics during the year, such as career choices, substance abuse, and friendship, and to design guidance activities in every class to focus on each topic for a specific period. In addition to offering your assistance and ideas, search for materials, kits, videos, and other resources to help teachers in presenting their activities. By locating useful resources, you expedite the teachers' integration of guidance in the classroom.

Locating Resources

Your preparation in school counseling has exposed you to numerous resources and ideas that will be helpful in designing guidance activities. Because teachers have much to do in preparing academic lessons, they will appreciate any assistance you give them in locating appropriate resources and materials. Recruit your school's media coordinator or librarian to help with the task of compiling guidance resources for each grade level. Some counselors develop resource guides listing activities and materials, such as learning kits, videos, music CDs, computer programs, and other media that are useful in classroom guidance activities. You can design a guide organized by grade level and align activities with the annual guidance goals chosen by the faculty. Ask teachers to devise activities and include these in the manual. In the past, loose-leaf binders made excellent resource guides for each grade level because teachers could update activities as they shared new ideas and found additional resource materials. With today's technology, this task might be accomplished by setting up a link on the schools' Web site or burning a CD of resources for every teacher.

Presenting Guidance Lessons and Activities

One way to share responsibility for guidance in your school is to present classroom guidance activities with teachers. This is an excellent process for winning the support of your teachers and, at the same time, for learning good instructional techniques from effective teachers in your school. By observing teachers, you hone your own large-group skills and improve the presentations you make to students, parents, and teachers.

Teachers sometimes prefer to have a counselor lead certain guidance lessons because of the sensitive nature of the subject matter. Ask teachers about which topics they are comfortable having you lead with their classes, and plan these presentations together. In these team-teaching efforts, teachers usually remain in class to observe and assist as needed. From their observations, teachers will be able to plan follow-up instruction. These team efforts also allow teachers and counselors an opportunity to exchange constructive feedback that is helpful in planning future guidance activities and in targeting services for students. Returning to Scenario 5.1, what role could the teacher play if you and she decided to use a team approach in helping students with appropriate classroom behavior?

In-service with teachers is another avenue for you to present guidance information during the year. You explored teacher in-service in Chapter Four in regard to the consulting function of counseling. By providing staff development for your teachers on topics of interest to them, you educate them about learning styles, developmental stages, student needs, and other factors related to guiding the whole child. You may not be able to do all these in-service programs yourself, but by coordinating them with the administration and bringing presenters into the school you can have a significant influence on the messages your teachers hear.

Another approach to guidance is through planning and coordinating events that foster healthy relationships and enrich school life. Schools can be difficult places in which to work. As a guidance-minded counselor, you can be a catalyst for positive ideas and activities that highlight student and teacher accomplishments and encourage a spirit of cooperation and togetherness in the school. In addition to encouraging and planning classroom guidance, take an active role in designing schoolwide guidance programs, such as Career Day, Citizen of the Week, Guidance Teacher of the Month, teacher advisement services, peer helper programs, and other worthwhile events. These kinds of activities help the entire school focus on total development for all students.

CHARACTER EDUCATION

Over the past two decades, a movement called *character education* has been active in our schools. In the twenty-first century it continues to receive attention by educators. If measured by the number of Web sites that market programs or provide information about character education, it remains a strong part of guidance initiatives. In preparing this revision of the *Survival Guide,* I searched the Internet for "character education" and found over 1.5 million Web sites. These included individual state and school Web sites as well as sites promoting resources, networking, lesson plans, and other information related to character education.

The basic concepts of character education consist of essentially healthy ways to help students develop good citizenship, self-responsibility, ethical behavior, and other virtues upheld by our society. Many of these same qualities were part of guidance programs of past years. Current character education information and materials available to teachers and counselors are worthy of adoption by schools as part of today's guidance curriculum.

You can take an active role in helping your school identify aspects of character education to use in both schoolwide activities, such as student assemblies, and in the guidance curriculum as integrated by teachers in the classroom. As with other guidance initiatives, you might want to enlist the assistance of your school's media specialist to locate appropriate materials, videos, kits, and other information to help teachers with character education. Some form of evaluation is appropriate and may help you and the school determine whether the emphasis on character education was effective in helping children learn concepts, alter behavior, develop healthy relationships, and succeed in school. You might also find the ideas for evaluating counseling services presented in Chapter Two useful in assessing the effects of character education initiatives in your school.

HOMEWORK

One component of the school curriculum that has received increased attention in recent years is student homework. As a school counselor, you can be helpful to your administration and teachers as well as to students and parents if you stay informed about the research on this issue.

America's focus on effective education and improving student academic performance in recent years has been intense. In part, the stimulus for this attention has come from No Child Left Behind (U.S. Department of Education, 2002), and the nation's anxiety that students are not competitive with learners in other countries. The fear is that the United States will lose its standing as a leader among nations, and increased homework for students has become a by-product of this concern. However, research results are, at best, mixed and inconclusive about the benefits of homework for all students. Some authorities have gone so far as to state that educators have abused research results, noting that the data pertaining to homework assignments do not support claims about the benefits (Kohn, 2006).

The Center for Public Education (www.centerforpubliceducation.org) is a joint initiative of the National School Boards Association and the National School Boards Foundation. This center is a clearinghouse for information and research about and analyses of public education and educational issues, such as student achievement and ways to promote support for public education. The Center for Public Education summarizes the current research on homework with these points:

- A relationship between student academic achievement and assigned homework from teachers is unclear.
- Research results concerning parental involvement with students to complete homework are mixed, and the findings are unclear.
- In general, older students may benefit academically from homework more than younger students.
- Students from higher income homes may benefit more from homework than students from lower-income homes.
- Students with learning disabilities may benefit from homework if certain supervisory and monitoring conditions are met.
- Asian American students might benefit more from homework than might American students from other ethnic groups.
- Too much homework may reduce its benefits.
- Homework may have some nonacademic benefits, particularly for younger students, such as learning time management, assuming responsibility, staying on task, and developing good study habits.
- Homework assistance in after-school programs may have some benefits related to student motivation and work habits, but not necessarily academic achievement.
- The amount of homework that a student completes may correlate more strongly with achievement than the amount of homework assigned by the teacher.

As with other summaries of research, you want to use caution in interpreting the above findings. Group data, for example, do not necessarily apply to individual students. Consequently, the finding that lower-income students may not benefit as much as higher-income students from assigned homework does not mean that an individual student from a low-income family in your school would not benefit as much as other students. The important point in sharing these findings is for you to help the school and teachers adopt sound policies and procedures for assigned homework. At the same time, you want to work with students who struggle with completing their homework assignments.

EDUCATIONAL PLANNING AND PLACEMENT

In U.S. schools, with their diverse student populations, it is challenging to address the needs of every single child. Yet research tells schools to consider individual learning styles, abilities, and needs if they want educational programs to be successful with diverse, multicultural populations.

As an elementary or middle school counselor, you share responsibility for ensuring that every child receives adequate attention in his or her educational planning, academic placement, and overall educational development. True, there will be many social and personal concerns brought to you, and at times educational development may appear secondary to some of the critical issues you face with students. Nevertheless, if you lose sight of your fundamental purpose as a counselor in the school, your overall effectiveness with students, parents, and teachers will diminish. For this reason, every case you handle, regardless of the nature of the problem or concern, should tie into the student's educational development and academic success.

Several of the activities and ideas presented in this and earlier chapters will help you foster a relationship with your students and teachers that will keep the educational mission of the school at the forefront of the counseling program. Here are a few additional suggestions:

• Periodically meet with teachers from each grade level to ask them about the educational progress of individual students, particularly those who are receiving counseling services.

• Form a child study committee or a student assistance team consisting of teachers and other student services personnel to examine cases of students who are not progressing in school but who do not qualify for special education or other support programs. When a group of professionals looks at a situation, it generates more ideas and solutions than if a single teacher or counselor tackles the same problem. Encourage team building as a process for effective educational decision making.

• Plan study skills groups for students who are not doing their homework or not performing well on tests. Work with the parents of these students to help them structure study time at home.

• Meet with every student in small guidance groups during the year to give each one an opportunity to talk about educational goals, what he or she wants out of school, and his or her desire for academic success. Bring in guest speakers, parents, and other volunteers who can share views of what an education has meant in their lives.

• Organize field trips to local high schools, community colleges, and trade universities. It helps students aspire to higher educational goals when they visualize what they will be doing in the future. Many elementary and middle school students will never have the opportunity to see a college or university unless someone takes them for a visit. Young boys and girls discover heroes and heroines in athletes, movie stars, and entertainers because these are the models seen on television, on the Internet, and in the movies. You can help students similarly identify educational role models. You need only to show students where to look for them.

• Use peer tutors. You will find some of the most powerful resources in schools among students who are willing to tutor peers and younger students. Ask teachers what training these tutors will need, and find out whether any of them are willing to work with you in forming and training this group of helpers.

• Encourage teachers to "teach to pass." William Purkey, a professor, friend, and mentor, once said that all teachers, regardless of the level at which they instruct, should be motivated by the desire to see all students progress satisfactorily in their studies (Purkey & Novak, 1996). Sadly, some teachers delight at the prospect of failing their students. This is tragic, but it usually happens when teachers become frustrated and feel unsupported by the school, parents, and counselors.

• Help your school and colleagues feel genuine support. Give out awards for teachers to boost their morale. Organize an appreciation luncheon with the help of parent volunteers. Tap your business community to donate merchandise that the school can give as rewards for teachers who go the extra mile and who "teach to pass" every student. One middle school counselor established a "Teachers Are Terrific" monthly drawing at staff meetings to introduce a fun activity and feelings of togetherness to the faculty. This is one of limitless ideas you can implement to encourage and support your teaching colleagues.

• Help your school establish programs for students in academic distress who do not qualify for special services, and create awards for students who overcome odds, make significant gains, and greatly improve their standings in their classes and the school. Start a secret "Red Alert" team for students in danger of failing and a "Code Blue" club for students who make significant progress. Although it is appropriate to recognize and honor students who are "high fliers," it is equally important to reward those who survive despite seemingly insurmountable obstacles. Exhibit 5.1 illustrates an award for continuing progress.

EXHIBIT 5.1

The Edinburgh Middle School Continuing Progress Award

Felicia Ramos is hereby recognized and highly commended for her superb progress in Mr. Hatchback's math class at Edinburgh Middle School on this date, January 4, 2005.

Principal: _____   Teacher: _____

The suggestions in the above starter list help you and teachers stay focused on educational planning, placement, and development of all students in the school. Use it as a jumping-off point for your school to design and implement other strategies unique to your student population.

TEST RESULTS AND IMPROVED INSTRUCTION

Scenario 5.2: Test Results
A father has called you about a student's test results. He explains that the results are confusing, and that although he scheduled a conference with the teacher, he remains confused about the results, the purpose of the test, and the school's testing philosophy. What steps would you take in responding to this parent? Whom would you involve, if anyone, in helping answer the father's questions?

Another way that the curriculum and the school counseling program interact is through the roles you assume to help teachers interpret and use achievement test results and to help students perform at optimal levels on standardized tests. Student achievement in school relates to the adequacy and appropriateness of the curriculum and the student's placement within the instructional program. These two factors often relate to teacher understanding and the use of test data.

In recent years, media and political emphasis on the status of education in the United States has increased attention on school testing programs and student results. In every grade, including kindergarten, schools are testing students to evaluate their readiness to learn or to assess the progress they are making in school. Whether or not you agree with this proliferation of standardized testing, it is the reality in many schools, and all signs indicate that it will remain so for the time being. Citizens and elected officials want schools to be accountable and expect, rightly or wrongly, that effective schools will have improved test scores.

Capitalize on this testing movement by helping teachers use the results to improve their instruction and helping students increase their learning. To do so, you must first help teachers, students, and parents understand what standardized achievement tests really are. They are merely tools with which to gather information about student learning to compare with the results of other students in the same grade, at the same age, and in the same areas of the curriculum.

You can also help teachers use testing summary data to examine how the present instructional program relates to the learning objectives assessed on the standardized tests. (Worksheet 4.5 in Chapter Four illustrated one way to conduct an analysis of class summaries of annual test results.) The next sections give you additional information to help teachers, students, and parents understand and use testing for positive purposes.

Teachers and Testing

An understanding of how test results relate to instruction may relieve teachers of the pressure of seeing student performance as a reflection of teaching effectiveness. At the same time, teachers will be able to learn what impact they can have on student achievement scores by tailoring their instructional objectives to match the published objectives measured by the tests. Of course, this raises other issues, such as who chooses the test and whether or not the objectives match the school's curriculum. You can provide in-service information for teachers about the state-mandated or school district testing program, the test selection process, and the specific objectives addressed on the tests administered to students. In most cases, the results that schools receive on achievement tests include classroom summaries to show how well students performed on specific learning objectives. In-service with teachers about these school summaries is valuable in two ways.

First, in-service allows teachers the opportunity to examine the objectives stressed on the standardized test and determine whether these are the same objectives stressed in the instructional program. If discrepancies exist, teachers have the right (and perhaps the obligation) to question the selection of the achievement test or to change their instructional focus. Changing instructional objectives is not the same as "teaching to the test." By adjusting instructional objectives, teachers bring the subject matter and learning goals of the classroom in line with the content of the test chosen to measure student progress. If these two elements do not match, teachers should question the validity of using the test to assess student achievement.

Second, in-service for teachers to learn about school summaries removes the mystery of testing and test results by allowing teachers to take an active role in learning about the instruments used to measure student achievement. People tend to be afraid of what they do not understand, which is the case with testing. When teachers learn more about the testing program, the specific tests administered, and the methods of reporting student results, they are better informed and less likely to be intimidated by the process. They may also feel that they have more control over the assessment process.

In large school systems, counselors can be spokespeople for their schools when teachers and administrators conclude that the tests, chosen by central office specialists or other personnel, are not in line with the schools' instructional programs. To be a competent spokesperson, you want to be informed about the curriculum in your school and about the standardized testing program of your school system and state.

Students and Testing

Student attitudes and feelings about taking tests can influence the results. To achieve optimal scores, students need to feel as comfortable as the teachers do with the testing program. Naturally, there are few people, adults included, who view test taking as a positive experience. No one enjoys being compared to other people, on tests or in other ways. You can help students and teachers by designing guidance activities that focus on test-taking skills, relaxation techniques, and other test preparation procedures.

One program used in elementary and middle schools is Bowman's popular *Test Buster Pep Rally* (2004), a kit consisting of more than one hundred activities, games, songs, and skills to improve attitudes toward testing, teach useful test-taking interventions, and help overly anxious students. The program provides material for a half-hour assembly program and pep rally to focus on student performance on standardized achievement tests. The pep rally includes skits, cheers, and songs that encourage students to do their best on tests. A recording of *Test Buster* cheers and songs plays in the background during the assembly skits. The kit also contains preparation worksheets, practice tests, games, songs, and exercises for teachers and counselors to use in classrooms during the school year.

In middle schools, students are aware of the importance of tests and as a result may feel more anxiety than elementary students. If you include group sessions on test-taking skills in your counseling program, middle school students will benefit from basic helpful hints about answering questions on standardized tests. Some students will also profit from learning relaxation techniques or other skills to control their testing anxiety. The following are some guidelines for choosing and applying relaxation, systematic desensitization, or other strategies in your school:

1. *Know the approach well.* Study and learn each of the techniques you plan to use with children in your school. Read the professional journals, study textbooks, attend workshops, and enroll in seminars to become proficient in these strategies. It is particularly helpful

to experience the techniques yourself. If you want to use systematic desensitization, for example, you should learn it from a competent counselor or therapist who can walk you through the process to focus on concerns of your own.

2. *Eliminate the mystery and magic of these techniques.* Inform administrators, teachers, and parents about the approaches you use with children. The more secretive you are about what you do, the more suspicious people will be of your practices. Most stress reduction approaches used by counselors in schools are simply educational exercises that anyone can learn when taught by people who have sufficient training. Educate your school about these approaches. For example, if you use relaxation techniques, demonstrate the approaches at a PTA meeting with student volunteers. Invite your faculty to the counseling center on a Friday afternoon for snacks and beverages, and take them on a guided fantasy tour to the Bahamas! The point is to show people that these techniques are strategies for learning new behaviors and coping with everyday stresses.

3. *Inform parents about the approaches you plan to use with their children, and invite them to discuss these strategies with you.* Elementary and middle school children can make significant progress with assistance from an effective counselor, and parent commitment and support will increase the counselor's ability to facilitate student development and resolve identified concerns.

4. *Know your local school policies regarding the use of particular counseling and learning techniques.* If there are no specific policies, discuss your ideas with the principal and teachers whose opinions you value. These professionals know the community and can guide your decisions appropriately.

5. *Use new approaches with individuals and small groups of students before attempting to use them with larger audiences.* Some techniques can be helpful to students in classes and large groups, but it is best if you begin small. After you have practiced and honed your skills with individuals and small groups, you will be able to move into larger settings.

6. *Always practice with the best interest of the student (or other client) in mind.* Sometimes new techniques and strategies interest and intrigue us so much that we just want to try them! Monitor your enthusiasm about new ideas and, in addition to the guidelines mentioned above, always choose them primarily to help students and other clients.

Parents and Testing

National emphasis on accountability and standardized testing to measure student progress and school effectiveness has left some parents confused, anxious, and angry, while others express approval and even delight. As a counselor, you want to assess, formally and informally, parents' attitudes about the school's testing program. From this assessment, you will be better prepared to guide administrators and teachers in delivering information to parents about the testing program and how the results are used to improve instruction. Worksheet 5.1 is a sample survey to use in designing an assessment of parents. You could post the survey on the school's Web site or send it home in paper form.

Test interpretation with parents is an important function. As Scenario 5.2 indicates, understanding test results is frequently challenging to parents, and help from school counselors, teachers, and administrators enables parents to convey the results accurately

Parent Survey of the School's Testing Program

Instructions: Our school gives several tests during the year to different grade levels. If your child's grade level is scheduled to take one or more of these tests this year, please complete the survey below by circling your responses to each question. The information we collect from this survey will help us work with parents to provide information and make the testing program work for all children in our school. Thank you for your help!

1. I know about the tests my child will take this year.   Yes   No   Unsure

2. I usually understand the scores my child receives on standardized tests.   Yes   No   Unsure

3. I believe the testing program is helpful to my child.   Yes   No   Unsure

4. I want information about how to prepare my child for taking tests and performing well.   Yes   No   Unsure

5. I wish parents had more say about the testing program.   Yes   No   Unsure

6. I feel the school does a good job reporting my child's testing results to me.   Yes   No   Unsure

7. I think the school spends too much time and emphasis on the testing program.   Yes   No   Unsure

8. I would like my child to receive services from the school so he or she will be more relaxed and ready for the tests.   Yes   No   Unsure

to their children. Without services to help parents and students understand the purpose and results of the testing program, the tests and their outcomes are meaningless. As a counselor, you can help your school establish an open dialogue with parents about the testing program and plan individual and group services to inform parents about their children's performance and how the school uses the results to improve or alter instruction.

The ideas in this chapter—integrating guidance into the curriculum, achieving results to improve learning, using homework effectively, planning educational goals, and coordinating schoolwide guidance—have a common purpose: they each contribute to the development of the whole student. This, in brief, is the essence of a comprehensive school counseling program: to ensure that each student has every possible opportunity to develop to his or her potential. One final area of learning that completes this wide-angle focus on the whole child is career development.

CAREER DEVELOPMENT

Some elementary and middle schools focus on learning basic skills and personal growth so intensely that they neglect to give attention to career development. At best, this area of learning may receive a cursory glance with a unit on career exploration taught in some grades or a Career Week planned for students to learn about occupations in their community. Although these activities are excellent learning opportunities, alone they do not give sufficient emphasis to the process of career development and decision-making processes students can learn so as to focus and strengthen career exploration and future choices.

In practice, we often delay career decisions until the last years of high school or several years later. It is common to hear adults joke about their own lack of career awareness, saying, "Now that I'm thirty-five, I wonder what I'll be when I grow up!" Made in jest, these comments often reflect a degree of truth. Despite many advances in American society, choosing a career track does not appear much easier than it was years ago. People have not become adept at planning their careers or life goals. Students at every level of learning—elementary school, middle school, high school, and college—are placed in educational tracks or choose their courses with little thought or guidance for lifelong planning.

Help your school maintain a balanced focus on career development by encouraging teachers and other professionals to include career information in the integration of guidance activities. Plan schoolwide career exploration activities and incorporate decision-making skills into your counseling groups.

At the elementary level, offer students frequent opportunities to receive information about different occupations and changing male and female roles in the world of work. Classroom activities and group counseling can explore personal interests, develop group cooperation skills, and teach how schoolwork relates to career development and future life plans. Ask your advisory committee or another school committee to evaluate how well the instructional program and counseling services address the career needs and aspirations of elementary children. Although elementary students are young, and career choices seem years away, it is not too early to begin setting a foundation upon which vocational decisions eventually will be made.

Career awareness is equally important at the middle school level. Decision-making skills become vital as students learn to cope with family, personal, and social transitions in their lives. In middle schools, personal interests now can relate to broad occupational areas, and the spectrum of possibilities sometimes is overwhelming and confusing to the preadolescent.

Middle school counselors and teachers who integrate this vast area of learning into the everyday tragedies and accomplishments of middle school life will be successful in helping students with their career development. To do this, you and your teachers can plan schoolwide, classroom, and small-group experiences that focus on

- Decision-making processes
- Conflict resolution skills and conciliatory behaviors
- Communication with peers and adults
- Relationships between educational achievement and career success
- Changing job markets in the twenty-first century
- Technology's impact on career choices
- Examination of personal interests
- Information about various educational and vocational choices
- Gender stereotyping, discrimination, and other conditions that limit educational and vocational opportunities

As with other areas of student development, there are countless ways to integrate career learning into the curriculum. You alone do not own this responsibility, but you can facilitate this effort among the teachers, parent volunteers, business groups, and others who wish to make a difference in the choices available to children. At both the elementary and middle school levels, everything teachers and counselors do to foster learning, promote healthy development, and help students master basic skills contributes to career development.

A LIFETIME OF LEARNING THROUGH POSITIVE BEHAVIOR

One possible by-product of integrating affective education into instructional programs is students' appreciation of the power of learning and the impact it has throughout life. Teachers who instill this notion in all aspects of school life can have a tremendous influence on student development. They create schools and programs that promote success as an essential ingredient for learning and living. This may seem like a simplistic notion, but many schools fail to educate students because they rely on punitive regulations and requirements rather than promoting optimistic opportunities and possibilities.

Successful schools consistently strive to establish places, policies, and programs that treat students as capable, responsible, and valuable human beings. Administrators, teachers, counselors, and others who embrace these ideals are in a stronger position to help students accept the value of an education and maintain that value throughout their lives. You can apply these principles of learning to a wide spectrum of helping relationships. They might also be useful in responding to teachers' requests pertaining to classroom behavior, such as that in Scenario 5.1. Here are a few starter ideas for including these values of lifelong learning and positive behavior into your counseling program and the school curriculum.

1. *Give students responsibility to care for their school building.* Elementary and middle school students take pride in their education when they are proud of their schools. Ask the PTA to sponsor a tree planting or landscaping outing during a weekend. Invite students to help plan the event and become involved. Spruce up the school entrance with carpets, plants, and comfortable chairs for visitors. Ask local businesses to donate furniture, plants, carpets, paints, and other materials.

2. *Provide in-service education for teachers that emphasizes positive methods of student evaluation.* Help teachers focus on what students are able to do rather than what they are unable to do. Ask teachers to share both the methods of reinforcement they use to encourage student learning and their systems of evaluation. Persuade faculty to replicate the most successful approaches that colleagues have shared and to use them with students in their classes. Examples of strategies to consider for teacher in-service are

- *Emphasize what is right.* Help teachers focus on what students do correctly when grading homework, tests, and essays. For example, saying a student got 75 percent correct sounds much better than 25 percent wrong. Help teachers emphasize what children do well, not what they do poorly.
- *Use positive reinforcement.* Show teachers how to structure positive reinforcement systems and choose appropriate rewards. Search for teachers in your school who use reinforcement wisely and successfully, and ask them to be copresenters with you.
- *Observe and listen.* Teachers are the best observers in the school because they are with students daily, and many students confide in teachers they trust. Help teachers know what to look and listen for when interacting with students. Often, students who are in need of help, depressed, lonely, or feeling otherwise disconnected send signals that an observant teacher will notice.

3. *Advocate for positive discipline in your school.* Educational research has verified the benefits of appropriate classroom management and positive discipline strategies for student learning. With this knowledge, it is bewildering why so many schools cling to archaic and brutal methods of punishment in order to control student behavior. If your school does not have a consistent model for positive discipline for students and teachers to follow, ask your advisory committee to review some of the approaches that have been successful elsewhere. Some approaches found in educational and counseling literature are

- Positive discipline (Nelson, 2006). See www.positivediscipline.org for other resources.
- The quality school (Glasser, 1998; www.wglasser.com).
- Assertive discipline (Canter & Canter, 1992). Also see http://maxweber.hunter.cuny.edu/pub/eres/EDSPC715_MCINTYRE/AssertiveDiscipline.html.

- Logical consequences. (See, among many other resources, *A New Approach to Discipline: Logical Consequences,* by Dreikurs and Grey, 1993.)
- Invitational education (Purkey & Strahan, 2002).

Be proactive by showing teachers you want to be involved in school discipline and want to help them develop positive approaches that work. Plan in-service sessions to examine different discipline models and strategies. Organize support groups for teachers to share successful approaches and encourage their colleagues who are experiencing difficulties with students or classes. Promote parent involvement in the school (see Chapter Eleven). The more parents become involved with the school, the more likely they will know teachers and form ongoing relationships. Help administrators develop a schoolwide plan for positive discipline (see Chapter Ten).

4. *Use as many avenues as possible to learn about students who are struggling in class.* Although integrating guidance activities into the curriculum will help many children, some will need additional attention. Develop strategies to obtain this information from teachers on a continuous basis. Visit classrooms, eat lunch with students, drop notes in teachers' mailboxes to ask about particular students, and send thank-you e-mails or handwritten notes when teachers give feedback about student progress. Remember, all of us need reinforcement at times—teachers, too!

This chapter has described several ways in which a school counseling program cooperates with the instructional program to focus on the development of the whole child. The suggestions and ideas advocated here will benefit most students in elementary and middle schools. However, because today's schools include diverse student populations, some children will need special assistance and more intense counseling than will their peers. Chapter Six considers your role in reaching out to exceptional children and other students who require your services.

chapter 6

REACHING OUT *to* DIVERSE POPULATIONS

Scenario 6.1: Struggling Student

A new student at your school has been struggling academically. With the parents' permission, teachers have referred her for exceptional student assessment and identification. According to the assessment results, the student has no exceptionality that qualifies her for services. As the counselor, in what ways could you advocate for this student? What other options or programs might be relevant? What resources are available? How would you proceed?

This chapter considers diverse populations in elementary and middle schools and how to reach out to these students. Among them are students with learning difficulties and exceptionalities, social and behavioral problems, the challenge of learning a new language, and cultural differences. For these students, counselors make a special effort to ensure their optimal development, prevent long-term difficulties, remedy existing concerns, and include them in all school programs.

School counselors have a responsibility and obligation to intervene on behalf of students who have unique needs not always met by the regular school program. Some of these children receive services from specialists, including exceptional children's teachers, school nurses, social workers, English language teachers, and psychologists. Because exceptional children receive particular attention from these specialists, school counselors sometimes overlook them. This is unfortunate because, as emphasized in this guide, comprehensive school counseling programs serve all students. You want to provide a wide range of services to meet the needs of a broad spectrum of students, which includes being knowledgeable about other specialized services and coordinating these with the counseling and consulting services you provide in your elementary or middle school.

Students with unique needs enrich a school population and challenge each of its programs to provide services in an equitable manner. Before focusing on specific students with diverse needs, the next section offers a few general suggestions for you to consider.

GENERAL GUIDELINES

As an elementary or middle school counselor, you work with many specialists who have responsibility for students with particular needs. How you relate to these professionals, cooperate with them, and include them in a comprehensive school counseling program will largely determine the success you have with exceptional students. The following guidelines outline some areas to consider:

1. *Know the specialists who serve your school and keep them informed about your role as counselor.* Invite specialists who serve the children in your school to meet with you and share information. Learn about their programs of services and about their professional backgrounds. Give them information about your program and ask them for suggestions about how you can work together for the benefit of all children.

2. *Check for duplication of services.* Part of your role as a school counselor is to coordinate various student services. Because so much goes on in schools, it is occasionally possible to lose track of which students are receiving what services. When this happens, students may receive the same or similar services from different professionals. When duplicate professional relationships occur without the knowledge of each specialist, confusion results and progress is inhibited. Design a system of tracking and monitoring the services you render to the students in the school. Worksheet 6.1 shows a student services record to use when many school specialists serve the same students. This record should be in a separate, confidential file, accessible only to student services professionals: the school counselor, social worker, nurse, and psychologist. Individual records are a way that you can track and account for services provided to students, parents, and classroom teachers.

3. *Encourage communication among all the student services specialists who serve the school.* Set aside time to meet on a regular basis, perhaps monthly, to share cases. Regular meetings facilitate communication among staff members and provide professional support for each specialist. Student services teams can be expanded beyond school counselors, social workers, nurses, and psychologists to include exceptional teachers, English language teachers, and others. In this way, these teams bring together a variety of professional perspectives with which to consider the *whole* child, a concept discussed in Chapter Four.

Student Services Record

Student: _____ Grade: _____

Teacher: _____

Date	Service or Activity	Student Services Staff
_____	_____	_____
_____	_____	_____
_____	_____	_____
_____	_____	_____
_____	_____	_____
_____	_____	_____
_____	_____	_____
_____	_____	_____

4. *Know your competencies.* Serving a wide range of students, you may find that in certain instances your knowledge and skills are limited. Search for professional allies who are highly skilled and can assist with critical cases. If such professionals are not available in your school system or community, you may want to become competent to handle some of these critical situations, at least at an initial level of service. Worksheet 6.2 can be helpful in listing professionals in your school system and community and identifying their areas of specialty. Keep this list in an easy-to-locate area of your office, or on your computer.

5. *Be knowledgeable about and skilled with the strategies you choose.* Many techniques and strategies for assisting special students and students in crises are in the counseling literature. Choose which methods to use carefully and caringly by doing your homework. Read journals, attend workshops, discuss strategies with colleagues, and become proficient in the services you provide. In most cases, your search for knowledge and information in this regard will never end. Everyday medical science, educational research, and psychological discoveries lead to new information that enables professional helpers, such as counselors, to design effective ways of assisting students and others in need.

6. *Learn about yourself: your feelings and prejudices.* Working with children who are different due to exceptionality, physical disabilities, or their cultural backgrounds takes a high level of caring and respect. Examine your own values and beliefs about people with physical disabilities, minorities, gender stereotypes, sexual orientations, divorce, substance abuse, and other conditions that can identify students as being different from their peers. If your beliefs prevent you from forming beneficial relationships with students, reflect on these values and see how you might alter them before proceeding.

One caveat when working with culturally diverse clients is to beware of cultural encapsulation—the propensity to view the world through a narrow lens. It is difficult if not impossible to help people who have different worldviews and experiences from yours when you hold on too tightly to your perceptions, rendering you unable to fully understand and empathize with theirs. Worksheet 6.3 illustrates a brief self-assessment checklist to evaluate your cultural encapsulation. If you find yourself weak in some of the areas assessed by these statements, consider attending a diversity workshop, reading more about counseling diverse populations, or attending a university course on social and cultural issues in counseling.

The guidelines in this section apply to all relationships that you form with students and parents who face special challenges in learning, or who have language or cultural differences that present particular hurdles in adjusting to classroom and school environments. The next three sections examine specific aspects of each of these groups of students and present ideas for working with them, their families, and their teachers. Let us begin with students who present exceptional challenges related to learning and behavior.

School and Community Specialists

Name	Specialty	Location	Phone Number
_____	_____	_____	_____
_____	_____	_____	_____
_____	_____	_____	_____
_____	_____	_____	_____
_____	_____	_____	_____
_____	_____	_____	_____
_____	_____	_____	_____
_____	_____	_____	_____
_____	_____	_____	_____
_____	_____	_____	_____

Assessing Your Cultural Encapsulation

Answer each statement honestly, which may be your first impulse.

Sometimes I find myself

· Measuring all persons according to the same "normal" standards of behavior, notwithstanding their cultural differences

· Presuming individuals to be more important than the collective group in most settings and situations

· Presuming the collective group to be more important than individuals in most settings and situations

· Defining professional boundaries narrowly, and discouraging interdisciplinary cooperation

· Describing psychological health in mostly abstract terms (for example, "functioning normally"), with little or no attention to unique expressions of cultural differences

· Viewing dependency as always an undesirable trait or condition

· Ignoring the relevance of a client's support system to her or his overall psychological health

· Maintaining a narrow view of scientific processes by accepting only linear, cause-and-effect thinking

· Expecting individuals to adjust to and fit the system all the time

· Disregarding or devaluing the historical roots of a client's background and heritage

· Presuming that I am free of racial, social, and cultural bias

· Believing that all people can make changes in their lives through counseling if they are only willing to try

Adapted from Pedersen, 2002.

EXCEPTIONAL CHILDREN

The Education for All Handicapped Children Act of 1975, commonly known as Public Law 94-142, changed our schools and the lives of millions of children across the country. It defined exceptional children as all students with physical, educational, emotional, and other disabilities that interfere with learning. This law, and its subsequent revisions, has had significant impact both on the role of school counselors, particularly elementary and middle school counselors, and their professional preparation. Before passage of this law, few mildly to severely handicapped students attended public schools. Now these young people are an integral part of educational programs and they, like other students, face an array of developmental challenges. In addition, exceptional children in today's schools include students identified as gifted and talented, and they also face unique challenges to their development. All these students can benefit from the services of a comprehensive school counseling program.

Counseling books, journals, and other resources list various approaches to assisting exceptional students. From these resources, the following list summarizes general suggestions for counseling exceptional children:

1. Attain a basic understanding and knowledge of the child's exceptionality; learn about the characteristics of each exceptional condition and the limitations and strengths of the child.

2. Work closely with special education teachers to choose and plan appropriate counseling strategies. By coordinating services with special education and classroom teachers, your counseling services will be on target and the teachers, in turn, will provide supportive activities in the classroom.

3. Focus on the personal and social development of students and allow teachers to focus on appropriate instructional services. Choose counseling activities that focus on self-concept development, acceptance of the identified exceptionality, and acquisition of coping skills.

4. Emphasize the possibilities and potential for every child; encourage students to look beyond their disabilities and find positive ways to manage, overcome, and compensate in their lives; choose counseling activities that teach specific social and personal skills.

5. Use group approaches when possible and, if appropriate, include children without identified exceptionalities in these groups. Select group members carefully, being sure to include students who are sensitive to the differences of others and willing to form relationships with students from diverse backgrounds. Group activities are not the time or the place to help antisocial and prejudiced students become more sensitive to the challenges of being an exceptional person.

6. Become aware of community agencies and services that cater to the needs of people with different challenges. Coordinate your services with professional helpers in the community.

7. Support the teachers and parents of these students. Teaching special children, including gifted and talented youngsters, is a significant challenge, and parenting them has its own unique set of concerns and difficulties. Meet with teachers and parents on a regular basis. Form parent discussion and support groups.

8. Include awareness activities in the guidance curriculum to educate all students in the school about the exceptionalities of some children and what these unique challenges mean in terms of educational and career opportunities.

9. Provide information to teachers and parents to help them understand how cultural differences interact with certain exceptionalities, such as intellectual disability and giftedness.

10. Offer services that assist exceptional students with the numerous transitions occurring within the school, from one school to another, and from school to adult life in the community. In most elementary and middle schools, changes and transitions occur regularly, and sometimes children have difficulty with change. Design strategies to help children who have difficulty coping with adjusted schedules, changing programs, and newly adopted policies.

11. Include siblings in counseling services. Brothers and sisters of the exceptional student are often affected by or contribute to the challenges faced by the entire family. Help siblings by providing them with information about the exceptionality. Offer a safe environment in which children can explore their feelings of guilt, fear, and anger; establish their own self-identities; and learn coping behaviors.

These guidelines offer a framework with which to develop specific services for students in your school. Given the range of intellectual, emotional, and physical disabilities that children bring to elementary and middle schools, offering a wide selection of guidance and counseling approaches is reasonable in a comprehensive program. Before examining some specific strategies and approaches for you to use in your program, let us consider current implementation of laws pertaining exceptional children.

IDEA and Section 504

Today, the original 1975 law continues as the Individuals with Disabilities Education Act (IDEA), which the U.S. Congress reauthorized in 2004. In addition, the U.S. Department of Education continues to issue updates on regulations for implementation of this act. IDEA governs all services for exceptional students and designates some funding to schools and other education agencies to guarantee services for identified students. The law designates several categories of disability and corresponding criteria for eligibility for each category. It is a continuing challenge for schools to identify, assess, and meet the educational needs of students in all these categories. As a counselor, you have responsibility to help the school address these issues and ensure that all students receive appropriate services as designated by the law.

A further challenge for school administrators, teachers, and counselors is implementation of Section 504 of the Rehabilitation Act of 1973. In brief, Section 504, a civil rights provision, prohibits discrimination by school programs and activities that receive or benefit from federal financial assistance based on a student's disability. Many students that have difficulty in school but do not qualify for services under the categories and criteria of IDEA may be eligible for other services under Section 504 (Romano & Hermann, 2007).

For some students, providing appropriate instructional modifications and other accommodations is a way to ensure they will have successful school experiences. Knowledge and understanding of the provisions of IDEA and Section 504 will help you guide administrators and teachers to make appropriate decisions about the education of each student in the school. You also want to be informed and skilled about the use of appropriate responsive services to assist these students. The next section presents a few starter suggestions that cut across various counseling, guidance, and consulting activities that you might use.

Approaches with Exceptional Students

Many approaches and strategies are useful with a variety of exceptional students, including learning disabled, emotionally handicapped, educable handicapped, and physically challenged youngsters. I recommend individual and group counseling, social skills learning, behavioral contracting, career guidance, and parent education. The following sections consider a few of these approaches, starting with cognitive interventions and strategies.

Cognitive Interventions and Strategies

Some approaches to working with exceptional students encourage the incorporation of cognitive strategies into instructional programs for students and into interventions planned by school counselors. Having cognitive instructional strategies helps students

- Evaluate their present skills and abilities
- Assess the nature and difficulty of a specific task before attempting to do it
- Design a clear plan of action for approaching different tasks
- Explore all reasonable alternatives

Cognitive instructional goals also help students internalize their responsibility for achieving and succeeding in class. By giving students a cognitive focus, you help them alter beliefs and attitudes that inhibit learning while encouraging their confidence and self-reliance.

Cognitive strategies and interventions are also useful when you use individual and group counseling with exceptional students. The goals of these helping relationships are to improve understanding of individual differences, attack irrational beliefs, increase self-acceptance, design decision-making and problem-solving strategies, and encourage student participation in classes and schoolwide activities. In counseling these students, try a structured group counseling approach that introduces basic cognitive principles of self-acceptance, self-talk, and discerning between rational and irrational thinking. In these groups, instruct students about self-talk (that is, what they think and say to themselves) and its positive and negative influences on the behaviors they choose. Post examples of positive self-statements around the room and ask students to add to these statements. Possible statements include

- I can do this task.
- Math is tough, but I can learn it.
- I sometimes make mistakes, and that is OK.

After sharing and adding to these self-statements, students begin to learn the skill of positive self-talk. As an example, you might give a middle school student a sentence with a grammatical error to correct on the blackboard, while other group members gently provide encouraging, helpful statements. Then the same student attempts another problem, while this time saying positive self-instructions aloud. Finally, the student works on other sentences using self-talk quietly. This instructional process helps students internalize responsibility for their progress and enhances their appreciation for academic success.

When students have learned about self-statements, the group moves to a discussion of individual differences and the process of identifying as exceptional students. In this phase of group counseling, students explore their notions of "differences" and receive accurate information from the counselor about special education and placement in the program.

In various stages of this group process, students can learn about different aspects of being exceptional, which might include examining and debunking irrational beliefs, teaching problem-solving strategies, and encouraging experiences in which they attend classes and other programs with nonexceptional students (that is, mainstreaming). Each stage of the process extends and supports the learning begun in the earlier sessions of the group. The goal is to help students establish rational views of their abilities and capabilities and choose behaviors that reflect these views.

Using another cognitive approach advocated by Maultsby (1986), you can help students by teaching them to check the rationality of their thoughts using five basic questions:

1. Are my thoughts based on clear facts?
2. Do these thoughts help me protect my life and health?
3. Will these thoughts help me achieve my short-term and long-term goals?
4. Do these thoughts help me prevent unwanted conflicts with other people?
5. Do these thoughts help me feel the emotions I want to feel without using drugs or alcohol?

When students answer "no" to these questions, they reveal some cognitive conflict and irrational thinking. If students honestly answer "no" to some of these questions, you can help them identify irrational thoughts that they might want to alter. As they develop new rational thinking, they will be able to answer "yes" to these questions. Exceptional children can learn to use these rational questions to check their thinking, particularly the thoughts they have about their abilities and disabilities.

Token Economy Systems

A token economy system is one type of behavioral strategy that counselors and teachers use to increase desirable behavior and decrease undesirable behavior. It uses tokens (for example, stickers, points, poker chips, and play money) that are turned in by the student for a reward. Typically in a token economy system, students receive tokens immediately after they show a desirable behavior. After students collect an agreed-on number of tokens, they may exchange them for a designated award or privilege.

When designed and used appropriately, a token economy system can help elementary and middle school students stay on target when learning new behaviors, changing behaviors, or adjusting to new situations. When using token economy strategies, close communication between home and school is essential. To maximize parental involvement, try these steps:

1. *Identify concerns.* Ask the teacher (or other referral source) for specific behaviors he or she would like to see increased, decreased, or extinguished.
2. *Gather additional data.* In addition to the teacher's referral, gather information from your observations of the student and cumulative records. You may also find it desirable to interview the student.
3. *Collect baseline data.* Ask the teacher to collect baseline data on the identified behaviors. This involves gathering data on how frequently the behavior occurs during a specified time (a class period, in the morning, during a day, or all week).
4. *Meet with parents.* In a parent conference, have the teacher share the concern, the strategies that he or she has already attempted, and the results of collecting bascline data. Explain the token economy system, and if the parents agree, you, the teacher, and parents can design a plan, agree on responsibilities, choose an appropriate token and reinforcement schedule, and design follow-up procedures. You might design an agreement form, such as that shown in Worksheet 6.4, and give a copy to all participants. Follow up with the parents by phone unless there is an immediate need to reconvene in person.
5. *Implement the plan.* Each adult—the parent, the teacher, and you—takes responsibility and has a role in implementing the plan. All participants must carry out their responsibilities and roles as agreed if the plan is to be successful.
6. *Evaluate the outcome.* At the end of an agreed period, assess the progress made with the teacher and parent.

The goal of a token economy system is to help children experience initial success with external reinforcement (tokens) so that eventually they transfer this success and use the knowledge gained in handling other concerns and developing new, appropriate behaviors. If the outcome of this strategy is not successful, you want to reexamine roles and responsibilities and reevaluate selected tokens (reinforcers). Sometimes parents and teachers are inconsistent with the agreed reinforcement schedule, or the reinforcers lose their importance over time and no longer hold the power they once had. In these cases, a conference may be necessary.

Counseling Strategies

You can use several counseling approaches with exceptional students in either individual or group sessions. The following are a few strategies that you can adapt and use:

1. *Journal writing.* Have students keep journals of their actions and thoughts, and ask them to share their journals with you individually or in a small group. Students' levels of writing ability will affect your use of journal writing. Yet many children with limited writing skills enjoy this type of activity and frequently incorporate artistic renditions to illustrate their actions, thoughts, and words or to depict events in their lives.

Token Economy Agreement

Teacher: _____ Conference date: _____

Student: _____

Parent (guardian): _____

Teacher assignment: _____

_____

Parent assignment: _____

_____

Counselor assignment: _____

_____

Reinforcement schedule: _____

Follow-up conference date: _____

2. *Bibliocounseling.* Use storytelling and read books with students to facilitate the expression of their own feelings as they identify with story characters. Books and stories also can provide avenues through which students learn helpful problem-solving skills as they give suggestions of how story characters should resolve conflicts.

3. *Guided imagery.* In individual and group sessions, you can assist children by encouraging them to fantasize about how they would like to be. At the same time, they can visualize how they are, and how any self-defeating behaviors prevent them from achieving their goals. Once they imagine these debilitating behaviors, it is easier for them to choose more positive actions and relate in healthy ways to themselves and others.

4. *Role playing.* Exceptional children may sometimes have difficulty conceptualizing solutions to their problems. They also may struggle with language to express how they view these concerns. Role playing gives these students an opportunity to act out how they see their problems, how others behave toward them, and ways to resolve these conflicts. A type of role playing called the "Empty Chair" may be helpful with these students. In this role play, the child sits in one chair and talks to the "person" in the empty chair. Then the child changes positions, sits in the once-empty chair, and talks as the other person would to the now empty chair. As you discuss this process with the child, it may increase his or her understanding of relationships with others.

Consulting with Parents of Exceptional Children

Consulting with parents of exceptional students—and with the support professionals who assist them—is another major area of services for exceptional students. Consulting with parents of exceptional children begins at the point when the school informs the parents of their child's disability. Regardless of the social and educational backgrounds of parents, this is often a difficult task for counselors and teachers of exceptional children. Here are a few guidelines to consider:

1. *Be prepared.* Review all the assessment information carefully before meeting with parents. Have a clear understanding of all aspects of the program for which the child qualifies. Know the legal regulations according to which the school is placing the child. Anticipate questions the parents might ask, and prepare accurate responses.

2. *Set up a conference.* Establish an agreeable time and choose a private meeting place where the conference will not be interrupted by accidental intrusions or phone calls. Avoid placing barriers, such as a desk or table, between you and the parents. Maintain an open posture. Plan adequate time to cover all the information and answer all questions.

3. *Lead the conference.* One person, either you, a teacher, or an administrator, should be in charge of the meeting and lead the discussion. Those who are not leading the meeting are there to provide information when requested. Be careful not to overwhelm parents with a legion of professionals or with burdensome regulatory processes. Establish rapport, be open, and support one another. You can facilitate group discussions and coordinate action plans. Let the parents be the "experts" in giving support and advice.

Resource handouts and program updates offer two other effective ways to reach out to these parents. You can design and publish an annual resource guide listing community and state agencies that assist families and children. When new parents with exceptional children enroll at your school, place this information in their orientation packets. You can provide program updates through collaboration with children's teachers and by planning periodic meetings throughout the year for parents to receive information about their children's programs of instruction. Also give parents updates about new regulations or programs related to special education services.

ENGLISH LANGUAGE LEARNERS (ELL)

Learning challenges affect not only exceptional students but also students who come from other countries. Many students whose families immigrate to the United States enroll in school without any knowledge of English. Programs for English language learners, also known as English as a Second Language (ESL), exist in schools across the United States to help these relocated students.

The U.S. Department of Education's Office of English Language Acquisition (OELA) provides leadership to schools for English language learners and foreign language programs (http://www.ed.gov/about/offices/list/oela/index.html). Authorities estimate that people in the U.S. and its territories speak or sign over three hundred languages, including indigenous languages. In the coming years, programs for English language learners will serve about thirty percent of enrolled students in American schools. Some maintain that the population of ELL students is growing at a rate much faster than the English-speaking population. However, a few urban school systems have indicated a decline in ELL students. Such declines are debatable, however, and it seems that schools, teachers, and counselors in the future will continue to serve this important population.

For students who face coming to school without command of the primary language, school adjustment and academic achievement may seem like unreachable goals. Your support of ELL students in your elementary or middle school, in addition to following the general guidelines and strategies for exceptional students discussed above, may include the following suggestions:

- *Speak clearly and slowly.* Whatever language you use when counseling students, it is helpful only when students comprehend what you say. Avoid asking ELL students in front of others if they understand you. If you are uncertain whether students understand, ask them to tell you in their own languages, or in English, what you have said.
- *Plan accurate assessment of students' understanding and proficiency in speaking, reading, and writing English.* This is essential for proper placement of students in the academic curriculum and in the ELL program. In addition, this assessment will help with decisions about using interpreters.
- *Use nontraditional methods of assessment.* Students who are not proficient in English are unlikely to produce reliable or valid results on regular academic and psychological

testing instruments. If you are unfamiliar with alternative methods of assessment, consult with professionals who can assist you and the school with these procedures.

• *Create a sense of belonging for all students.* Students perform better in school when they feel as though they belong. ELL students need special attention and empathy. Design strategies with classroom teachers to help all students feel welcome.

• *Encourage bilingualism in the school.* Help your school soften the stance against bilingualism. Encourage all students and staff members to embrace the concept of learning other languages, which can become a goal of the entire school, not only the ELL students!

• *Collaborate with ELL teachers.* Form close working relationships with ELL teachers and learn techniques that will help you and the students establish rapport. Keep in regular touch with the ELL teachers in your school to be sure that you and the school are meeting the needs of students.

• *Establish a buddy system.* Assign each new ELL student a buddy from his or her grade level or class. English-speaking students you choose for this important responsibility should be selected carefully and prepared for the role. They could be some of your peer helpers. You might use more than one buddy for each new student so that a number of students benefit from this experience. Buddies can help their new friends learn their way around the school, understand school regulations, and find out who the counselor is and what the counselor does—and can generally welcome and support each ELL student.

• *Locate interpreters and translators.* Find out who the interpreters and translators are in your community and learn how to use interpreters appropriately. Select interpreters carefully to be certain they have language competencies and personal qualities that fit with the goals of the counseling program. Avoid using family members or other relatives as interpreters, and do not use students to interpret for their parents. The school might also employ translators to interpret documents from families given to the school and vice versa.

• *Cultivate pride and family involvement.* One of the most important roles you will play as a counselor to ELL students is that of advocate. Although ELL students are learning a new language and adjusting to a new society and culture, it is especially important that you allow them to retain and express pride in their native languages and cultures. At the same time, invite their families to become an integral part of the community. For example, a starting point may be to find out what special skills or talents family members have to share with the school and enrich the curriculum.

• *Increase cultural sensitivity and acceptance.* As you select interventions to use with ELL students, be sensitive to cultural nuances. Likewise, encourage your school administrators and teachers to examine school policies, programs, and processes to ensure that traditions of the school do not hinder the adjustment of students from different cultures. Most important, actively search for ways to help your school celebrate diversity throughout the year. By making an effort to appreciate and celebrate diversity, you demonstrate understanding and acceptance of students and families from varied backgrounds.

CULTURALLY DIVERSE POPULATIONS

Scenario 6.2: Differences

Comments you hear from teachers and administrators when talking about particular students cause you to wonder if some multicultural training might be appropriate for the staff. For example, you sometimes hear teachers or other staff generalize about groups of students. One teacher said, "Students from that part of town just don't have the ambition to learn." What first steps would you take to offer your colleagues in-service on multiculturalism?

In addition to learning challenges, exceptionalities, and different languages, children bring their diverse ethnic and cultural backgrounds to school. Across the United States, it is difficult to find schools that are not touched by our shrinking world or populated by children of Native American, Asian, African, Latino, Indian, Middle Eastern, or other heritage. With constant social and political upheaval and changes taking place in Africa, Asia, Europe, the Middle East, and other parts of the world, inevitable multicultural exchanges will continue to have an impact on American education.

As an advocate for all children, you accept responsibility for ensuring that the school addresses issues of equity, appropriate services, and adequate educational planning for students across cultures. Equally important is your role in helping the school increase its multicultural awareness, including the knowledge and skills of teachers and other professionals.

Multicultural awareness begins with an acceptance of the belief that cultural differences influence the needs, learning styles, and behaviors contributing to student development. Many authorities have noted that culture is not only external to the individual but also internal, and therefore is integrated with other learned experiences during a lifetime (Schmidt, 2006). For this reason, effective schools both design educational programs that accept the cultural diversity of students and make this acceptance visible in all school procedures and activities, including counseling services.

To help your school strive toward a higher level of multicultural awareness and acceptance, you require knowledge of the school population and the cultural subgroups within it. You also need to acquire counseling skills appropriate for children from different cultures, and information about community resources to assist culturally different families.

In a now classic article, Sue (1978) identified several characteristics related to effective multicultural counseling against which you might assess your attitudes. Worksheet 6.5 is an adaptation and expansion of these characteristics. Use it as a checklist to rate yourself and identify areas to strengthen so you can work effectively with children from different backgrounds.

An analysis of your values and beliefs will help you identify areas of concern for your school as well. By identifying these concerns, you are in a better position to design a program of services with a broad perspective on multicultural counseling. Multicultural counseling, broadly applied, is concerned with all the services you offer in your school.

A Multicultural Checklist

_____ I am aware of my own values and attitudes regarding the nature of people, and realize that some people differ in these views.

_____ I am knowledgeable of basic counseling skills that span different socioeconomic backgrounds, cultures, and ethnic groups.

_____ I am aware of social and political influences in my community, the country, and the world that have prejudices about cultural differences and negative attitudes toward people of different groups.

_____ I choose from different theoretical orientations and approaches when selecting counseling strategies, and tailor services to the cultures and needs of students, parents, and teachers.

_____ I am comfortable forming helping relationships with people who are different from me.

_____ I believe that all students are capable of learning.

_____ I include students from all groups in services of the school counseling program.

_____ I help identify areas of discrimination and inequity that exist in my school and in the educational program.

_____ I encourage my school to establish programs and services that reflect the school's population (for example, ensuring that the cultural makeup of the exceptional children's program, student council, peer helper program, and other services parallel the school's population).

Celebration of Cultures

As a counselor you can offer many services and programs in school to celebrate culturally diverse populations. These programs and services are educational and appropriate in small-group guidance, classroom guidance (integrated into daily instruction), and school-wide activities. Such activities with elementary and middle school students often begin with instruction about cultural differences. Incorporate this information into the school curriculum across all subject areas, including social studies, language arts, math, science, and health. Schools that recognize and celebrate cultural differences are more effective in establishing healthy learning environments.

Cultural celebrations include activities in the school that focus on cultural traditions, festivities, and historical events. Allowing students from different cultures to perform dances at assemblies, hang their own art in the hallways, write columns in the school newspaper, read literature to classes, teach classmates popular phrases in their native languages, and share other aspects of their cultural heritage invites them to become part of the school. Invitations that promote cultural sharing tell all students they are welcomed at school to continue their educational careers. By asking students to share parts of themselves with their peers, the school says, "We want to be with you."

Guidance and Counseling Services

Schools can design guidance units for students from diverse cultural backgrounds to encourage them to set educational goals, adjust to school customs and expectations without abandoning their own cultural traditions, and continue to attend school. Although these types of activities are important to helping students celebrate their differences, some of the counseling services you and teachers design for students from different cultures will focus on these students' developmental needs.

Students from different cultures who enter your elementary or middle school require the same attention to developmental concerns that other students do. In some instances, they may need more attention, particularly when they have language difficulties to overcome. When planning services for these students, you need to consider differing attitudes and beliefs associated with class and culture.

Activities you design as part of the counseling program should enhance culturally diverse students' personal, educational, and career development. You can use group counseling services and group guidance programs to help students develop essential skills and become successful in their educational and vocational careers. Specific group processes can focus on student self-confidence, career goals, human relationship skills, problem-solving skills, study skills, and test-taking skills. Here are a dozen suggestions for establishing relationships and counseling services across cultures in your school:

1. *Learn about and appreciate your own culture.* Such learning facilitates understanding and acceptance of other cultures.

2. *Be open and honest in your relationships with children, parents, and teachers from other cultures.* Be receptive to different cultural attitudes and encourage students to be honest and open with you about cultural issues.

3. *Demonstrate genuine respect for culturally diverse attitudes and behaviors.* Cultural differences, such as how people dress, eat, or worship, sometimes can be surprising when you first observe them. Remain open and receptive to learning about these customs and beliefs.

4. *Become involved and participate in cultural enrichment opportunities and activities in your community.* Invite representatives from different cultures to your school.

5. *Assess your perceptions.* Monitor your views accepting all people as unique individuals and as members of their respective cultural groups. Respect their individuality and encourage their group heritage.

6. *Examine and eliminate prejudicial and racist behaviors.* This begins with your own self-examination and extends to staff development and educational activities you plan for your school.

7. *Examine school policies and procedures for unintentional discriminatory practices.* Sometimes the most damaging behaviors and attitudes are those hidden in school policies and the curriculum.

8. *Reduce stereotyping behaviors.* Help teachers and students become more aware of their beliefs about race, gender, age, religion, and other aspects related to ethnicity and culture.

9. *Help your school plan ongoing cultural exhibits and exchanges throughout the year.* Whereas some nationally sponsored and celebrated events highlight cultural differences (for example, Black History Month in February), it may be appropriate to plan a variety of activities during the year so students of different cultures do not become associated with an obligatory calendar. If we truly accept people from all cultures, there is no need to limit our awareness and appreciation to a few designated weeks or months of the school year.

10. *Plan schoolwide cultural programs within the curriculum.* Choose curriculum materials that represent the diversity of students' cultural heritage.

11. *Encourage your colleagues and parents to set high expectations for all students.* Too often, a child's educational opportunities diminish due to an inaccurate assessment of ability based on biased perceptions of cultural differences. Help teachers and parents set high standards for student achievement that are determined by accurate assessments and reasonable expectations.

12. *Become involved with students from culturally diverse backgrounds.* Invite them to visit the counseling center. Go to lunch with them. Ask about their cultures, and share your culture with them.

Your objectives in designing the counseling services are to help all students remain in school, advance academically, and form friendships. These overlap with students' own educational, social, and career development goals. At the same time, you offer counseling services to help students correct situations, change behaviors, or overcome obstacles to learning and development. In all instances, it is imperative to be mindful of the difference between the processes of accommodating students from different cultures and assimilating them in your school. On the one hand, accommodating activities and services help students adjust to the school and encourage the school community to make adjustments for these students. Assimilation, on the other hand, is a process of absorbing the student into the majority culture while risking the loss of his or her own cultural identity. It diminishes the celebration of cultural differences and detracts from the developmental goals of your counseling services. Choose approaches that strike a balance between helping students adopt new behaviors that will facilitate their adjustment to school and allowing them to have pride in and respect for their heritage.

Although group processes, such as group counseling and group guidance, can be effective with culturally mixed groups to help them adjust to school, achieve academically, and alter behaviors, you want to screen members carefully to ensure that differences will not impede group progress or individual development. You might consider two factors when forming such groups. First, explain why you are inviting a student to join a group and describe the group's purpose. Help students understand that being part of a group means focusing on making changes in their lives. Second, you will want to examine these potential changes for culturally diverse students in relation to their unique cultures. The consequences of changing their behavior could affect their relationships with their community and family. You want to be sure that students fully and openly explore these possibilities and consequences.

Counseling culturally diverse students, either individually or in groups, requires accurate assessment of each student's present situation and level of functioning. To summarize points made earlier in this chapter, it means avoiding assessment instruments and processes that have socioeconomic and cultural bias. In addition, guard against making educational decisions for any student based on data from a single assessment instrument or process.

Individual and group counseling relationships with culturally different students place high importance on the development of self-esteem and self-worth of the individual. With the exception of modifying destructive, disruptive, and violent behaviors, the goal of altering behaviors should be secondary to one of fostering students' feelings of self-worth and belonging. At the same time, these helping relationships should value membership within a particular ethnic or cultural group.

This chapter has suggested ways for you to reach out to diverse student populations and children with special concerns. I suggest that, in doing so, you plan counseling services that satisfy preventive, developmental, and remedial needs of all students and include as many professionals as possible in this process. A broad focus across various student needs allows you to assist a diverse population. It also enables you to intervene accurately and effectively when crises occur in the school. Sometimes events happen that threaten the welfare of students, teachers, and the school community, and you want to be prepared to assist. Chapter Seven presents ideas and strategies for intervening in critical situations.

chapter 7

PREPARING *for* CRISIS INTERVENTION

Scenario 7.1: Bus Accident

A school in a neighboring district has experienced a terrible bus accident. Three students and the driver were killed. Many students were injured, and several are in critical condition. Although this accident did not involve a bus at your school, what steps could you take to provide assessment and services for students, teachers, and staff members in your school who might be affected by this event? How might you identify students and staff members who have friends or relatives involved in the accident? What signals would you and teachers watch for among students and staff members that might warrant intervention? What general, schoolwide services might be appropriate? What would you do in preparing your school to handle such tragic events as this one?

Schools face many challenges, and sometimes these challenges present themselves in critical situations. As used here, *critical* means sudden dangerous or traumatic events. Similarly, parents confront a variety of situations that can, at times, magnify into potentially explosive circumstances. Added to these emergencies are a multitude of social, economic, and environmental events that have an impact on schools, students, families, and the learning process. Family deaths, destructive tornadoes, war, factory closings, automobile accidents, substance abuse, and other traumas and tragedies contribute to crises that students, parents, and teachers face daily.

You have an important role, both as an individual counselor and as a team member, in assisting students and schools when crises occur. This chapter examines some key points to determine your role in crisis intervention. Among the suggestions in this chapter, one point is clear: be prepared. Successful resolution of crises in school will depend on your readiness to act in a direct and purposeful manner by doing the following:

- Gathering pertinent information
- Involving appropriate personnel
- Seeking supportive resources
- Formulating a plan of action
- Staying with the plan to its conclusion
- Following up with people affected by the crisis

This chapter includes suggestions for developing a crisis intervention team, designing a plan of action, implementing preventive staff development, and providing direct intervention for students and others who are in crisis. The ideas in this chapter suggest a framework within which you can work with your principal and teaching colleagues to design and implement crisis intervention strategies. In preparing for your role in crisis intervention, consider these preliminary suggestions:

- *Be informed.* Because we live in an ever-changing society with an ever-increasing storage house of information and knowledge, it is essential that you stay abreast of the latest techniques and procedures to use in critical situations. To avoid becoming outmoded, attend workshops, read professional journals, use the Internet to locate reliable and accurate information, and visit with other counselors to learn how to approach these situations.
- *Seek assistance.* In most crises, if you use the services and resources of other professionals you will be more successful than if you attempt to save the day on your own. Schools and communities often have professionals and resources that they can pool to resolve crises efficiently and effectively. A capable counselor is one who seeks collaborative relationships with other professional helpers.
- *Know your limits.* Regardless of the knowledge you possess and the level of skill you have attained, there will be times when your knowledge and skills are insufficient to help people who have critical needs. It is imperative in all helping relationships to monitor your level of competence and refer cases when you have reached the limit of your expertise.

By staying informed, seeking assistance, and knowing your limitations, you can establish effective helping relationships and formulate precise plans to meet most crisis situations head-on. The first step is to achieve an understanding of what a crisis is. A clear definition helps you distinguish between emergency intervention processes and other types of helping relationships, and enables you to choose appropriate strategies and techniques.

DEFINITION AND DESCRIPTION OF A CRISIS

A crisis is an intolerable situation, an unstable condition, or a sudden change in routine that disrupts the normal functioning of a person, group, or organization and requires immediate attention and resolution. For persons who are in a crisis, the surrounding events can be so emotionally or physically threatening that they believe they have lost control and are unable to cope.

Many different crises occur in schools and communities that can affect students, teachers, and others. Tragic deaths, violent assaults, chemical accidents, and natural disasters, among other events, can have serious impact on student behavior and the learning process in schools.

Characteristics of Crises

Although individual crises have their own unique traits, they also have some common characteristics. For example, in all crises you want to identify and address the immediate needs of people in order to resolve the situation. Usually, these needs involve physical welfare, emotional stability, and personal security. Crises generally consist of abnormal, uncommon, and extraordinary conditions that bring forth strong emotional reactions from affected populations. These reactions include high levels of fear, stress, and anger. Frequently, victims of crises become preoccupied with their situation and function in a state of disequilibria. Because of this high stress level, confrontations are common.

Many crises have the potential to upset entire school communities. Some are so traumatic that they alter the consciousness of schools and communities for years to come. Americans will remember for decades the shock of the World Trade Center's towers in New York City being hit by hijacked planes and crumbling to the ground, killing thousands of innocent people. Old news videos or pictures of this attack remind us where we were and our reactions to this national tragedy. The explosion of the *Challenger* spacecraft in 1986 and the sudden breakup of the *Columbia* shuttle in 2003, witnessed by schoolchildren across the country, are other examples of tragic events that disrupted the educational process. School counselors, social workers, psychologists, and teachers at all levels of education assisted in the wake of these disasters.

Similarly, premature deaths of students, teachers, or community leaders can have a significant impact on schools. Suicides, homicides, and tragic accidents result in feelings of loss, hurt, and anger that extend beyond the immediate family and close friends. Classmates and teachers who have had relationships with the victims also experience these feelings. In such crises, the welfare of all involved is an important consideration for counselors and other helping professionals.

Types of Crises

Sometimes crises are sudden and traumatic, such as accidents and suicides. Other times, they may be terminal, long-term, contagious, or chronic illnesses. On occasion, the illnesses themselves are not as critical to the school as are the fears raised among the school and community populations. Uncertainty about AIDS, herpes, infectious hepatitis, and flu viruses, for example, can feed unfounded rumors and exaggerate the threat to personal safety and well-being. Instances of irrational fears sometimes create a crisis.

Social and economic events also can be disruptive to schools. Such events include violent crimes, imprisonments, sexual deviance, substance abuse, sudden unemployment, industrial closings, and bank failures. Likewise, natural disasters, such as hurricanes, tornadoes, floods, and fires, can have a debilitating effect on students, parents, and teachers. People are also at risk of such environmental disasters as industrial accidents, chemical leaks, and nuclear incidents that place large segments of the population in jeopardy. In some cases, the aftermath of a major disaster requires long-term intervention and counseling to help students and others regain their momentum and stability.

A CRISIS TEAM AND PLAN

Because each crisis has its own unique characteristics as well as traits that are common to other crises, many different types of expertise can assist in handling tragic and traumatic events in schools. Crisis teams can provide such valuable assistance. Before exploring ways to establish a team and choose team members, we will first consider some general issues when handling a crisis in your school.

Factors to Consider

In preparation for designing a plan to handle various crises, you want to focus on such factors as safety, media, communication, emotional and physiological stress, and authority. Let us examine each of these briefly.

Safety

During a crisis and its aftermath, your school will want to ensure the safety of students and staff. The exact steps taken to protect people and secure the building will vary from crisis to crisis, but one point is essential: the basic needs of security, shelter, and safety from physical harm must be met in all critical situations.

Media

When tragedies occur in schools and communities, the media—press, television, Internet, and radio—want information to broadcast and distribute to the public. In most instances, the media takes this "need to know" stance in the interest of public welfare. In some crises, furthermore, schools may rely on the media to seek relief and assistance for students and teachers. For example, if a rare blood type were needed for transfusions, the media would be most valuable in broadcasting this emergency. Likewise, if there were a serious chemical spill in the neighborhood and people needed to evacuate, media sources would announce appropriate procedures.

Although the media can provide beneficial services to your school, they can sometimes be a hindrance during crises. For example, a reporter's aggressiveness in creating a newsworthy story might impede the school's progress toward calming an explosive situation and resolving the crisis at hand. The public's right to know needs to be balanced with an individual's right to privacy and protection. An appropriate plan for handling crises in your school will address this need for a balanced perspective. You can help your school write specific guidelines for the dissemination of information and media access to school personnel and present these procedures to the school staff and local media.

Communication

Specific procedures for disseminating information depend on the nature of the crisis, but schools should establish general guidelines to address how to distribute information, in what form, and through whom. The most important reason for controlling the flow of information in a systematic and reasonable way is to ensure that all announcements and requests are accurate. Misleading and inaccurate information has the potential to exaggerate a crisis, hinder attempts to help, and fuel an already volatile situation.

Emotional and Psychological Stress

Estimating how much the overall impact of a crisis will heighten the emotional and psychological stress of students, teachers, and others is another feature to consider. Such factors as the seriousness of the crisis, the number of people directly involved, and people's initial reactions to the event will serve as indicators by which you and other professional helpers will be able to estimate the scope of the problem and begin taking steps to provide assistance.

A school bus accident that kills several students, such as in Scenario 7.1, is one example of a crisis that touches everyone in a community as well as in nearby communities. Helping a large number of people deal with loss in these circumstances is challenging to everyone involved. At the same time, a tragic bus accident may raise various other issues during the peak of emotional stress. Extraneous issues, such as employing competent and qualified bus drivers ("This never would have happened if the system hired better drivers") could become emotional topics that, if not contained, might fuel an already critical situation and, more important, hamper the assistance being offered to students, parents, and teachers. The emergence of such issues presents an additional challenge for school administrators and community leaders to handle. With a comprehensive crisis plan, your school and community are prepared for all possibilities when crises occur, including the expression of a wide range of emotional responses.

Authority

Another factor to consider in a crisis is authority. During a crisis in your school, who will be in charge? This is not simply a question of who runs the school or school system. It strikes at fundamental issues, such as parents' rights, the legal jurisdiction of the police department, and the authority of other community agencies. For example, in the event of an explosion in a school, fire marshals, police officers, medical personnel, and the school administrators want to coordinate their decisions and recognize the parameters of their authority in dealing effectively and efficiently with the situation.

It makes sense to establish cooperative channels of communication and authority between schools and communities before crises occur. A well-publicized crisis intervention plan helps make strides in this direction. The first lines of authority for crises in schools must be established among school personnel who will be coordinating services. For this reason, a team approach, examined in the next section, can be helpful in dealing with most critical situations.

The Crisis Team

When determining crisis team members, your school might consider three areas of crisis management and intervention:

1. Management of the situation
2. Direct intervention strategies
3. Post-crisis procedures

Successful outcomes in each of these three areas will require appropriately trained and competent professionals. Management, communication, intervention, and other skills are organized and used to facilitate the most beneficial solutions and assistance for individuals, the school, and the community.

The first area, crisis management, requires people to make organizational decisions, handle communications, and arrange hospitalities (for example, food and beverages) if needed. Management personnel include people who will

- Be in charge of the overall operation
- Notify other team members of their responsibilities
- Respond to the news media according to established procedures
- Manage the crisis headquarters
- Notify the appropriate authorities
- Keep logs of incoming and outgoing phone calls
- Prepare news releases for publication and broadcast
- Arrange for refreshments and appropriate facilities if a prolonged crisis is expected

Some people on the crisis team have the primary function of intervening and assisting students, parents, and teachers. These team members are counselors, nurses, social workers, rescue technicians, and other available professionals. They are responsible for

- Assessing immediate needs of the people in crisis
- Determining what services to deliver and who will deliver these services
- Identifying and referring cases to appropriate agencies and professionals
- Establishing an assistance center in the school or community
- Deciding about classroom interventions, services, and strategies

After a crisis has ended, the team assesses the post-crisis environment and makes decisions about

- Returning to a normal school schedule and routine
- Continuing assistance for people in need of services
- Determining the appropriateness of special events; for example, memorial services, fundraisers, and recognitions of valor and heroism
- Examining causal and contributing factors

- Evaluating management and intervention strategies
- Planning preventive measures to avoid or deal with future crises of this nature

As you can see, a crisis team consists of several professionals and support staff. Your school may have a large crisis team designated each year, but each crisis will dictate which team members need to be involved. Possible crisis team members include the principal, assistant principals, counselors, nurses, social workers, psychologists, campus security, staff trained in CPR, staff to handle communications, and one or more teachers. In addition, crisis teams might include local police officers, mental health counselors, medical personnel, rescue squads, and others. Because of the emotional and psychological stress associated with most crises, it is reasonable to assume that you would be involved during and after the event in providing necessary counseling services.

When many team members are involved, leadership is essential. For example, if school counselors, social workers, and psychologists provide assistance during a crisis, one of these professionals needs to lead this team of helpers and coordinate services for students, parents, and teachers. Adequate coordination avoids confusion and duplication of services. Because you work daily with students and coordinate student services in your school, you are probably in the best position to provide team leadership during crises.

The Crisis Plan

In addition to designating a team, a crisis intervention plan often includes general guidelines and specific procedures to follow. The school evaluates the plan each year and revises it as needed. After the plan has undergone appropriate revisions, staff in-service at the beginning of the school year should include an overview of the crisis plan and the designated responsibilities of each team member.

Your school can design an individual crisis plan, but it should coordinate efforts with plans developed at the school system level. This is particularly true in large school systems in which several elementary schools feed into particular middle schools, and the middle schools feed to one or more high schools. In such systems, consistent crisis procedures are necessary to facilitate communications among all the schools and community agencies.

General Guidelines

In helping your elementary or middle school develop crisis plans, you may want to present general guidelines as an initial step in the process. Here are ten starter steps for handling crises:

1. *Define the type and extent of the crisis as soon as possible.* Be cautious about the information you collect and release. Accurate information is essential.

2. *Contact the superintendent or other designee and inform that person of the current situation.* Let the superintendent know the specific steps taken thus far.

3. *Notify the school staff about the situation as soon as possible and inform them of appropriate actions to take.* Depending on the crisis, you may find it is not necessary to notify all staff. Only those with an immediate need to know warrant notification.

4. *Contact the person or people affected by the crisis.* For example, call parents and guardians of students involved in the incident.

5. *Identify a central location as a communications center.* Appropriate personnel who coordinate all communications in and out of the school will staff this location. All school personnel should receive instruction as to how to refer information and questions regarding the crisis to the communications center. Assign staff members to answer phones and to call for additional information and assistance.

6. *When appropriate, contact the news media and provide accurate information about what is known about the crisis.* Release information when facts are verified and the school's position regarding the crisis is clear. Read all news releases from prepared statements. Avoid speaking "off the cuff." In critical situations with emotions high, statements can sometimes be misinterpreted and misunderstood. A prepared text is a safeguard against miscommunication.

7. *Maintain a record of all incoming and outgoing phone calls and personal contacts regarding the crisis.* This guideline is particularly important in crises that involve criminal activity, but it also is helpful in other situations to demonstrate that staff acted responsibly and reasonably during a difficult incident.

8. *Relieve key people from their normal duties.* Design strategies to allow crisis team members and the communications center staff to delegate their normal duties to other staff members. Use all available personnel.

9. *Provide refreshments for employees, rescue workers, media, and others if the crisis is prolonged.* Hunger, fatigue, and similar conditions add to an already difficult situation. Having nourishment and adequate facilities available will help keep emotions in check.

10. *After the crisis has ended, express appreciation to all individuals and agencies that helped resolve the problem.*

Exhibit 7.1 provides a checklist that may be useful in monitoring the preceding guidelines. Use it as is or adjust it to fit your school's situation.

EXHIBIT 7.1

Checklist of Crisis Guidelines

	Completed	Incomplete
1. Identify the crisis and obtain accurate information.	_____	_____
2. Contact and inform the superintendent or designee.	_____	_____
3. Notify and inform appropriate school staff.	_____	_____
4. Contact those affected by the situation.	_____	_____
5. Set up and staff a communications center.	_____	_____
6. If appropriate, contact and inform the media.	_____	_____
7. Set up a system for recording messages.	_____	_____
8. Have a plan to relieve people.	_____	_____
9. Provide refreshments, if needed.	_____	_____
10. After the crisis, express appreciation to all involved.	_____	_____

Specific Procedures

A crisis plan or manual specifies procedures for all school staff to follow in responding to a crisis. The following list offers sequential steps that schools can follow in responding to a crisis.

1. The first individual who observes the crisis alerts the principal or designee.
2. The principal notifies appropriate crisis team members and gives the location or locations to which they should report. Schools might consider a crisis signal that indicates the nature of the crisis, such as the following example of a color-coded signal:

   Blue: sudden illness (heart attack, severe fall, seizure)
   Red: suicide threat
   Yellow: hostage taking, kidnapping
   Brown: physical attack or abuse
   Green: evacuation needed
   Orange: social disturbance
   Black: accident
   White: hostile intruder on campus

   (*Note:* a caution about crisis codes and signals is appropriate here. If your school chooses to use a signal, such as the color code suggested above, consistent staff in-service is necessary. Train staff members at least once a year to inform them about the code. Teacher transfers and retirements will make crisis signals obsolete unless you regularly share updated information with the staff.)
3. One member of the crisis team supervises the communications center. This center is usually in the principal's office and has various communication capabilities.
4. The coordinator of the communications center relays a message to the superintendent's office immediately (see Exhibit 7.2). The coordinator contacts appropriate persons affected by the crises (for example, parents, spouses).

EXHIBIT 7.2

Communication with Superintendent's Office

Instructions for sending a crisis message to the central office:

1. Identify who you are and your school.
2. Identify the type of crisis.
3. Give pertinent facts regarding any individuals or services that have been called—for example, the fire department, rescue squad, and police.
4. Give facts regarding individuals involved in the crisis—for example, names of students, parents, and teachers.
5. Follow the instructions of the superintendent or designee regarding
   a. Information to be released to parents and family members
   b. Information to be given to others (the media, neighbors, concerned citizens)

Specific procedures enable the crisis team to follow consistent steps in each type of crisis. You might develop these procedures in a handbook for crisis interventions.

STAFF DEVELOPMENT

When preparing general and specific procedures to follow during crises, the school staff will need adequate in-service training. You can assist in planning, coordinating, and delivering in-service opportunities to teachers and other staff members in your school.

In-service workshops for teachers and other school personnel in regard to crises can include both prevention and intervention strategies. This section explores topics for administrators, teachers, staff, and you to consider when planning staff development for the school year. We will first examine some general information related to crises in schools and a few procedures that could influence staff development plans.

At the beginning of the school year, it is appropriate to assemble the school staff and openly discuss the types of crises that have occurred in the school and community in recent years. During this discussion, as crises are identified, you, the principal, or another leader could ask the staff to determine how the school should respond to similar crises in the future. This discussion helps identify the essential elements of an annual crisis plan for the school—and the role of school staff therein.

One topic that could come from a discussion of past crises in the school is the need for emergency medical intervention. For example, teachers may decide that they need training in CPR procedures. If so, a representative of the American Red Cross or similar organization could provide this instruction. Similarly, the staff may want to learn basic procedures for responding to other medical crises, such as seizures, fainting spells, and lacerations. Medical organizations in most communities will cooperate in providing schools with basic information about how to respond to these types of crises until professional medical assistance arrives. You can help by determining how many staff members want this type of training and by locating appropriate professionals to present the workshop. A quick survey, like that in Worksheet 7.1, can gauge teacher input.

The legal and ethical implications of crises in schools are also points for discussion with staff. Principals, teachers, counselors, and other school personnel frequently are concerned about their personal liability when assisting in critical situations. A school board attorney or other local law practitioner can assist with information. In addition, you probably are concerned about confidentiality in your counseling practice and how you handle privileged communications in crises. If you have these concerns, you should first become familiar with local and state policies and statutes regarding privileged communications for school counselors. You also should be knowledgeable about the code of ethics of the American School Counselor Association, the American Counseling Association, and the National Board of Certified Counselors, which are among the codes most professional school counselors follow. Note, however, that you do not maintain confidentiality when clients threaten themselves or others, or when students are in imminent danger. Chapter Twelve provides additional information about these legal and ethical issues.

Crisis In-Service Survey

Name: _____   Date: _____

Teachers:

At our recent faculty meeting, we discussed many different ways for us to be prepared for and ready to handle various crises that could occur in our school. As a follow-up to that discussion, we are asking for your ideas about specific in-service and preparation you would like to receive for dealing with critical situations affecting our school.

Please give us your suggestions about the topics that follow and return this form to the counselor. Thank you for your input!

First aid: _____

_____

Group management: _____

_____

Handling the media: _____

_____

Dealing with specific crises: _____

_____

Natural disasters: _____

_____

Other skill areas: _____

_____

Learning about procedures for contacting rescue squads, the fire department, or other agencies is another area you can address through staff development. What may appear to be simple procedures sometimes become major ordeals during a crisis because people have not received the necessary preparation and information beforehand. Gather important phone numbers and post emergency numbers in suitable locations around your school. Coordinate with your principal to invite representatives from agencies that can assist schools with critical situations to present at faculty meetings about procedures for including these organizations in crisis interventions. Teachers and staff members may also want to review the general and specific procedures outlined in your school's annual crisis plan.

Planning ways to respond to the news media and other inquiries into the school during and after a crisis is another avenue for staff development. When crises occur, it is difficult to think of what to say, how to say it, and to whom. If teachers receive this information and training at the beginning of the year and practice these procedures in mock situations, they are better prepared to handle communications appropriately in the heat of a crisis.

PREVENTIVE ACTIVITIES AND PROGRAMS

Many activities that you organize and deliver in the counseling program help prevent crises or limit the impact of inevitable and uncontrollable crises. In most cases, prevention takes the form of instructional services. One such activity is classroom guidance, which, as noted in this survival guide, is an ongoing component of the school curriculum.

Classroom Guidance

Classroom guidance activities help students learn about their development; their relationships with peers and others; and the personal, educational, and career decisions they will make during a lifetime. You and teachers can plan classroom guidance to help students identify indicators of stress and danger in their lives and the lives of their friends. At the same time, you can encourage children to help their friends by referring them to you or a teacher for assistance. Children often notice changes in their peers before problems become apparent to teachers, counselors, and even parents. Encourage them to share these observations through appropriate channels so that their friends and classmates can receive help.

A by-product of classroom guidance activities is your ability and that of teachers to identify students who need special attention. Sometimes teachers do not identify students who are quiet and withdrawn as ones needing a counselor's assistance. Through classroom guidance, you and teachers are able to determine whether a particular behavior warrants referral for counseling or contact with the student's family.

Developmental Counseling

You can also use developmental counseling as a preventive measure. Developmental counseling, defined earlier in this *Survival Guide,* frequently uses instructional processes similar to those used in guidance. Its purpose is to help students explore developmental concerns and issues and learn appropriate ways of handling and coping with them.

Developmental counseling helps students learn about a variety of issues, including peer relationships, feelings, assertiveness versus aggressiveness, loss and grief, educational planning, and stress management. Through developmental counseling, in groups and individually, you help students acquire skills to cope with normal, everyday problems before these concerns become overwhelming crises. This is the basic purpose for using developmental counseling with students. It provides learning experiences so students can learn coping skills to respond appropriately to difficult situations.

Peer Helper Programs

Peer helper programs incorporate some of the aspects of guidance and developmental counseling into a variety of helping processes and can thus be included among preventive approaches for dealing with crises. Typically, counselors, teachers, or both organize and supervise peer helper programs, selecting and instructing students in basic helping skills. In middle schools, students become peer helpers to tutor fellow students, act as "buddies" for new students, present guidance activities with teachers and counselors in the classroom, or become listeners for classmates who need a friend. Middle school students who are peer helpers also assist in elementary schools by tutoring younger students, reading to kindergarten and first grade groups, and assisting teachers and counselors with classroom guidance. Not all these services link directly with crisis situations, but the broad purpose is to give students basic behaviors and skills that will strengthen their ability to respond appropriately when crises occur.

Instruction in basic helping skills is essential for peer programs to be successful. In particular, peer helpers need to learn how to refer to you for counseling students who are in critical need. In this way, peer helpers are the "meteorologists" in your school, helping the staff stay informed about the school's atmosphere, climate, and critical issues affecting students.

Parent Education Programs

Education programs for parents presented in large sessions, such as PTA meetings, or in small, ongoing groups, are another example of instructional and informational services that you can use to prevent crises. In these programs, you assist parents with communication skills and help them identify early warning signs in the behaviors and developmental patterns of their children. Chapter Eleven has detailed information about establishing such programs.

Safety Education

Safety education offers another area of prevention topics that you and teachers can plan and present to students and parents. Safety lessons, although applicable at all grade levels, are particularly important in the elementary grades, in which young children are curious yet unknowing about the world around them. Safety issues you might present include information about riding the bus, walking to and from school, talking to strangers, walking in the hallways, and playing on the playground. In some communities, the local police department has a special program on safety, and officers come to school and present to classes of students. You can help by contacting community agencies and locating these services for teachers to use as resources for classroom guidance activities or school assembly programs.

Elementary and middle schools can prevent accidents and preserve student safety if faculty and staff adequately supervise students. This is not always an easy task, particularly on campuses with several buildings and expansive grounds, but even so, close supervision is necessary. Small elementary children can sometimes disappear before a teacher realizes it. Their curiosity and enthusiasm frequently lead them astray and into areas of the classroom or schoolyard that could be hazardous.

Staff development to help teachers learn strategies and techniques to increase their supervisory abilities will prevent some crises from occurring. One way to plan this type of in-service is to ask experienced teachers to share ideas and suggestions they have found to be successful in student supervision. A related skill is that of observing and referring students who are in need of services beyond classroom guidance and instruction. Offer your teachers instruction on some of the observable, behavioral indicators that, if left untreated, could evolve into major crises. This topic is of particular importance at the middle school level, at which students are entering transition years, which present limitless challenges to their physical, social, emotional, and educational development. Helping teachers learn about crisis indicators places your school in a stronger position to plan prevention activities and strategies.

The observational skills of teachers relate to their listening and communication skills. For this reason, staff development activities on student supervision for crisis prevention might also address such topics as active listening, reflection of feelings, and attending skills (for example, making eye contact). When teachers acquire these basic helping skills, they accurately respond to the needs and concerns of students in crisis. Furthermore, by effectively handling crises during the initial stages, teachers are better informed to make referrals to you or other student services professionals.

CRISIS COUNSELING

At times, you might receive referrals of crises from students, parents, and teachers, and need to determine whether you should provide direct counseling services in these instances. No clear or easy formula exists to help you decide what crisis cases you should or should not handle. Sometimes you might answer this question simply by assessing the fact of whether or not there is a more qualified professional to serve the student. For example, in a large urban area with a wealth of mental health practitioners in the public and private sectors, a counselor may decide to refer all crisis cases. In many rural areas, however, with few services for students and families, school counselors may be the only professional helpers available. Whatever the decision, you always provide services within the scope of your professional competencies and abilities. At times, this may mean going back to school or attending seminars to learn new information and skills.

When you receive a referral for crisis counseling, the following questions may help you explore the situation and make an appropriate decision:

1. *Is the situation such that you need to inform the school crisis team?* In all critical situations, you should inform the school principal. Together, you and the principal will be able to determine whether other team members need to be involved.
2. *What steps do you take immediately?* Depending on the nature of the situation, you and the principal will make decisions regarding the safety of the child; notification

of parents or guardians; and referral to other community agencies, such as the health department or social services.

3. *Do you have the training and knowledge needed to counsel effectively in this case?* If you have the skill, will you have the time necessary to see this case through to a successful resolution? If you do not have the skill or time, are other agencies or professionals available to accept this case?

4. *If another agency accepts the case, what support services should you and the teachers provide in the school setting?* You will want to keep in contact with the outside agency as the case progresses to learn the best approaches for the school to take with the child and family.

When you receive a referral and decide to handle a critical situation, taking a few clear steps will help establish an appropriate counseling relationship. These steps involve (1) assessing the nature and severity of the crisis, (2) establishing and implementing a plan of action, and (3) following up by evaluating the outcome of the counseling process.

Assessment

When assessing crisis referrals, you first determine the *degree of risk* for the student's welfare and safety, which enables you to decide who needs to be contacted about the situation and whether or not you have the skills to intervene. When possible, include other professionals in the assessment process.

Use assessment procedures that include interviewing the student, parents, teachers, and peers; observing behaviors of the person in crisis; screening the individual by using standardized as well as informal measurement instruments; and gathering data from other available sources. In making accurate decisions in crisis, the axiom "leave no stone unturned" applies. There is no such thing as too much information.

Of course, some crises do not permit enough time to do a thorough assessment. When a student is having a seizure, it is not the time to check the health record. First, you must handle the immediate medical emergency. Later, when the student stabilizes, you might perform a more thorough gathering of data.

If you determine that a student is at high risk to harm himself or herself, or is at risk of doing imminent harm to another, you must bring in all resources and appropriate authorities on the case. You immediately inform the principal and notify the parents.

In addition to assessing the scope and severity of the situation, you eventually will want to assess causal and contributing factors. When the case is referred to another professional or agency, such as a mental health center, it is still appropriate for the school to be involved in this assessment process and informed about factors that may have contributed to the crisis. You will want to examine and alter school-related factors if any are found to have been detrimental to a healthy learning environment.

Whatever assessment procedures you use to determine the extent of the crisis and contributing factors, they are simply the first steps in the crisis counseling process. Once you have decided to intervene through a counseling relationship, the next step is to determine an appropriate plan of action.

Plan of Action

Crisis counseling in most situations is direct and action oriented. This is not the time for self-reflection and exploration on the part of the student. For the same reason, in critical situations you will not have the luxury to sit back and allow the counselee much freedom to make decisions, particularly in life-threatening situations. Typically, students in crises want direction, and it is only after they stabilize and feel secure that they are able to assume some decision-making responsibilities. This responsibility to make increasingly difficult decisions comes gradually, after you have established an initial plan of action, and the student has experienced preliminary success.

A sample plan of action for crisis counseling is as follows:

1. Identify the problem.
2. Narrow the focus.
3. Formulate specific steps for action.
4. Agree on a plan or contract.
5. Refer the student for other services.

Identifying the problem means helping the student recognize and verbalize what his or her concerns are. The essential question for the students is, "What do you want to have happen?" Sometimes the answer to this question may be broad and difficult to pinpoint. When this is so, help the student narrow his or her focus. For example, the student might respond, "I'm not happy." By helping the student narrow the focus and clue in on specific factors, you might learn that the student's best friend has moved away, he or she just failed a test, or the student shows indications of abuse in the home. These facts, rather than global feelings, will enable you and the student to decide on a precise plan of action.

A plan of action in crisis counseling includes a commitment to what the student will and will not do, and what you will do in the helping relationship. Sometimes in crisis counseling it is helpful for the student and counselor to write a contract and sign it to seal their agreement. Chapter Eight includes information on using contracts with students. If the contract is broken, the relationship continues, but you negotiate a new contract. As mentioned earlier, when a counseling relationship is not improving or you have reached the limits of your expertise, it is time to refer to other agencies and professionals. Students may balk at this prospect, particularly in elementary and middle schools, because they fear forming new helping relationships. Assist them through this referral process by going with the students for their first visits and by continuing to see them at school by agreement with—and with the approval of—the other mental health professionals. Be honest with students about the reason for the referral: "We need to find someone who has more knowledge about this and is better able to help you than I am."

Follow-Up and Evaluation

Whether you provide services or refer to another professional, you have a responsibility to follow up and evaluate the outcomes. In this way, your school assesses the programs and professionals to whom you refer students and families. This is necessary both to ensure that the student continues to receive supervision and is safe from harm and to measure the progress you are making in the counseling relationship. When you have been involved in a crisis relationship for a period of time and little or no progress is seen, it is time to examine the direction and approaches chosen in the helping process and to consider the option of referring to another professional or agency.

Following cases takes time, particularly in elementary and middle schools in which student-counselor ratios are often quite high. Phoning community agencies, other professionals, and parents ensures that the services you expect are delivered by the relevant professionals and received by students and families. Sometimes all the work you do to refer a student and family to an agency falls through because the family fails to keep the appointment. By staying in touch with referral agencies, you are in a better position to remedy the situation when other people neglect their responsibilities.

By following up with the family, you let parents know that the school cares for the child and is not simply passing him or her off to another agency. This demonstration of concern encourages the family to continue therapy and lets students know that the school is looking out for their best interests. In addition, it allows you to gather information about student progress and to evaluate the strategies and approaches chosen to handle critical situations. Through informal and formal evaluation processes you will become better equipped to choose effective approaches efficiently and expeditiously when future crises occur.

AFTER TRAUMA OR TRAGEDY

When a trauma or tragedy has ended, crisis management has been successful, and you have completed any counseling necessary, your work on this situation may not be over. As devastating tornadoes, horrific floods, and senseless shootings have taught us, the residual effects, anniversary dates, and new tragic events present ongoing challenges and opportunities for schools and communities (Bodenhorn, Moore, Obenshain, & Knott, 2008; Hebert & Ballard, 2007; Kennedy, 2008b).

After a tragedy or trauma, counselors, teachers, administrators, and other personnel remain cognizant of signals that psychological stress continues to affect students, staff members, and others in the community. Anniversary dates may be particularly difficult for some people to handle. A proactive stance that establishes safe routines, plans appropriate commemorative activities, and offers guidance and counseling services for students and others seems suitable in helping people deal with stress, as does encouraging them to take charge of their emotions, move forward with their lives, and empower themselves to learn from these experiences.

Ongoing counseling services after traumatic events can include several activities. Hebert and Ballard (2007) mentioned several, including play therapy, art therapy, and other activities that encourage children to express feelings, deal with their grief, handle anger, relieve stress, and become empowered. As a counselor in the school, you will find many counseling approaches in the literature that can help students in the aftermath of tragic or traumatic events.

In this and the preceding chapter, you have learned about general guidelines and approaches to working with students with special needs and diverse cultural backgrounds, as well as about being prepared for crises that occur in schools and communities. Chapters Eight and Nine highlight several areas of student concerns and present ideas and strategies for assisting in particular cases.

chapter 8

SELECTING RESPONSIVE SERVICES *to* ADDRESS STUDENTS' CONCERNS

Scenario 8.1: Head Slapper

A teacher has referred a student because of his perfectionist behaviors and self-hitting when upset with himself. The teacher reports that at times, when the student is angry about something he has done, he will slap himself with both hands on the sides of his head. The teacher is not only worried about this behavior but also concerned because it is disruptive to the class. Other students laugh at the student when he does this. When the student in question slaps himself on the head, he does it for a few seconds. No physical harm seems apparent, except his ears sometimes are red from the hitting. How would you proceed with this case? Would you contact the parents? If so, on what basis? If not, why not? What responsive services, if any, would you use in helping this student and teacher?

Most elementary and middle schools include children who, although not identified with specific exceptionalities, have concerns that require the attention of teachers and counselors. Scenario 8.1 illustrates one such example. Conflicts and concerns are part of everyday life, and helping students deal with their difficulties is an important part of your role as a school counselor (Purkey, Schmidt, & Novak, 2010). Some concerns place children at risk of school failure, contribute to poor peer relationships, or relate to other conditions that negatively affect student development. For example, a student who has lost a close grandparent may need assistance through the grieving process. Such help may ensure that school attendance does not suffer and the student returns to a normal routine within a reasonable amount of time.

This chapter presents noteworthy student concerns that, in most instances, do not present critical situations. Although the list of concerns addressed here is not exhaustive, the examples, ideas, and strategies might be useful in selecting approaches to help students with a wide range of common developmental issues. You will have undoubtedly handled many of these concerns, or will confront them as an elementary or middle school counselor. (Chapter Nine will explore more critical issues that some students and families bring to school, as well as events in the community that have an impact on the school.)

In many instances, student concerns arise because of social forces, such as a parent's loss of a job, over which children have little or no control. Other times, children themselves instigate the difficulties. This chapter considers the following childhood and preadolescent issues: bullying, cyberbullying, divorce, after-school child care, loneliness, relocation, stress, underachievement, and technology.

BULLYING

Bullying is a phenomenon that appears at many levels of schooling. Although considered a significant problem in U.S. schools, bullying is also a noted problem in other countries, such as England, Australia, and Japan, to name a few. Research in the United States indicates that between 30 and 80 percent of students, depending on the region of the country, suffer from bullying at some point in their educational careers. About 160,000 students remain home from school each day to avoid being the victims of bullying. These data show that bullying in schools is a persistent problem that requires attention from counselors, teachers, administrators, students, and parents.

The effects of bullying often leave students with long-term physical, emotional, and educational scars. Victims of bullying frequently have problems focusing on their schoolwork; perform below levels of expectation; show symptoms of anxiety, depression, and poor self-confidence; and have higher absentee rates. All of these consequences take a tremendous toll on students and, equally important, on the school as a community. Taking a proactive stance against bullying can also be a preventive step to help the school avoid legal entanglements with parents and students.

School counseling literature and research have documented the scope of the bullying problem. These articles and studies also offer insights about ways to identify bullies, provide counseling services for bullies, plan and deliver programs for teachers and staff to address bullying, provide guidance lessons across the school to help understand bullying, and deliver counseling services to victims to help them learn assertive behaviors and other skills to cope appropriately (Bradshaw, O'Brennan, & Sawyer, 2008; Carney, 2008; Cole, Cornell, & Sheras, 2006; Hall, 2006; McAdams & Schmidt, 2007; McLaughlin, Laux, & Pescara-Kovach, 2006).

Bullying is a specific type of aggressive behavior that does the following:

- Harms or disturbs another person or persons
- Repeatedly and over time willfully exposes others to negative behaviors
- Creates a harmful relationship in which power is exerted over another person

Bullying comes in many forms, ranging from name calling and other verbal put-downs to physical abuse. Jacobsen and Bauman (2007) identify three types of bullying: verbal, relational, and physical. Among these types, schools find a range of behaviors that might include blatantly discriminating against or excluding another person; deliberately ignoring someone; taunting, teasing, or taking or damaging property; coercing someone to do something he or she does not want to do; or a combination of hurtful and harmful behaviors. (The next section considers the impact of advancing technology and the newest form of bullying, called *cyberbullying*.)

The literature also mentions two main types of bullies—aggressive or passive. You might expect the aggressive bully to overtly and actively taunt, tease, abuse, and bother others. In contrast, passive bullies usually associate with aggressive bullies but rarely take the initiative to bully others. They are "hangers-on" who support the aggressive bully.

As necessary as it is to identify types of bullying and design interventions to prevent bullying, it is equally important to know why bullying occurs for those interventions to be effective. Students bully other students for a variety of reasons, and some researchers have noted that understanding these underlying dynamics and the relationship between bullies and their victims is important in choosing successful strategies (Roberts & Morotti, 2000). One critical point to remember is that bullying in schools is everyone's problem. These destructive behaviors not only have a negative impact on the victim, they also inhibit the healthy development of the bully and create frightening, uninviting schools.

What can you do as an elementary or middle school counselor to help address bullying? The first step is to recognize the problem when it exists. Too often, adults dismiss bullying as a normal part of child development. Be proactive. Let your administration and teachers know when you observe children in bullying relationships, and offer specific suggestions to address the situation. Also, create reliable ways to identify bullies before problems escalate. For example, Cole, Cornell, and Sheras (2006) found that peer nomination methods, whereby students at-large name those who bullied others, identified far more bullies than did methods when students self-reported whether they had bullied or had been bullied.

Another early step is to help your school develop a clear code of conduct that spells out appropriate behavior and dictates what to do when faced with repeated inappropriate behavior. This code needs to be available and easily understood by everyone in the school. Simply publishing the code without a systematic procedure for introducing and explaining it to the student body is insufficient. As counselor, you can help develop and explain this code of conduct.

You and other school personnel can assess the school's physical environment to diminish opportunities for bullying. Search areas of your school where inappropriate behavior is likely to take place, and help teachers and administrators address and change these sanctuaries of hostility. At the same time, look for ways to increase student supervision without needlessly burdening teachers. Consider using volunteers, such as parents or retired citizens, to help with this initiative.

Incorporate information about bullying into your school's guidance curriculum and assist teachers in delivering this content. *Bully Busters* (Horne, Bartolomucci, & Newman-Carlson, 2003) is a research-based approach for teachers of grades six through eight that aims at controlling and preventing bullying. The program is for teachers to increase their awareness, knowledge, and skills to address the root causes of bullying and handle the problem with confidence. The manual includes eight learning modules with a total of thirty-six classroom activities. You also want to teach students what to do when faced with bullying situations. Help them learn appropriate assertiveness and coping skills as well as where to turn for assistance when they become frustrated or fear for their safety. Establish small groups in the counseling program to give added attention to victims who need it. As students learn various assertiveness and coping skills, ask teachers to provide feedback about student behaviors. Exhibit 8.1 is an illustration of how to obtain such feedback. Observations from teachers would help you evaluate the student's progress and assist the student with behaviors that need further attention.

EXHIBIT 8.1

Monitoring Student Assertiveness and Coping Skills

Student: _____ Dates: _____

Teachers: _____

Please observe the above student throughout this week. When you meet with your unit or team, share and discuss your observations of the student's responses to bullying behaviors. Use the checklist below to summarize your observations. When you have finished, please provide a summary to the counselor.

_____ Student looked directly at the bully, spoke clearly and firmly, and told the bully to stop the behavior.

_____ Student told the bully to stop and then conferred with the teacher.

_____ Student told the bully to stop the behavior, paused for a moment, then turned to other tasks.

_____ Student showed good judgment in avoiding situations where bullying would likely occur.

_____ Student did not do any of the above behaviors. Instead, the student:

_____

_____

_____

Teacher's Summary:

_____

_____

_____

Adapted from Hall, 2006.

Finally, address the concerns of the bully. Encourage teachers and administrators to make contact with bullies in nonthreatening ways. Provide individual and group counseling so bullies can have a safe place to speak openly about their concerns. Listen carefully and be sure you understand the full dynamics of what the bully is saying. Create guidance and counseling services to help these students learn ways to make changes in their behavior, become more tolerant of others, and use their power in constructive ways to help others. Let bullies know that you are there for them just as you are for all other students, and you will be there for the long haul whenever they need you.

Gathering data to verify if bullying prevention strategies and intervention programs are working is an important part of your comprehensive school counseling program (Young et al., 2009). The time and energy you and your colleagues expend in providing prevention and intervention programs need assessment in terms of the effectiveness of these services. Have antibullying programs and strategies been effective in your school? Do students report fewer instances of bullying? Do students feel more empowered to cope successfully in bullying situations? These and other questions can help you frame an evaluative process and collect useful data to measure the value of these services.

CYBERBULLYING

With continuously advancing and expanding technologies, the nature of bullying has a new appearance. Today's students have access to e-mail; Internet platforms, such as MySpace and Facebook; blogs; cell phones; text messaging; and countless other technologies. Many of these technologies can be tools for bullying, commonly referred to as *cyberbullying*.

Although traditional bullying and cyberbullying both have the capacity to harm someone directly or indirectly, researchers have noted that cyberbullies may include school leaders who are viewed favorably by teachers and administrators (Willard, 2006). It may be that easy access to new technology has increased the population of potential bullies. At the same time, students bullied through such technology are reluctant to report these instances for fear of forfeiting their access privileges.

You may want to help your school develop appropriate policies and procedures to address cyberbullying specifically. You might also design and deliver parent awareness sessions about cyberbullying. Finally, you should use the counseling strategies you have developed for traditional bullying to assist victims and perpetrators of cyberbullying (Chibbaro, 2007). In this regard, group work may be helpful in bringing students together to talk openly about bullying and specifically about cyberbullying. Through group processes, you offer students opportunities to inform and help one another about actions to take when being bullied.

DIVORCE

Divorce continues to affect a high number of children and families. It is stressful and painful for all involved, and teachers and counselors usually see the effects manifested in children's behavior in school. Divorce results in the collapse of a supportive and protective home structure, without which a child feels alone, frightened, and insecure in an uncertain, often terrifying world. The effects of divorce are readily apparent with some children, whereas others may not exhibit developmental reactions for several years after the breakup.

Very young children of preschool age have limited understanding of divorce and, as a result, often feel insecure and frightened, experiencing nightmares and behaving in an infantile manner. Elementary children with advanced cognitive development frequently view the divorce as their fault and hope the family will reunite. As children approach middle school, they experience feelings of loss, shame, rejection, and anger over the divorce, yet they strive to adjust to the change and usually cope satisfactorily. Judith Wallerstein (1983, 1996) studied children from divorced families for many years and, based on her research, established six tasks that children of divorce must accomplish to achieve healthy development in their lives. Although she undertook this research years ago, the findings are still useful in working with today's children of divorce. Counselors and teachers who understand these tasks are able to design intervention strategies—preventive, developmental, and remedial—to assist elementary and middle school children of divorced families. Here are Wallerstein's six psychological tasks, accompanied by ways you can intervene as a counselor:

1. *Acknowledge the reality of the marital rupture.* It is essential that the child move from a state of fantasy, fear, abandonment, and denial to an acceptance of the divorce. The sooner the child confronts the reality of the breakup and receives assistance with his or her feelings, the earlier a resolution of concerns is possible. Relationship-building skills, such as listening, clarifying, and reflecting, combined with stress reduction and relaxation techniques, may be helpful when counseling children of divorced families.

2. *Disengage from parental conflict and distress and resume customary pursuits.* Withdrawal from normal activities and neglect of schoolwork are common concerns with children of divorce. They have difficulty distancing themselves from the stress and conflict between their parents and as a result tend to lose interest in school and other activities. Counselors and teachers want to be understanding and respectful of children's desires to be concerned and involved with their parents during this stressful time. At the same time, services should be available to assist students so they can eventually distance themselves from the conflict and resume normal childhood activities. Group counseling is one approach that has been a successful intervention strategy in helping children of divorce confront these issues and learn coping behaviors.

3. *Resolve loss.* This task requires children of divorce to resolve several factors related to loss. These factors include the obvious departure of one parent, often felt as rejection and worthlessness, as well as the possible loss of neighborhood, school, friends, and place of worship if the divorce precipitates a family move. In addition, abstract characteristics, such as status, security, and family traditions, may diminish or disappear in the eyes of the child. Individual and group counseling sessions to focus on self-esteem and the value and worth of the individual child will be helpful. When children of divorce have irrational thoughts of how the divorce is "catastrophic" to their lives and lifestyles, cognitive behavior modification and restructuring techniques are helpful.

4. *Resolve anger and blame.* Children and adolescents sometimes resort to anger and blame in their search for "answers" to the family divorce. They might blame one or both

parents, themselves, or their siblings. Very young children fault their own "badness" for the breakup, whereas older children blame themselves for an inability to keep their parents together. Older children also might direct intense anger toward one or both parents for "wanting" or "causing" the divorce. These feelings of blame, guilt, and anger can be resolved, and children can forgive themselves and their parents for the family breakup. Bibliocounseling in groups or individual sessions can help children come to terms with these feelings.

5. *Accept the permanence of the divorce.* In dealing with tremendous feelings of loss, a child will hold on to the fantasy that his or her mother and father will eventually reunite and the family will again be together. These feelings persist even in the face of remarriage by one or both of the parents. Children will benefit from counseling and guidance activities that encourage them to test the reality of the situation, accept their parents' decision to divorce, and continue forward with their lives. During counseling, children can make choices, such as whether to continue hoping that their parents will reunite, that will enable them to accept the permanence of the divorce and move ahead with their own development.

6. *Achieve realistic hope regarding relationships.* For middle school children entering their adolescent years, a divorce can influence how they view their own relationships, their ability to love and be loved, and their willingness to take risks in establishing relationships. Teachers and counselors can encourage these children to take the risk of becoming involved in relationships with other people, realizing that not all relationships will succeed. When relationships end, it may be painful but all right nevertheless. When students never attempt relationships, however, they have absolutely no chance of succeeding.

Counselors who help children through parental divorce must, as when addressing any special concern, have adequate skills and demonstrate appropriate acceptance and understanding of the situation. The following guidelines will help you when working with children who are dealing with divorce:

- *Examine your own values and views regarding divorce.* Children are perceptive. They will identify any negative responses that you convey.
- *Avoid using abstract explanations and offering sweeping generalizations.* Use concrete examples to help children understand their feelings about the divorce.
- *Give children time to express their feelings* of hate, anger, fear, sadness, and relief. Encourage them to look toward the future and identify their strengths for dealing with challenges that lie ahead.
- *Emphasize that the children are blameless for the divorce.* In general, avoid labeling anyone as a "bad guy" or "good guy" in the situation.
- *Make only the commitments you can keep,* and avoid promises you cannot deliver. Further disappointments for divorced children could be devastating.
- *Offer children the opportunity to meet in groups* with other students experiencing divorce. They can gain strength by identifying and sharing with others.
- *Refer children to local practitioners and agencies* when you think more intensive or long-term counseling is necessary.

In addition to these guidelines, you might consult with teachers and administrators about school factors (for example, attendance regulations, classroom guidance) that will aid children and parents of divorced families. As a counselor you can help your school by doing the following:

- Review forms and regulations that demonstrate biases toward traditional families. Such policies discriminate and potentially embarrass single parents and children of divorce.
- Collaborate with the media coordinator to establish a section of the library for materials on divorce. Ask your advisory committee to correlate these materials with grade-level curricula.
- Help teachers plan classroom guidance activities to include information on various family structures in society and integrate these lessons with daily instruction.
- Coordinate staff development opportunities for teachers to learn effective strategies when working with divorced parents and their children.
- Maintain classroom structure and a consistent school routine. Consistency in school schedules and discipline provides security for children whose families are going through a divorce.
- Be available to children who need to confer with you during periods of severe stress and conflict at home. By being available in such situations, you help prevent disruption in the classroom.

When working with parents who are going through a divorce, encourage them to focus on the children's needs rather than on past problems with the former spouse. Reassure parents that although their children may have trouble, most children rebound and overcome the negative aspects of divorce. Provide them with community resource information and suggest that they be open and honest about the divorce with their children. It is not necessary for parents to burden their children with unnecessary details, but an honest explanation at the child's level of understanding can facilitate the healing process. Here are some other suggestions you may make to parents:

- Avoid using children as messengers between partners or as "investigators" into the life of the other parent.
- Permit children to remain children and not become miniature adults. Resist the temptation of having them become "the man of the family" or "the big sister" for everyone else.
- Respect the parent-child relationship. Do not seek counseling from your child for your own problems.
- Keep your commitments and promises. Do not make promises you cannot keep.
- Talk with your children about their future. Include them in plans for the family.
- Give children appropriate responsibilities and chores to help them feel like an essential part of the family. Everyone in the family should have responsibility.

Assign chores that are developmentally appropriate and expect children to accept responsibility and follow through.

- Avoid conflicts and put-downs with your ex-spouse in view of the children.
- Cooperate with your ex-spouse in arranging suitable visitations. Demonstrated love on the part of both parents will overcome most obstacles in difficult situations.

AFTER-SCHOOL CHILD CARE

Elementary and middle school counselors and teachers want to both identify family factors that inhibit learning and development and assist children and parents with these hindrances. One factor associated with families of working parents is the issue of child care, particularly after school, when many children go home and care for themselves while their mothers and fathers are at work.

Many students leave school at the end of the day and go home alone to an empty house, or they stay with an underage brother or sister for a significant portion of the day. It is difficult to estimate the number of children who care for themselves and younger siblings after school and at other times when their mothers and fathers are working. Some estimates claim that over 30 percent of children between the ages of five and thirteen care for themselves after school. The number of mothers in the workforce, the rise of single-parent households, and burdensome economic pressures have all contributed to this phenomenon.

These students often experience higher levels of worry, fear, boredom, and loneliness. Children who care for themselves have shown lower academic achievement than those with parental supervision, and children who care for their younger brothers and sisters show a decrease in school performance.

Your school could develop programs to help children reduce the feeling of isolation that frequently accompanies self-care. It can also encourage neighborhoods to establish networks of community resources and organizations to assist what we sometimes call *latchkey* children. In addition, schools can sponsor programs to help children learn about self-care and protection, and they can organize after-school activities that allow children to spend additional time at school with adequate adult supervision.

Counselors and teachers could develop guidance units to present to all students about being responsible for self-care. The lessons might include information about arranging systems of communication, establishing home rules, practicing safety, handling emergencies, coping with fears, overcoming boredom, and talking with parents about concerns. In addition, students would receive information about how to care for younger children.

Another role for you in assisting children who spend a significant amount of time at home alone is as a presenter at PTA or PTO meetings and other parent gatherings. Encourage parents to establish set routines with their children, provide safety checklists, know their children's friends, monitor the use of technology, and keep open the lines of communication so children feel free to raise their concerns and feelings about staying alone. Also, remind parents of their responsibility to come home immediately after work. Children worry when their parents do not heed family schedules.

LONELINESS

Another issue you might encounter as an elementary or middle school counselor is children's feelings of loneliness. Some estimates of loneliness are as high as 25 percent for the population in general, and there is no reason to expect that it is lower for children.

In helping lonely children, you should work cooperatively with teachers. Often, teachers can alter the classroom environment to facilitate the inclusion of these children in social and learning activities. Classroom structure and size can enhance or inhibit the social isolation of children. When teachers arrange their classrooms and plan activities to encourage student interaction, friendships develop, cooperation increases, and isolation diminishes.

Help children develop social skills by using modeling and role playing to teach them how to approach people, begin conversations, give and receive compliments, send notes, and improve their personal appearance and grooming habits. You might try cognitive approaches to counseling to help students develop positive thought processes about themselves and overcome fears of social interaction.

Shyness sometimes goes hand in hand with loneliness. Shy children will express their feelings more readily when you use puppets, drawings, storytelling, unfinished sentences, or play therapy techniques. Here are five specific activities that may help when you are working with shy and isolated children:

1. *Involve children in peer helper services.* Have them assist other students through tutoring or other active means.
2. *Invite children to participate in small-group activities in the counseling center or as members of other school programs.* Have them take on such roles as student media aids, school spirit committee members, or office helpers.
3. *Locate a "pal" for a shy child and team the two together.* The friend you find should not be a domineering and overpowering type of student, and he or she will need instruction about the concerns of shy children.
4. *Give shy and isolated children responsibilities in the school.* Let them run errands for the school secretary, bring supplies to the custodian, hand out materials in class, answer the counselor's telephone, and help the media coordinator by showing other students where to locate books and materials or use technology.
5. *Use bibliocounseling and other media to help isolated students learn new coping skills and relationship-building techniques.* By using books and other media in a nonconfrontational approach, you will encourage students to adopt positive methods of gaining acceptance from their peers.

Some children who are naturally shy can be encouraged to become involved and belong with others in the school through such programs and services as those listed above. Other children become quiet and withdrawn when they experience a personal tragedy. At these times, you and teachers need to show concern and understanding toward the child by allowing time to grieve and by being available when he or she needs support and comfort.

RELOCATION

Countless families move each year, thus affecting millions of children who relocate and change schools. This is particularly true for children of military families when parents are deployed, promoted, or transferred to another base. Elementary and middle school children sometimes have trouble when they transfer to a new school. In most cases, children who move are able to adjust to their new school and establish new friendships when given time. Sometimes family moves are even beneficial, because they offer children a wider perspective and additional challenges in life. Moving too many times, however, is rarely helpful to a child's educational and social development.

As a counselor, you can ease children through their relocation by helping teachers and parents understand the stress and loss that children may experience when moving away. Teachers and parents also can learn about behavioral signals children send when under stress. These signals include withdrawal, aggressiveness, chronic ailments, and infantile behaviors. At times, a child will also exhibit irrational fears about a new house or the school he or she will attend.

The following are a few strategies that teachers, parents, and you can use to help children with relocation:

1. *Have classroom discussions to focus on positive aspects of the impending move.* Recognizing the loss is important, but it is equally helpful for the child to focus on the future: new experiences and friends. Class discussions in the school the child is leaving can bridge the old with the new. For example, teachers in the sending school could encourage children in their classrooms to correspond with their former classmates. In return, children who have left the school can send letters and e-mail messages about their new surroundings and photographs of their new home and friends.

Counselors and teachers at the receiving school can also assist with the transition. Holding similar classroom discussions in the new school is helpful in making the child feel welcome. Assist in this process by establishing peer welcomers who are trained to meet new students, orient them to the school, and be their "buddies" for the first few weeks or months while they learn their way around. For a new student, having someone his or her own age show him or her the ropes is much better than being guided through a tour by a counselor, principal, or other adult who cannot possibly see the school in the same way students do.

2. *Meet with parents to prevent a difficult move from becoming catastrophic.* If parents have children who are leaving your school, help them understand the difficulties the child may experience. Do some planning and have discussions so parents can help the child survive the initial scrutiny of new peers. At the same time, parents can encourage their children to maintain links between the old and the new. For example, buying new clothes and school supplies might seem appropriate for a new start, but some children may feel more comfortable with familiar clothes and a favorite backpack. Students will feel awkward enough just being new to the school. They may not want to be "freshly wrapped," announcing their arrival to the whole world! Encourage parents to let their children keep a low profile if they choose to.

If you are a counselor in the receiving school, you can meet with parents to find out about children's interests, the subjects they like, and the activities they pursue in and out of school. At the same time, parents can learn about the school procedures that may differ from those of the sending school. With this information, they can guide their children in knowing what to expect from the new school environment.

Help parents become familiar with the community and its resources. Prepare parent orientation sessions periodically during the year to assist new families. Arrange to have community leaders speak about social opportunities, financial assistance, municipal facilities, medical care, and other community resources. The more information and assistance afforded to parents, the less stressful the move is for them, and in turn the easier the move is for their children.

3. *Hold individual or group sessions with children whose families are leaving the community or have moved into town.* These preventive relationships can give children accurate information, allow them to express their feelings in a safe setting, and help the counselor identify children who are going to need special attention. Using bibliocounseling and other media with individuals or groups also will give children information and allow them to identify role models illustrated in the books or stories. Books and videos about relocation can similarly be used in classroom guidance to help all children learn ways to welcome new students to their school.

4. *Call the new school or send a postcard and let the school know that a student of yours is coming.* If you have been counseling the student, ask to speak with the new school's counselor (or principal if there is no counselor) and let that person know the student may need some special attention and support. Exhibit 8.2 illustrates a sample postcard to send to the new school. You could also transmit such a postcard as an e-mail.

EXHIBIT 8.2

Sample Postcard for Student Transfers

Dear Washington Elementary School:

We understand that one of our students, Jack Rogers, a fifth grader, is transferring to you this month. Please know that we are available to help you with this student's transfer and adjustment to your school. If you need additional information, you may call our counselor, Mr. Robert Hastings, at (020) 555–7000; write to him at Downtown Middle School, Railroad Street, Anywhere, U.S.A.; or e-mail hastingsr@downtownmiddle.usa.

Let us know if we can be of assistance.

Downtown Middle School
www.downtownmiddle.usa

STRESS

Stress is widespread among children and adolescents in American society. For children and adolescents, several stress factors emanate from a number of sources. For example, the freedom resulting from having working parents often influences childhood and adolescent decisions about sexual activity, drugs, and other inappropriate behaviors. Family divorce, relocations, and deaths, as already discussed, also add to the stress children and adolescents experience. Added to these factors are the expectations of the school and the increased emphasis on testing and achievement.

Various strategies are available to help children deal effectively with stressful situations. Systematic desensitization, relaxation, and cognitive behavior therapy, among other approaches, are methods that can be helpful with young people. In helping children handle stress appropriately and effectively, the following suggestions may be useful:

1. *Choose strategies carefully.* Know whether your school's community is receptive to different types of counseling approaches. Terms such as *systematic desensitization, biofeedback, cognitive behavior modification,* and *guided imagery* are sometimes suspect because they are mysterious and unknown to most people, including teachers and administrators. Use language that is clear and understandable to children and parents. For example, *cognitive behavior modification* is translated as "learning to tell yourself to do good things."

2. *Learn your techniques well.* Obtain the necessary training through coursework, seminars, and readings to be proficient in the approaches you choose. Incorrect use of strategies may result in outcomes quite opposite from what you envisioned. As one example, by using relaxation techniques forcefully and awkwardly you might increase a child's stress rather than reduce it! The same is true for other misused and misguided approaches.

3. *Consult with teachers and parents to help them become familiar with stress factors among children.* Parent education programs and teacher in-service activities can educate adults about the indicators of childhood stress and appropriate stress management strategies.

4. *Coordinate classroom guidance activities with teachers and health educators in your school to include information about stress reduction.* Plan schoolwide physical activities so children learn the relationship between appropriate exercise and stress management.

5. *Learn ways of managing stress in your own life.* Counselors face the same frustrations and challenges as others and need to be equipped to handle stress effectively. Take care of yourself. Chapter Thirteen of this guide emphasizes in more detail the importance of self-care.

UNDERACHIEVEMENT

One of the most frequent referrals counselors receive from teachers concerns students who are not doing their work or do not complete their assignments. In many cases, these students are not performing up to their capabilities as measured by educational assessments and teacher judgment.

Although not as alarming as such other problems as substance abuse, depression, suicidal talk, and physical abuse, student underachievement is a critical problem in American education. Often it is a symptom of unique, serious dysfunctions in a student's life, but increasingly these instances of underachievement are a combination of personal, psychological, intellectual, and social concerns inherent in a large number of students.

Sometimes underachievers are students who act out in class, disrupt the learning process, and rebel against school and classroom regulations. Other times, however, they are quiet students who simply appear apathetic, disinterested, or lazy. Teachers and parents frequently describe these students as behaving immaturely, giving up easily, being overly critical of themselves, or lacking self-confidence. Whatever the characteristics, the results are the same: poor academic performance in class, lower-than-expected scores on achievement tests, and increased frustration among teachers and parents.

When schools allow underachievers to continue without intervention, the result is often complete failure and lack of interest in learning, contributing to school dropout levels in the upper grades. For this reason, you want to place high priority on assisting these students. To do so effectively, it will help to know what strategies and interventions with underachievers have been most successful. A review of studies that examine the effects of counselor interventions with underachieving and low-achieving students in elementary, middle, and high schools shows that

- Group procedures appear to be more effective than individual counseling with these students. In addition, groups that use structured, behavior-oriented sessions as opposed to unstructured, person-centered approaches tend to be more effective in improving student performance.
- Longer treatment programs, those lasting more than eight weeks, are more effective than short-term interventions. This finding indicates that you should not expect a quick fix of student attitudes and behaviors related to school achievement.
- Voluntary participation is essential to program effectiveness. When students agree to join a group, they are more likely to commit to change than if they are forced into a program.
- Counseling in combination with study skills instruction is effective in helping students raise their achievement.
- Programs that include parent participation tend to show positive results.

In addition to these findings, instructional strategies and counseling approaches to consider when you are working with underachieving students include the following:

1. *Individualize homework assignments.* Underachieving students may need tailor-made homework assignments that gradually increase requirements as earlier assignments are completed successfully. Homework assignments should be clear to students. Teachers might take these students aside and ask each what he or she will complete as a homework assignment.

Occasionally, teachers might resist treating some children differently than others. Through staff development, however, teachers might learn about and discuss the importance of fostering student uniqueness and giving individual attention in the educative process. When we refuse to recognize individual qualities and the unique concerns of students, we condemn many children to certain failure. By individualizing educational approaches, teachers offer every child equal opportunity to join other students in realizing academic success.

2. *Focus on success.* Underachieving students will climb the highest mountains, swim the deepest oceans, and take on the most threatening challenges to avoid class assignments

or homework that set them up for failure. Encourage teachers to begin with assignments and projects that interest students and offer them a reasonable chance of success. When grading students' work, emphasize the positive and de-emphasize the errors. Teach students to capitalize on their strengths in order to compensate for and overcome their weaknesses.

3. *Be consistent and hold up your end of the deal.* When students renege on agreements they have made with you, do not lower your expectations. Gently remind students of the agreement they made (for example, to change a behavior) and let them know that you always keep your end of a deal because you care about them. You also want them to care for themselves, so you expect them to keep their agreements with you. Sometimes you may decide that the agreements you have made with students are too stringent or unreasonable. When this happens, it is appropriate to renegotiate with students and draw up new plans.

4. *Keep lines of communication open with the home.* Report frequently to parents about the progress of students. Let parents know that their input and opinions are valued. Show parents how to establish a study time at home and identify an area where the child can be alone during this time to complete assignments. Lead groups in which parents can share strategies they have found to be successful in their families. In these groups, you can facilitate learning and offer positive approaches to help parents communicate with their children and preadolescents.

5. *Use volunteers, such as retired citizens, to establish study partners for underachieving students.* Schedule times during the week when students and their partners can meet, read together, review assignments, and establish healthy working relationships.

6. *Establish a peer-tutoring program.* For elementary school students, contact middle or high schools to identify student helpers who can offer services to younger children after school. Middle school peer helpers can learn to tutor in classes, during lunchtime, or after school.

7. *Write behavioral contracts with students.* Let them work toward in-school rewards, such as a trip to the school's media center, an extra half hour on the playground with the counselor, a free ice-cream bar after lunch, or other special treats. Exhibit 8.3 illustrates a sample contract.

EXHIBIT 8.3

Sample Student Contract

(Student) agrees to complete all assignments in (class) for the next (number) days. The teacher will determine whether assignments are complete and will give the student a receipt for each day that work is handed in. At the end of (number) days, the student will submit receipts to the counselor. The student and counselor agree that (number) receipts can be exchanged for (reward).

Student's signature: _____ Counselor's signature: _____

8. *Share test data.* Students in upper-elementary and middle school grades should learn where they stand in academic achievement and ability. Many children do not realize their potential and may not see themselves as capable. Test results explained in understandable language can be a powerful antidote to self-deprecation.

In some cases, students who are not achieving may need additional assessment. Communicate with teachers and, when appropriate, seek the assistance of other student services specialists, such as the school nurse or psychologist. By gathering as much information as possible, you are more likely to plan and implement effective helping strategies.

TECHNOLOGY

As noted in Chapter Three, today's technology offers limitless opportunities for counselors and teachers to provide expanded services. In addition, it can contribute to elementary and middle school students' learning and development, and most of these students are ahead of adults when it comes to learning about, using, and adjusting to new technology. The rapid speed at which inventors and companies introduce new methods of communicating, while recent technology becomes obsolete and disappears, can be challenging. Think about the items that exist today for which we did not have a term a few years ago—for example, iPods, iTunes, MP3 players, personal play stations, PalmPilots, smart phones, apps, SMART boards, wireless connections, high-definition TVs, broadband, text messaging, twittering, instant messaging, webinars, blogging, downloading, Googling, MySpace, Facebook, Wii, YouTube, and the list goes on. For students born into this information age, new technology and the language it creates are a given. Such innovation is a natural part of their world, just as automobiles, microwave ovens, television, and space travel may be to their parents and teachers.

With each new technology comes many challenges for parents and schools. As noted in an earlier section of this chapter, advanced technology has contributed to the phenomenon of cyberbullying. In addition, parents and schools face the challenge of monitoring how children use the Internet and other technology in appropriate ways. Supervising students and educating them about safety issues when they are online or using cell phones is also important for schools and parents.

Use the following ideas to create school procedures, guidance lessons, parent education groups, and other activities that will help students take advantage of new technology in appropriate ways.

1. *Survey students about the Internet sites they visit*, what attracts them to these sites, how much time they spend on the computer each day, and whether they register for particular sites. Gathering data about student use of technology gives the school and parents a starting point for prevention and intervention.

2. *Help your school establish reasonable policies and procedures* about what technology students may bring and use during school hours. Parent and student input during this process will be essential.

3. *Form parent education groups or plan programs* to help parents learn and discuss how to talk with their children about using technology and how to supervise that use. As with other developmental issues, parents often learn from other parents, so facilitating such groups and programs can be an important role for you, the counselor. If meeting face-to-face is not possible for many parents, consider using the latest technology to deliver services online.

4. *Provide resources to parents* about ways to keep in touch with their children's use of technology. Place these resources in the media center, list them on the school Web site, or use other methods to help parents access them. Use technology to learn about technology. You may find the Internet a useful tool in gathering books, DVDs, Web sites, and other resources that might be helpful to parents.

5. *Establish guidance lessons to integrate into the curriculum.* Please note that technology is such an integral part of students' lives that they may not understand the value of these guidance lessons. For this reason, it is valuable to get students' input and perspectives about what they need to learn.

6. *Keep up with the new technology available to students and the new language created by it.* Being an informed counselor always keeps you a step ahead of your clients—students, parents, and teachers.

The concerns examined in this chapter represent commonplace issues that elementary and middle school students bring to school every day. These concerns are commonplace in that many of them are part of normal childhood and preadolescent development. Chapter Nine considers more serious and critical concerns that fewer students experience, but that often pose challenges for school administrators, teachers, and counselors.

chapter 9

RESPONDING *to* CRITICAL CONCERNS

Scenario 9.1: Socioeconomic Disparities

Your school serves a wide audience of students who come from extremely poor families as well as from affluent families. The socioeconomic differences are sometimes obstacles to achieving a harmonious school environment. For example, after the holiday season, some teachers ask their classes to tell about the presents they received. Unintentionally, these teachers highlight the disparities that exist among students and bring about resentment from some students. More significantly, the socioeconomic differences are evident when the school sponsors field trips and other activities for which students have to pay a fee.

As the counselor, what would you do and what would you encourage the school to do to address this concern? What responsive services, if any, would you use? What preplanning at the beginning of each school year would be helpful?

In many ways, schools reflect the concerns of the communities surrounding them. Therefore, students and teachers often feel the impact of crises in the community. Similarly, when critical events occur in the school, the community to some degree experiences alarm, grief, anger, and other residual, negative feelings. Sometimes, as Scenario 9.1 suggests, some concerns are ongoing and affect every facet of school life.

This chapter includes several areas of critical concern that schools and counselors frequently face: child depression and suicide, self-injury, child abuse, chronic and terminal illness, substance abuse, loss, poverty, violence, and school phobia. As you can see, the concerns covered are not all-inclusive, but by combining the ideas concerning crisis intervention from Chapter Seven with strategies for critical cases in this chapter, you will be better prepared to help students, parents, teachers, and the school with difficult situations.

Each of these concerns presents a different set of circumstances and dynamics for you and your counseling program. In the following sections, you will find specific information and guidelines about these types of crisis.

CHILD DEPRESSION AND SUICIDE

News reports of teenage suicides in epidemic numbers make it one of the leading causes of death among adolescents. To complicate matters, fatal accidents, usually cited as the prime reason for teen deaths, may frequently be instances of suicide. Added to these tragic statistics are a number of child fatalities of suspicious origins. Young children who attempt suicide are rarely successful because they usually do not choose lethal methods. Nevertheless, some experts believe that suicidal thoughts, attempted suicides, and deaths from suicide are higher than available statistics indicate. If this is true, the dynamics and conditions associated with suicide, particularly depression, should be a major concern in our schools and communities.

In years past, society gave little attention to childhood depression, perhaps because we think of childhood as a carefree, happy period of life. In American society, with its changing conditions and added pressures, the perception of childhood is becoming less favorable: separated and divorced families, physical and sexual abuse, increased attention to school success, drug use, violence in the media, and other phenomena have drastically altered the face of childhood. Most of these social stressors have existed forever, though not to the same degree as today. These conditions increase the likelihood that students in schools will experience depression. Depressed children see many of their problems as related to outside forces that are beyond their control. Their depression may lead to suicidal thoughts and attempts when the pain of rejection and feeling of hopelessness reach unbearable proportions.

The first step in assisting depressed or suicidal children and adolescents is to assess the extent of their despair. Interviews with the child, parents, and teachers will help determine the consistency of the depression and the degree to which a child's behaviors are affected. If a child's unhappy state is pervasive, affecting many aspects of school and home life, the depression is severe.

Assessment also examines causal factors. Sometimes children become depressed due to specific events that have occurred at home or school. The death of a relative or pet, a family relocation, an argument with a friend, or a failing grade on a test, for example, may contribute to feelings of loneliness, worthlessness, and hopelessness. In these cases of temporary feelings of grief and despair, you want to examine ways to alter events, teach coping skills, and provide other short-term relief and support for students.

Other times, child depression may be more frequent and not related to any single event. This kind of chronic depression is more severe and requires more in-depth assessment and treatment. On these occasions, it is appropriate to consult with parents about referring the child for a complete medical and psychological examination. At the same time, you may want to confer with other student services team members, such as a nurse, social worker, and psychologist, about appropriate intervention strategies in the school.

Common indicators of depression include emotional, physical, cognitive, and behavioral characteristics. Emotional traits associated with depression are sadness, guilt, anxiety, anger, fear, pessimism, mood swings, unhappiness, feelings of worthlessness, and a sense of helplessness. Physical characteristics may be fatigue, eating problems, upset stomachs, headaches, sleep disorders, constipation, high pulse rate, and menstrual irregularities. Cognitive indicators are poor self-concept, pessimism, self-doubt, self-blame, loss of interest, poor concentration, apathy, and indecision. Some behaviors associated with childhood depression are withdrawal from normal activities, excessive time spent alone, slow speech, soft intonation, group avoidance, lower school achievement, frequent crying, procrastination, preoccupation with death, lack of interest in personal appearance, and rarely smiling or laughing.

When you find that suicidal indicators are present, contact parents immediately, and protect and monitor the student at all times. In these cases, always maintain helpful, protective, caring relationships with students, while taking steps to meet your ethical and legal obligations.

The literature reveals several motives and behaviors associated with child suicide attempts. Exhibit 9.1 illustrates some of these behaviors of children and adolescents, and Exhibit 9.2 includes further adolescent motives and behaviors.

EXHIBIT 9.1

Child and Adolescent Motives and Behaviors Associated with Suicide Attempts

- Signaling distress, a "cry for help"
- Being angry with another person
- Escaping from an unbearable situation
- Attempting to manipulate others
- Wanting to join a loved one who has died

- Behaving impulsively
- Punishing oneself for misbehavior
- Avoiding punishment for misbehavior
- Seeking revenge
- Hoping to be rescued

EXHIBIT 9.2

Additional Adolescent Motives and Behaviors Associated with Suicide Attempts

In addition to the list of child and adolescent motives in Exhibit 9.1, adolescent factors related to suicide include the following:

- Family problems
- Loss of a relationship
- Sexual and physical abuse
- Financial difficulties
- Despair about one's identity
- Academic competition
- Rejection
- Value conflict
- Decline in communication
- Lack of support

Sometimes people who contemplate suicide give signals that indicate their present state of mind and plans they are making. Some of the verbal clues that teachers, parents, students, and counselors might hear from children and adolescents in schools are

- "I am going to kill myself."
- "This is so bad, I could just die."
- "My family doesn't care about me."
- "I won't be seeing you anymore."
- "I can't stand it any longer."
- "If this doesn't change, I'll kill myself."
- "No one needs me anymore."
- "Life doesn't mean anything to me anymore."

Behavioral clues are

- A previous, unsuccessful attempt at suicide
- Giving away valued possessions to friends
- Writing a suicide note
- Sudden happiness following a time of despair
- A new interest in guns or other lethal weapons
- Resigning from clubs, teams, and other groups
- Loss of appetite
- Impulsive abuse of alcohol or drugs

The preceding clues and indicators are a sample of signals that you and others may see from children and adolescents who are contemplating suicide. One behavior or verbal clue may not mean anything, but you need to check it out. A combination of indicators is a definite reason for concern. When you notice a pattern of these behaviors and traits, or when other students or teachers bring them to your attention, establish a relationship with the child as soon as possible. It may be that the student will not want to talk with you, but do not let that hesitancy dissuade you. Maintain contact with the student and continue to establish rapport. With a young child, you might have lunch together, go for a walk outside, play a game in the counseling center, or read a book. At the same time, you will contact the home and inquire about what the parents or guardians have seen there. When the student becomes more comfortable in sharing concerns with you, he or she may disclose suicidal thoughts. If so, you will want to structure an assessment to determine the severity of the situation and the lethality of the student's plan. It is best to include another professional who has experience in this type of assessment. Exhibit 9.3 lists some questions for school counselors to ask students who express suicidal intentions.

EXHIBIT 9.3

Questions to Ask Suicidal Students

- How much do you want to die right now?
- How do you plan to kill yourself? How will you do it?
- How much do you want to live right now?
- How often do you have thoughts about dying or killing yourself?
- When you think these thoughts, how long do they stay with you?
- Have you ever tried to kill yourself? What happened?
- Did you write a suicide note, or do you plan to write a note?
- Has anything happened to make life not worth living?
- Is there anyone or anything that would stop you?
- Do you have close friends? Do you feel alone or isolated?
- On a scale of one to ten, how likely are you to kill yourself?

The student's responses to these and other questions will enable you to assess the seriousness of the student's threats, and with the crisis team you will be able to plan strategies and interventions accordingly. Remember these important steps in handling any level of suicidal threat:

- Notify the school principal.
- Collaborate with another professional in the assessment process.
- Supervise the student.
- Contact the parent or guardian.
- Confer with other student services team members.

When you establish a counseling relationship with a student who is experiencing depression or contemplating suicide, the following approaches will be helpful:

- *Be action oriented.* Self-destructive students need more than passive affirmation from you. Let these students know what can and will be done to protect them and help them learn coping behaviors.
- *Focus on self-concept development.* Students can be encouraged to discover the power to make good things happen. Although not everything in life is controllable, they can learn to capitalize on positive events and prevent negative outcomes.

- *Take charge of the helping relationship.* A directive process is required in suicidal cases. Students should know that you are going to do everything in your power to keep them safe and help them choose appropriate behaviors, now and in the future.
- *Help students learn the art of compromising with oneself.* Sometimes the goals we set for ourselves are unrealistic and unreachable. Students can learn to negotiate with themselves to set attainable goals.
- *Teach the concept of time, as it relates to the past, present, and future.* This will help students lessen their focus on immediate events and crises. Young children and adolescents need assistance in stepping back from critical situations and placing these significant events in balance with their entire life spans.
- *Demonstrate your trustworthiness.* Although you cannot honor confidentiality about suicidal thoughts and attempts, you can show your trustworthiness in relationships with students by not revealing intimate feelings and thoughts they disclose. Students need someone in whom they can believe and trust.
- *Show your confidence and patience.* Be optimistic about the future. Let students know that together you will overcome obstacles and meet the challenges that lie ahead. At the same time, accept their confusion and inconsistencies by patiently guiding them back on track when they falter. Their unrealistic expectations do not need to be confounded by the impatience of others.
- *Require a commitment from students* that they will not harm themselves or attempt suicide. Stay in contact with suicidal students and give them a systematic plan to handle depressed feelings when they occur. Although there is controversy about the use of no-suicide contracts and their effectiveness, they are widely used among counselors and other mental health professionals (Range et al., 2002; www.suicide.org). See Exhibit 9.4 for a sample of a self-protection agreement. If you decide that a no-suicide or other self-protection agreement is appropriate, be sure to design one that is developmentally suitable, containing language and concepts that the student will understand. In addition, the use of self-protection agreements may not reduce your legal liability in the event that a student attempts or commits suicide—they are not legal contracts.

When working with these students, keep in touch with their families, maintain contact with classroom teachers about student progress and behaviors, confer with other student services specialists when progress is stalled, and be prepared to refer the case when you have gone as far as time and competency allow. In summary, the following guidelines will help you and the students' teachers approach and support students who are experiencing severe depression and expressing suicidal thoughts in school:

1. *Recognize the clues to depression and suicide.* Take these signs seriously and contact appropriate personnel.
2. *Trust your judgment.* Act on your suspicions and beliefs when you think a student is in danger. Do not ignore the evidence. You may be wrong about the severity of the situation, but it is much better to take action than to hesitate and witness a tragedy.
3. *Ensure the short-term safety of the student.* If immediate danger exists, stay with the student and send for assistance. Remain with the student until help arrives.

EXHIBIT 9.4

Self-Protection Agreement

While I am in counseling with (school counselor's name), I, (student's name), will do the following things:

1. I will live a long and happy life.
2. I will come for counseling at my scheduled times to learn how to be happy and understand my feelings.
3. I will not hurt or kill myself while I am seeing my counselor. I know it will take time to learn how to be happy.
4. I will tell _____ immediately when I am feeling sad and wanting to hurt or kill myself. If I cannot find _____, I will call _____ or tell the nearest adult in my neighborhood or at school.
5. I agree to the bedtime and eating schedule planned by my parents (or guardians).
6. I will keep this agreement until _____, when I see my counselor again.

Student: _____ Counselor: _____ Date: _____

4. *Tell authorities and parents.* As mentioned earlier, there is no confidentiality where suicide is concerned.
5. *Listen to the student.* Encourage the student to talk about the situation. Be nonjudgmental and avoid responding with unsubstantiated assurances, such as, "Everything will be all right." Use reflective listening and empathize with the student.
6. *Show support.* In these situations, the most important ingredient a counselor or teacher can offer is care and understanding. Let students know you are with them and want them to be well. Help them feel worthwhile and valuable. Tell students you are there for them and will stick by them through this rough time.

Sometimes students who have feelings of depression and low self-worth may resort to self-injurious behaviors that are not life threatening. Although they may have similarities with suicidal students, they will be discussed separately in the next section.

SELF-INJURY

Self-injurious behavior (SIB) is purposeful action that harms one's body without intending to cause death. For elementary and middle school students who self-injure, behaviors include biting, burning, cutting, hair-pulling, picking at skin, scratching, self-hitting, and other self-mutilating actions. These behaviors are usually directed at a student's head, arms, wrists, or legs, but can also affect other parts of the body (Moyer, Haberstroh, & Marbach, 2008; Moyer & Nelson, 2007). According to self-report surveys, the incidence of self-injury among adolescents is over 10 percent (Kress, Drouhard, & Costin, 2006), so you will likely encounter students who have exhibited one or more of these types of behaviors.

In many respects, you handle a self-injurious student in the same direct manner that you would a suicidal student. The alarm may not be as great, but it is nevertheless a serious situation. For this reason, confidentiality may not be an option for you as a counselor. When helping a student who has self-injured, give serious thought to contacting the parents and guardians, even when you do not believe that imminent danger exists.

Students who self-injure want help and want someone to listen. Therefore, counseling and referrals are important services to consider. As with other problems that students face, you can assist with self-injurious behaviors if you have the knowledge and competencies to be successful. Even though you may be competent in this area, however, you may not have the time to devote to such serious issues as this while directing a comprehensive school counseling program. Perhaps the best you could offer the student and parents are initial services, followed by a referral to another practitioner or agency.

In working with self-injurious students, you may find no-harm contracts, similar to the self-protection contract in Exhibit 9.4, to be useful. Such contracts may include instructions that the student shall not bring specific objects to school that might be used to inflict injury. At the same time, no-harm contracts may suggest appropriate alternative behaviors for students to choose when they are having self-injurious thoughts.

In addition to counseling and referral services, you could share with students and parents appropriate resources in the community and on the Internet. There are limitless resources online, but parents and students will want your guidance to avoid sites that may be misleading, inaccurate, or destructive in their focus (Moyer et al., 2008).

Lastly, if your school does not have specific policies to address these behaviors, you could help develop some (Kress et al., 2006). Established policies and procedures could help you and your colleagues understand responsibilities and parameters in identifying, assisting, and referring self-injurious students. The following are some questions to ask when developing policies and procedures:

- What do you do when you suspect a student is self-injuring?
- To whom do you report the suspicion?
- What is the involvement of school administrators in such cases?
- What is the involvement of the school counselor?
- What is the involvement of other student services professionals (nurse, psychologist, and so on)?
- Who contacts parents or guardians?

CHILD ABUSE

Child abuse is the tragedy of children and adolescents' victimization by adults who are their caretakers. Abuse comes in different forms, including physical harm, sexual attacks, emotional and physical neglect, and psychological torment. As community caretakers of children, schools have a legal, professional, and moral obligation to offer protection and appropriate services to students who are victims of physical, sexual, or psychological abuse.

Your first step as counselor is to learn about local policies and state laws regarding obligations and procedures for reporting abuse cases. In some schools, crisis teams examine initial evidence, make a determination about the suspicion of abuse, and contact the appropriate investigation agency. Reporting instances of suspected abuse can be a stress-producing responsibility for a teacher, counselor, or administrator who has to contact the agency. For this reason, a team approach helps by (1) assessing the information observed and obtained from the student, (2) determining appropriate steps to ensure the safety of the child, and (3) delegating responsibility for reporting the suspicion of child abuse to the authorities.

One difficulty for school personnel is defining *suspicion* and determining whether or not there is reason to report a case to the authorities. The question that arises is, What if we are wrong? The fear of wrongfully reporting suspected child abuse sometimes inhibits teachers, counselors, and administrators in following through on their legal obligations. Crisis teams can help by instructing school staff members about indicators of abuse, reporting procedures, legal and liability protection for reporting in good faith, and the extent of the school's role in the investigation. In any event, the school should always follow the practice of "when in doubt, report." Let the investigation agency have the responsibility of substantiating the case. If there is sufficient doubt about the likelihood of abuse, trained professionals from an appropriate agency are the ones to make that determination.

Another area of staff development for teachers and staff lies in understanding the legal process when a case goes to court. Occasionally, school personnel are called to testify about their observations of the child in school. In-service workshops can help teachers and counselors become comfortable with court appearances. You can plan instructional and informational sessions by recruiting the services of a local school board attorney or other lawyer who is willing to share expertise.

The next step to take as a counselor is to determine your role in assisting the child after the abuse has been discovered and reported. As with other crises, your decisions relate to your knowledge and skills, the availability of appropriate services in the school and community, and the amount of time you have available to assist the student. Your knowledge and skills will include an understanding of the family dynamics involved, information about traits and characteristics of abusers, an awareness of the child's perceptions and feelings, and a command of effective counseling approaches and techniques.

When you refer a child to another professional or agency, such as a family counseling center, you want to maintain contact with this referral source so you and teachers are able to determine what supportive services, if any, to deliver at the school. Coordinate these school activities with the professional or agency providing the primary care to the child and family. Adequate coordination prevents contradictory and confusing relationships from developing that would thwart the child's progress.

Abused children are not easy clients. Their trust has been shattered and, understandably, they are often unwilling to establish close relationships. To be effective, immerse yourself in the helping relationship and show the child that responsible people are trustworthy. At the same time, understand that abused children often will stretch the limits of their trust by testing your patience and empathy. You meet this challenge by consistently demonstrating caring behaviors toward the student and interacting in the most positive manner.

The following guidelines are compiled from various resources and may be helpful if and when you become involved with cases of child abuse:

1. *Establish a trusting, empathic relationship with the child.* Begin by examining your own feelings and beliefs about the issue of physical and sexual child abuse. If you have difficulty with the subject, your reactions may inhibit the child in freely expressing feelings, and your relationship could be counterproductive by affirming the guilt and shame the child is experiencing. Interview the child in a quiet, safe, and private area. It may be best with young children to hold initial sessions in a playroom rather than an office, which usually has all the trimmings of an "adult world."

2. *Use approaches and techniques that help children overcome feelings of worthlessness.* Because abusive relationships damage a child's esteem, you want to create and deliver responsive services that help improve self-worth. Such services could come from an array of strategies, including informal personal contacts with the student, group guidance to solicit support from other students, and consultation with teachers to discuss ways that everyone can focus on the child's well-being, to name a few.

3. *Distinguish between an empathic relationship and a sympathetic stance.* Empathy is the ability to identify with and understand a student's perspective and feelings about a situation. By empathizing with the child's perspective, you increase your comprehension, become closer, and gain credibility, and your opinions become valued and accepted. Sympathy, in contrast, merely expresses sorrow and pity, neither of which elevates the child to a position of self-assurance.

4. *For young children and preadolescents, use individual sessions to establish helping relationships.* Because of ambivalent feelings toward their abusers and their own feelings of guilt and shame, children are usually not ready to share their experiences in groups.

5. *Be prepared to provide support for the family of the abused child.* Teachers, counselors, and other members of the school often feel anger and repulsion over the hurt the child has experienced. Although these reactions are understandable, the school cannot allow such feelings to impair its working relationship with the home. Once the legal process has determined the status of the abuser, the child and remaining family members will need support if progress is to be realized.

6. *Design preventive activities and programs for all students in the school to help them learn about appropriate "touches" and achieve a better understanding of their own bodies.* Students in classroom guidance and small-group discussions can learn assertiveness skills for saying "no" and handling potentially harmful situations. Classroom guidance can also teach children about their rights, the procedures for reporting abusive situations, and how to seek help when they need it.

CHRONIC AND TERMINAL ILLNESS

Unfortunately, children are not immune to various chronic or terminal illnesses that can debilitate them or lead to an early death. Children who suffer from chronic conditions or terminal illnesses often experience emotional and psychological adjustment problems that interfere with their schooling.

As the counselor in an elementary or middle school, you strive to serve all children, including those suffering from illnesses that may make their school attendance inconsistent and sporadic. Here are some points to consider in providing guidance to these children and their families:

- Let parents and students know that you are available to assist students whose illnesses may prevent regular school attendance.
- Work with school administrators to monitor policies, such as strict attendance guidelines, that may hinder or interfere with helping particular students.
- Learn about medical centers, support groups, hospice facilities, and other community services that are referral sources for students and their families.
- Stay in touch with parents through phone calls, e-mail messages, and home visits to assure them that the school is doing its part to help. Send students friendly notes and greeting cards when they have missed long stretches of school days.
- Present guidance lessons about illnesses that some children may have. Through such lessons, their classmates can understand and empathize with them.
- Select counseling approaches to use with chronically or terminally ill children and work closely with parents and other helping professionals in selecting these interventions. For example, play techniques might be appropriate for use in short-term counseling to help children understand, accept, and cope with their illnesses. Counseling might also help these children deal with loneliness, a common concern for children with chronic and terminal illnesses.

SUBSTANCE ABUSE

Alcohol and drug abuse in our society continues to affect every aspect of our lives. For elementary and middle school children, substance abuse is an issue that is related to their own personal choices as well as to the choices made by their parents. In many families, children are the victims of substance-abusing parents. Millions of children, for example, live in families with problem drinkers. According to some estimates, the children of these parents are four times more likely to become alcoholics during their lifetime. Many of these children are under eighteen years of age, attending elementary, middle, and high schools across the country.

Children of alcoholics often report strong feelings of hostility and anger toward their parents, have lower self-images, and show a higher incidence of learning disabilities. Children whose mothers drink or use drugs during pregnancy tend to be more likely to become drug dependent and demonstrate lower performance on standardized ability tests. Substance abuse in families also correlates with child abuse.

Although these children often suffer emotional and physical abuse in their relationships with their parents, they tend to protect their parents by not talking about the problem. Very few children talk about substance abuse with their own parents at home. This unwillingness to discuss the substance abuse issue makes it difficult for you to identify the nature of the concern and offer assistance. A combination of behaviors and characteristics may indicate a family drug- or alcohol-related problem. Use caution to avoid making hasty judgments about a single, observed behavior, but when a child exhibits several of these signs, you and the school may have reason to be concerned. Exhibit 9.5 lists some factors and behaviors to monitor.

EXHIBIT 9.5

Indicators of a Family Drug- or Alcohol-Related Problem

- Indication of low self-esteem
- Feelings of rejection
- Withdrawn and isolated demeanor
- Lack of trusting relationships
- Poor eating habits
- Signs of physical abuse
- Overly responsible behavior

- Extreme self-criticism
- Antisocial behaviors
- Passiveness
- Frequent school absences
- Poor school achievement
- Missing or incomplete homework assignments

As noted in the previous paragraph, there appears to be a connection between student use of drugs and alcohol and family situations. Upper-elementary and middle school children who experiment with alcohol and drugs may be reflecting a chemical dependency found in the home. As children of alcoholics grow older, they have a stronger tendency to abuse alcohol themselves. In planning responsive services to address substance abuse, you want to think in terms of both intervention and prevention.

Intervention

To help students from substance-abusing families, schools can provide a wide range of educational experiences and counseling services. Even if you yourself are unable to invest the time or do not have the expertise to assist the family with much-needed therapy, you can coordinate services in the school. It is essential that you know the agencies and professionals in the community that are best equipped to help alcoholic and other families. You also want to be familiar with such programs as Alcoholics Anonymous (http://www.aa.org), Al-Anon, and Alateen (www.al-anon.alateen.org), as well as public and private centers that provide crisis intervention for alcohol and drug abuse.

Interventions, programs, and procedures that schools can provide to help students whose families may have drug or alcohol problems include the following:

1. *They maintain a consistent school environment.* In substance-abusing families, rules are inconsistent and schedules often are abruptly altered. Schools offer stability by letting students know they can depend on teachers and counselors. By avoiding schedule changes and keeping promises, schools minimize disruptions and disappointments that add to children's stress.

2. *They offer alcohol and drug abuse education.* Children will learn that they are not alone with this problem, and that they are not responsible for their parents' drinking or other abuse. Alcoholism, for example, is an addictive condition, which is why some alcoholic parents have such difficulty quitting, even to the point that they lose all control over their lives. When drinking heavily or using other drugs, these people cannot stop themselves. They are out of control.

On the upside, children also can learn that alcoholics and drug users can overcome these problems. The abusers first recognize and admit the problem exists, and then seek help. In the same way, children from alcoholic and drug-abusing families must come to understand the problem and seek assistance for themselves.

3. *They assess neglect and abuse in the family.* When children are being physically or sexually abused, emotionally traumatized or neglected, or deprived in other ways, the school is required to report these findings to the proper authorities. Because alcoholism and substance abuse are such emotional and secretive issues, people are hesitant to report abuse that stems from these addictive diseases; however, the school has a primary obligation to protect the child in abusive situations, regardless of the underlying causes.

4. *They hold instructional support groups for parents.* Group programs help parents learn appropriate ways to remedy the destruction caused by the alcoholism and substance abuse in the family. You might not be able to run these groups as part of your school program, but you can cooperate and coordinate efforts with community agencies, such as churches and civic clubs.

5. *They provide group counseling for students.* Children are more willing to share feelings and discuss family situations in a safe environment where they identify with one another's concerns. When you begin a group, you may want to lead students through several icebreakers to become acquainted before discussing the nature of their concerns. Usually a small, comfortable room for group work is conducive to establishing a trustful, secure environment.

Most children will need to see a counselor by themselves before agreeing to join a group. When establishing individual counseling relationships with these children, a few guidelines may be helpful:

1. *Focus on the student first.* Learn about the student's interests, what he or she likes to do, and what the student thinks he or she does well. Show genuine interest in his or her accomplishments. Reflect the content of the child's message and the feelings expressed by paraphrasing information and emotions back to the child. This is essential in this stage, especially because young students often struggle to express themselves concerning difficult situations.

2. *Confront the issue of drinking or drug use in the family clearly, but gently.* As noted earlier, children and adolescents will be protective of their parents. Take it slow, and consistently show your concern for the student. Look for reflex recognitions and reactions to statements you make. A raised brow, changed body posture, pursed lips, or other behaviors may indicate that a student understands but is unwilling to discuss the issue. Proceed patiently in these instances and take time to develop trust.

3. *Avoid asking questions.* Give the student illustrations and examples of concerns of children and adolescents in general. Offer specific situations regarding alcoholism and drug abuse. Let the student react, either verbally or nonverbally, to these scenarios. With some children, a book or video may be appropriate as a stimulus for further discussion in the counseling relationship.

4. *Inform the student about group counseling.* After the student becomes comfortable and begins sharing concerns with you, introduce information about group counseling and invite the student to join a group. Tell the child or adolescent about groups you are forming and the types of concerns that group members have in common.

Some middle school and elementary students will become involved with drugs and alcohol even though no such addiction exists in their families. A peer, older student, or unrelated adult, for example, may introduce them to alcohol or drugs. Help teachers become aware of changes in children's behavior that may point to drug and alcohol use. Consultation with parents usually will identify additional behaviors of concern when alcohol and drugs are involved. Exhibit 9.6 lists some possible indicators.

EXHIBIT 9.6

Indicators of Possible Drug or Alcohol Use

- School absence and tardiness
- Lower academic performance
- Loss of interest in school or extracurricular activities
- Chronic lying
- Stealing
- Preference for being alone at school and home
- Secrecy about friends and where-abouts
- Sudden change of friends
- Emotional outbursts and mood swings
- Change in dress
- Mysterious and unexplained phone calls
- Changes in speech, eye functions, and coordination
- Defensive behaviors and constant denial of wrongdoing
- Apathy, absence of ambition, and general lack of interest

With middle school and upper-elementary students whom teachers or parents have referred for counseling due to suspected substance abuse, you want to follow consistent procedures. Here are a few guidelines when counseling students about substance abuse:

1. *Know school policies concerning reporting substance abuse.* Usually school systems have clear regulations regarding substance abuse and parent notification. Learn about your ethical responsibilities to the counselee and how they relate to local policies.

2. *Assess each case thoroughly and accurately.* Get all pertinent facts from the student about actual drug use. When was the alcohol or drug taken? How was it taken? Who was present? How often has the student done this? Where was the alcohol or drug obtained?

Your assessment of the degree of use will guide you in determining whether to refer a case to another professional or agency. Exhibit 9.7 is an interview questionnaire for middle school students about alcohol and drug use.

EXHIBIT 9.7

Middle School Drug and Alcohol Assessment

1. Tell me about the drug or alcohol you took, and how you took it.
2. When did this happen? Where did you do this?
3. Were you alone or with someone?
4. How much of the drug or alcohol did you use?
5. Have you done this before? Tell me about those other times.
6. Where did you get the alcohol or drug?
7. Have you told your parents about this? What have you told them?
8. Have you ever talked with a counselor or other person about drug or alcohol use?
9. What do you think about this drug or alcohol experience?
10. Do you want help with this problem?

---

3. *Be directive.* Cases involving substance abuse are not the time for passive listening. Take charge of the relationship. Be respectful and show concern for the student, but at the same time convey the seriousness of the matter and be firm in letting the child or adolescent know that the behavior must stop.

4. *Inform the parents.* When your assessment indicates that the abuse is frequent and substantial, the student's welfare and life are at risk. In this case, the destructive behaviors preclude confidentiality. You must tell the parents. Even in cases of drug and alcohol experimentation, counselors of young children always involve parents. The student needs to understand the seriousness of these types of behaviors, and parental support is essential.

5. *Obtain commitment from the student to desist from further abusive behaviors.* If the counseling relationship is to make any progress, the student must show good faith in wanting to stop the drug or alcohol abuse. Without this commitment, the relationship is tenuous and threatened from the start.

6. *Become knowledgeable about the drugs currently being used in the community.* Learn about expected reactions to these substances. Attend workshops to acquire skills in handling substance abuse cases. Learn about reliable resources in the community to which you can refer students and families.

Prevention

Because drug and alcohol abuse continues to be a destructive force in American society, elementary and middle schools want to take an educative role in helping young people understand the dangers. Preventive activities are essential to a comprehensive school counseling program, and your role includes planning and coordinating such educational services.

Help your school establish a broad philosophy and basic premises for drug education and prevention programs. From what we already know about drug and alcohol prevention, the following beliefs will serve as starter points for addressing this concern:

- *Community and family involvement are essential.* Schools do not exist in isolation. Commitment to drug prevention is a community and family affair.
- *Drug information is insufficient for prevention.* Awareness programs, information brochures, and wellness events can supplement comprehensive educational programs, but information alone does little to help people change behaviors.
- *Effective drug prevention programs complement a healthful living curriculum, community youth activities, a public commitment to education, and family involvement.* A single focus on drug problems without an emphasis on improving the quality of life for young people is an unproductive approach.
- *Drug prevention requires a commitment of time and resources.* Effective programs take more than one class period or a weeklong community campaign to demonstrate positive results. Prevention requires an ongoing program reflected throughout the community and school, and this entails adequate funds and sufficient time to be successful.
- *Drug and alcohol prevention in schools can be best implemented by professional educators who care about children, plan effective teaching, create emotionally healthy learning environments, and invite parental involvement in schools.*

Drug prevention programs are most successful when they de-emphasize peer pressure and teach students assertiveness skills. You therefore want to develop programs that include strategies to help students make important life decisions, expand their alternatives, identify essential information, and act on the choices they make.

LOSS

Students in elementary and middle schools sometimes face the death of someone close to them—a grandparent, parent, sibling, or friend. Occasionally, it is an expected loss due to a long-term illness; other times it results from unexpected tragedy. In either case, the student needs support and understanding from the school community. Through cooperative and careful communication, you and teachers can help children and adolescents come to terms with a death, experience their grief, and move ahead with their development.

When counseling with children who have experienced a loss, you want a clear understanding of how each student perceives death. Children in first grade and younger rarely conceptualize the finality of death when it first occurs. They perceive death as something that happens to others, not to oneself or even to those one is close to. Very young children often take an egocentric view of death that involves magical thinking and fantasies. (Of course, you modify all developmental assumptions by considering diverse cultural backgrounds.) As students move into middle childhood (approximately ages ten and older), they begin to conceptualize specific ways that death occurs. Preadolescents are able to think about death in abstract terms and construct logical causes of death. Helpful counseling techniques in individual and group settings include bibliocounseling, role playing, puppetry, storytelling, and drawing.

When helping a student cope with a recent death, consider these guidelines:

1. *Openly express your sorrow and regret for the loss the student has experienced.* Let the student know you are available if he or she would like to talk about it. When a child or adolescent agrees to discuss the death with you, maintain an open posture and avoid judgmental responses to the information being shared. Send gentle invitations to the student to become involved, and resist coercing the student into a counseling relationship. Sometimes a child needs time to himself or herself before being able or willing to talk about the loss. In these cases, you may want to have contact with the student by eating lunch together, playing games, or reading a story, without forcing the issue by talking about his or her loss.

2. *Accept the student's right to mourn the loss.* Some children cope with death by behaving in unusual ways—behaviors often noticed by their peers. When teachers and counselors show understanding and acceptance of these changes, other students will show support for the bereaved child.

3. *Maintain as normal a schedule as possible for the student.* At the same time, allow avenues for the child to cope with the loss, such as a safe place to go when emotions are high; accept some behavior changes; and understand lower-quality schoolwork during the grieving period.

4. *Avoid surprised or shocked reactions to the student's expression of grief.* Children, like people in general, show their grief in a variety of ways. When a student is aggressive, withdrawn, or uncooperative, genuine concern and gentle reminders about class and school behavior may help. You can assist by showing him or her appropriate ways to cope with anger, grief, and other feelings.

Classroom guidance lessons can provide preventive measures as well as remedial approaches to helping students cope with death and dying. For example, an instructional unit about death could focus on the following concepts, depending on the developmental level of students:

- All living things die.
- People often need help when someone dies.
- People feel different emotions when they suffer a loss, such as death.
- Death is final, and this makes it sad.
- Certain activities follow a death.
- Life is worth living.
- We all leave things behind when we die.

POVERTY

Students from impoverished and low-income homes provide many challenges to schools. Studies indicate that they have fewer positive experiences in school, more behavioral problems, increased levels of anxiety and depression, developmental concerns, and an increased likelihood of school failure (Amatea & West-Olatunji, 2007).

As a counselor you have some responsibility in helping the school address the effects of poverty. This is important in ensuring that all students stand on a level academic playing field and have equal opportunity to succeed. Studies indicate that the sooner society addresses poverty and recognizes its effects on development, the more likely communities will support the development and implementation of educational and other services that will help all students be productive (Schmidt, 2008).

You have special knowledge and skills that can help your school and teaching colleagues address the needs of students who are economically disadvantaged. Here are some starter ideas:

1. *Use your leadership position to help the school focus on the issue of poverty* and its impact on students' development and success. Examine school policies and procedures that may unintentionally discriminate against students due to their socioeconomic positions.

2. *Design staff development activities to explore multicultural differences within the school.* Often, students in minority groups are among the poorest financially. Staff development activities can enlighten people to the sociopolitical influences that have an impact on students from low-income families and their involvement in school life. Such in-service can also highlight the advantages that students from more affluent families have in the school and community.

3. *Help teachers and administrators explore alternative instructional approaches with disadvantaged students.* Disparities among students due to family income often translate into different learning styles and perspectives about school. When schools insist on teaching all students in the same manner and with the same curriculum, they ignore significant individual differences.

4. *Help parents from low-income families find resources in the community.* At the same time, encourage them to be involved with their children's education at whatever level is possible. Families that experience economic hardships want their children to experience success, even though parents may not demonstrate this openly. Encourage your school to open doors for these parents and learn constructive ways to communicate with them.

VIOLENCE

Violence is a broad phenomenon in American society that has a significant impact on schools and student learning. Too many students resort to aggressive and violent behavior when faced with conflict. The number of fights, murders, and suicides among our youth is alarming.

As a school counselor, you have a responsibility to help prevent and remedy senseless violence on the part of students and against students in our schools. Simply implementing policies to punish students for possessing weapons and fighting in school is not the full answer. Schools need to be proactive in providing counseling and educational services for students. Here are some starter ideas:

1. *Be alert—listen to what students are saying and how they are treating one another.* Stay abreast of what is taking place in the school and out in the community among students. As noted earlier in regard to bullying and cyberbullying, the first step to thwarting violence is to pay attention and not ignore behaviors that will lead to altercations.

2. *Find conflict resolution material that you and teachers can use in the school's guidance curriculum.* Help students handle conflict and hostility in appropriate ways while maintaining an acceptable level of assertiveness. Add conciliation to your conflict resolution lessons and strategies (Purkey, Schmidt, & Novak, 2010). Invite law enforcement officers and other professionals into the school to talk with students about their rights and how to prevent violence in the community.

3. *Use peer helpers to help identify students who are victims of violence or who are threatening to harm themselves or others.* Elementary and middle school students will frequently confide in their peers before they approach a teacher, counselor, or even their parents.

4. *Instruct teachers and other staff members on how to observe indicators and precursors of violent or self-destructive behavior.* Suicide attempts and other self-harming behaviors are private forms of violence, and fellow students, teachers, counselors, and other school personnel are often in position to recognize when students are in serious distress. They observe symptoms that sometimes relate to these behaviors.

5. *Help parents identify symptoms and signals their children are sending them.* Teach parents to monitor television programs, movies, music, Internet sites, and computer games that emphasize and glorify violent behavior. At the same time, encourage parents to spend time talking with their children about these media forms, some of which are inescapable in our society.

SCHOOL PHOBIA

Suicide, child abuse, extreme poverty, violence, and substance abuse are situations and crises that may pose immediate danger to students' physical or emotional welfare. By comparison, although school phobia—the fear of attending school—presents a crisis of immediate concern, it lacks the threat of imminent danger. Children who suffer from school phobia are considered critical cases because of the long-term implications to their personal, social, and educational development. Rational and irrational fears that continue will thwart normal student progress. Left untreated, the school-phobic student may develop multiple phobias, such as the fear of being alone, fear of the outdoors, and fear of people.

Estimates of the incidence of school phobia range from 1 to 8 percent of the population. Concerned teachers and counselors develop approaches and procedures to assist these students about this critical anxiety. This is particularly true in elementary and middle schools, where school phobia generally occurs.

School phobia is often associated with being emotionally upset, complaining of illnesses for which there is no physical cause, and having temper tantrums. Although a number of factors may be involved, school phobia in young children is often associated with fear of separation from a mother who has nurtured an overly dependent relationship. Older children, some of whom have never exhibited fear of school during their first few years, become phobic when they change schools, move from elementary to middle or high school, or begin a new school program.

Many children resist going to school on occasion, or they express fears about changes in school schedules and routines, but school-phobic children experience levels of fear and anxiety that approach panic. The problem can be one of incapacitating trauma, and this is why teachers, counselors, and parents want to intervene as soon as possible.

Among the intervention strategies you will find in the counseling literature, three schools of thought encompass the major approaches to treating the school-phobic child: psychodynamic, behavioral, and cognitive. If you intervene with school-phobic students, you want to be familiar with different views and approaches, choosing methods that fit your philosophical beliefs and those of your school and community.

Psychodynamic approaches focus on the child's separation anxiety and the parents' overprotective behavior. By helping parents understand their contribution to the phobia, giving them alternative strategies for handling the separation anxiety, and helping them learn to cope with their own emotional reactions to the child's going to school, you and the teachers will be in a stronger position to help the child accept the school experience. Play therapy, conducted individually and in groups, can help young children express their fears about school and discover appropriate ways to handle their anxieties. Older children may benefit from drama techniques, storytelling and story writing, or direct verbal counseling to formulate a plan of action.

Cognitive approaches, such as Rational Emotive Behavior Therapy (REBT), are appropriate with middle school students. With these methods, you and the student examine his or her irrational and illogical beliefs about school, explore the student's responsibilities, and plan the best ways to handle the situation so that the student alters his or her thinking about school.

Behavioral approaches call on a variety of techniques, including relaxation, systematic desensitization, positive reinforcement, and removal of secondary (conditioned) reinforcers. In most cases, you combine behavioral techniques with other therapeutic approaches. For example, middle school students receiving individual counseling can learn relaxation strategies to help themselves when anxiety is high.

Whatever the approach, you will want to establish guidelines for yourself and for teachers when working with school-phobic students. Here are some suggestions:

1. *Give immediate attention to cases of suspected school phobia.* The more time that elapses, the more difficult it will be to help the student and family turn around the situation.

2. *Insist that the parents take the child for a medical examination if he or she is exhibiting physical symptoms and illnesses.* Although the probability of a physical manifestation is minimal, it is important to check it out.

3. *Include the crisis team in severe cases of school phobia, and make referrals when appropriate.*

4. *Establish open lines of communication with the parents.* Maintain regular contact with them to check on progress at home and report about progress at school. Individual consultation or parent education groups are appropriate for helping parents examine their feelings, address their own behaviors, and establish constructive routines for getting their children to school. In extreme cases, family counseling may be necessary.

5. *Consult regularly with classroom teachers.* A warm, caring, and pleasant school environment is essential in helping children overcome their fears. Teachers can be firm yet gentle when helping a student understand that he or she must remain at school.

6. *Avoid placing children in uncertain situations that may cause fear or embarrassment.* Children who are prone to anxieties can be carefully guided through and informed about all new experiences.

7. *Provide appropriate reinforcements* to let students know they are being successful in overcoming their fears and accepting responsibility for attending school.

8. *Give the school-phobic child an alternative choice when he or she feels extremely anxious and is unable to cope in the classroom.* Perhaps the student could go to the counseling center to sit for a few minutes alone or talk to you, or he or she could call home to check on his or her mother and make sure everything is all right.

For all of the concerns addressed in this and the preceding chapters, effective school counselors establish clear guidelines and approaches to helping students, parents, and teachers. Beyond the critical and special concerns presented in these chapters, you probably will help children on a regular basis with peer relationships, stealing, cheating, conflict resolution, tattling, lying, school attendance, daydreaming, hyperactivity, inattentiveness, and a host of other behaviors. Handling each of these issues requires specific knowledge and skills.

To be effective in all helping relationships, establish a resource file of approaches and strategies to handle a wide range of concerns. You might also compile a list of useful Internet sites for each concern. These resources not only will assist you in your counseling relationships but also will be helpful to classroom teachers who interact with these students every day. By helping teachers with these interactions and relationships, you establish an essential role for yourself as an elementary or middle school counselor. Equally important, you establish relationships within the school and community that consistently communicate this role. Relating to your school's professional staff is the subject of the next chapter.

chapter 10

BELONGING *and* BEING *with the* SCHOOL

Scenario 10.1: Ongoing Challenges

Your school has been going through a difficult time. A student's death, a faculty member's car accident, and lower performance on state mandated tests, among other issues, have contributed to a solemn year. You have talked with the administrators and some teachers about the school climate, and everyone shares the concern. Based on your knowledge of the school, where would you begin to offer expertise and assistance? What types of services or activities do you think would be responsive to the school's situation? What are some services and activities that you, the counselor, might instigate?

This *Survival Guide* emphasizes the development of strong working relationships with teachers and other personnel in your school. The school counseling program belongs to the entire school—students, parents, teachers, administrators, specialists, and you. For this reason, it is essential that you become an integral part of the school staff and the program. To do so, you want to make a conscious and purposeful effort to relate personally and professionally with your colleagues in the school.

The ultimate success of your program will be influenced by the personal and professional relationships you establish with administrators, teachers, students, parents, and others involved with your elementary or middle school. In turn, developing personal and professional relationships fosters positive public relations, which are essential for any program, particularly one that relies on a high level of trust and respect from the populations it serves. However, maintaining beneficial relationships is not sufficient to establish effective elementary and middle school counseling programs.

This chapter takes the idea of positive public relations a step further by advocating that you as a counselor are an essential part of the school program. To function effectively, moreover, you want to be accepted and sought after by the school community. Effective counselors are proactive, telling people that the counseling program belongs with the educational program rather than being a separate and distant service. Elementary and middle school counselors who are successful in creating this type of relationship respect the role of parents and teachers in the education and development of all children.

ESTABLISHING RELATIONSHIPS

As a successful school counselor, you demonstrate equal respect for the counseling profession, the teaching profession, and the role of parents in the education of children. In addition, you realize that it is through cooperative efforts that schoolchildren overcome obstacles to learning and development. The following are some guidelines and principles to follow in establishing a proactive and respectful stance as an elementary or middle school counselor.

• *Counseling services are an extension of the instructional program.* School counselors who see themselves as strictly therapists, delving deeply into the realm of unconscious motivations of their clients, tend to distance themselves from other professionals in the school. Counseling and consulting relationships, however, are essentially educative and instructive in nature. Delivered by highly prepared professionals who understand the importance of facilitative skills in developing effective helping relationships, these processes supplement and complement the school curriculum and classroom instruction. When you successfully help students, parents, and teachers alter behaviors and choose new directions, the approaches and strategies you use ultimately can have a therapeutic effect. Such a therapeutic outcome can be true for your counseling relationships, consultations, and guidance activities in the classroom.

• *School counselors, although not always trained as teachers, are an integral part of the school staff.* Counselors want to be included in all aspects of the school's program and professional responsibilities. This means sharing responsibilities for student supervision and administration of school services. Similarly, classroom teachers perform many duties beyond the realm of instruction and learning—they collect book fees; monitor hallways and restrooms; supervise cafeterias; and perform an array of functions that have little to do with language arts, mathematics, physical education, or other curricular areas.

As an elementary or middle school counselor, you enhance your working relationships with teaching colleagues by sharing some of these responsibilities. At the same time, know when to limit your participation so that these ancillary functions do not interfere with responsive services for students, parents, and teachers. Work closely with your school administrators to ensure that you do not compromise the integrity of the counseling program for the sake of administrative efficiency.

• *School counseling services are most beneficial and accepted by school communities when they relate to the educational progress of students.* In some schools, teachers are under tremendous pressure to demonstrate that students are achieving academically by how they perform on standardized tests. For this reason, teachers are understandably reluctant to allow their students to miss instruction in order to see a counselor. If you advocate the important relationship between academic success and positive self-worth, you will be able to convince teachers of the benefits of counseling. Make a concerted effort to share information about your services and illustrate how these services enable students to study better, attend class, behave appropriately, and achieve academically. When you demonstrate successful helping relationships and subsequently persuade your teaching colleagues of the connection between helpful individual and small-group services for students and their academic achievement, you will have little difficulty getting their permission for students to visit the counseling center. Individual and small-group services are especially vital in overcrowded schools, in which teachers strive to provide attention to students who need it most.

• *Collaboration with teachers and parents is essential.* Although you respect your ethical and legal responsibilities regarding confidentiality and privileged communication, you are most effective when you establish relationships with the adults who are closest to the children with whom you are involved. In your elementary or middle school, students will make progress with their personal and educational adjustment when you include teachers, parents, and administrators in the process of helping. In your efforts to facilitate healthy relationships from the start, you should inform teachers and parents about the importance of confidentiality in student-counselor relationships. At the same time, convey to teachers and parents the value of their input and involvement in the helping process.

• *Teaching is an admirable, vital, demanding, and challenging profession in today's schools, which have widely diverse student populations.* The overwhelming majority of teachers practice at a high level of professional expertise, which is indispensable in helping students succeed in school. Respect the role of your classroom colleagues and accept the professional knowledge and expertise these professionals offer in designing intervention strategies for children. Maintain frequent contact with teachers whose students are receiving counseling services and listen to their observations and recommendations.

• *School principals have ultimate authority and responsibility in the school.* For this reason, close communication and cooperation between you and administrators is essential. Inform your principal about prevalent issues and trends you observe in the school. Establish healthy working relationships with assistant principals. Share particular concerns expressed by a number of students, common family issues experienced in the community, teacher frustrations, and other observations, so that administrators can provide appropriate leadership in addressing these issues. In a sense, you are the eyes and ears of the school community, helping administrators stay in tune with the needs of students, parents, and teachers. To accept this role and perform it in an ethical and beneficial manner, you and the principal must establish a positive relationship with each other.

• *School counseling services offer one of several opportunities to assist students and their families.* Middle and elementary counselors rely on professionals within the school system, such as social workers, nurses, psychologists, and teachers of exceptional children, as well as agencies outside the school, to provide additional services. To ensure that you refer students and families to competent professionals, become informed about available services and inquire about the effectiveness of professionals in the school system and community. In addition, cultivate professional relationships with other practitioners to facilitate referral processes. Personal and professional relationships established with other practitioners can help expedite referrals to a number of community resources when students and parents are in need of services. By doing so, you will be perceived by social workers, physicians, and others as a competent professional.

Each of the preceding guidelines involves the use of competent skills when establishing effective helping relationships. Developing personal and professional relationship skills, in particular, is necessary to be successful with the many populations you serve. The next two sections consider these two types of skills and how they foster successful staff relationships.

RELATING PERSONALLY

Beneficial professional relationships are possible when you demonstrate helpfulness and caring as part of your persona. By personally showing concern and regard for others, you set the stage for your professional invitations and interactions to be accepted by those you seek to assist. Through these personal contacts, you establish a solid foundation for your professional helping relationships.

The approaches you choose and the styles you adopt in forming personal relationships affect the level of success you achieve. In most cases, the helping behaviors you choose are either visible or invisible styles of functioning. Visible behaviors describe those that people know you have performed. They have observed you doing them. In contrast, invisible behaviors are actions you take on behalf of other people without their awareness or knowledge. You perform such behaviors quietly and invisibly. To be successful in establishing professional relationships, you should be able to use either style, appreciate the value of each, and know the rationale and purpose behind both. Know when it is appropriate to be visible with your relationships, and learn to appreciate the value of discretion and lack of visibility when it is best for others to receive recognition and attention. The following paragraphs examine ways to be visibly and invisibly helpful in your personal relationships.

Being Visible

You want people in the school community to know what you do as a counselor. It makes sense to want them to know about the personally helpful relationships you establish with students, parents, and teachers and how those relationships benefit students. In many situations, you will want these relationships to be visible. By openly demonstrating your concern, respect, and regard for people, you enable others to identify you as a caring, helping person. This kind of identity, as you know, is essential for effective counseling.

Consistency is paramount in establishing a genuine identity as a caring person. Some people turn their personal charm on and off depending on the situation at hand or the clientele with whom they are working. Such a discriminating, inconsistent posture is destructive to human relationships and incompatible with professional counseling. Effective counselors do not determine their level of concern or regard for individuals based on people's circumstances, values, or other conditions. They view all students, parents, teachers, and others as having value, being capable, and being able to be responsible. In this way, you consistently demonstrate respect and trust for those you serve.

There are limitless ways that you can be visible in your school and reach out personally to others. The first step is literally to let people see you. This may seem obvious, but many school counselors are unsuccessful with their colleagues because they never leave their offices to venture out into the life of the school. This section contains some starter suggestions to increase your visibility. Although some may not be universally applicable, you can use this list as a point of departure to create personal invitations and become visible in your school program. Use the ideas that work for you; discard those that do not; and develop your own style of relating personally to students, parents, teachers, and administrators.

Offer a Morning Welcome

In most schools, teachers have responsibility for meeting the buses in the morning and escorting children onto departing buses in the afternoon. Unfortunately, these personal opportunities are often perceived as demeaning and arduous obligations. As a result, these functions are called "duties" and viewed in a negative light, making it impossible for anyone to appreciate their positive benefits.

Help your school take a positive stance by changing the language associated with these events. Chapter One stresses the importance of language in identifying and defining who you are as a counselor. The same is true for other aspects of your school. If you refer to functions as "obligations" and "duties," you will perceive them in negative ways. By finding a language that accentuates the positive, you encourage helpful personal interactions.

Begin by visibly helping with "morning welcomes," "meet and greet," "afternoon farewells," "hall safety," "lunchtime relief," and other aspects of student supervision around the school. For example, you can view bus duty as an opportunity to "meet and greet" students and parents as they arrive at school each day. Some counselors are reluctant to assist with these responsibilities because they place them in roles of monitoring student behaviors and correcting misbehaviors. Who better than counselors, who are skilled in human relations, student development, and helping behaviors, however, to help teachers learn positive ways of relating with students? By visibly relating to students, parents, and teachers in personal ways, you demonstrate positive behavior for other professionals to emulate.

A beneficial by-product of visibility is the incidental data that you observe and record when out and about in the school. When students arrive in the morning, enjoy recess on the playground, eat lunch in the cafeteria, and leave for home at the end of the day, you can gather valuable information to assist them and teachers. An observant counselor uses these occasions to watch for signals from students who are experiencing difficulties at school or home. In this way, you use ordinary, unobtrusive functions and activities to assess students and help parents and teachers focus on the personal, social, and educational needs of children.

Exchange Greetings

Take time each day to see as many of your teaching colleagues as possible. Early in the morning, visit their classrooms and stick your head in the door to say, "Hello. How are you today?" When you pass teachers and students in the hallway, make an effort to recognize them in some way. A smile, nod, pat on the shoulder, and similar gestures, when personally and culturally appropriate, tell people that you are aware of their presence and value their company. These apparently simple behaviors are sometimes the most powerful invitations you can send. Counselors who fail to attend to the presence of others become phantoms in their schools. People do not know who they are or what they do. It is hard to imagine that such personally invisible professionals would be effective helpers. In contrast, when you openly display acceptance and acknowledgment of others, people seek you out for assistance.

One caution about personal greetings is appropriate here. Always be intentional and aware of your behaviors to avoid discriminating against certain students and teachers. Because counselors are also human and face all the challenges and conditions that other people confront, they sometimes harbor biases, prejudices, and negative attitudes that inhibit personal relationships. It is essential to offer yourself personally in an equitable manner to everyone in the school. To do otherwise paints a fraudulent picture of yourself as a helping professional and alienates people who feel shunned by your discriminating behaviors.

Celebrate Events

Encourage your school, students, and teachers to celebrate life. Send birthday cards to colleagues, announce student achievements over the intercom or through closed-circuit TV, and post announcements of upcoming events on the bulletin board and school Web site. A visible counselor is one who actively promotes the celebrations and accomplishments of others. When students achieve their goals and improve their school performance, send notes home letting parents know about their children's progress. Show parents that you appreciate their support for the school. By choosing this type of visibility, you take a positive stance as a counselor, rather than constantly being a purveyor of bad news. All parents appreciate hearing about positive events in their children's lives.

Host a Party

Schedule a party in your counseling center for the staff after school. Offer beverages and snacks, and plan relaxing, fun activities for teachers and support staff. To ensure a pleasant, positive atmosphere, enforce one simple rule: no shop talk. Encourage teachers to relax, laugh, and enjoy one another's company.

If the week has been particularly harried and stressful for your colleagues, walk the teachers through a few relaxation exercises and take them on a fantasy trip to Tahiti! Find a soothing tape of music and ocean sounds as a background for your "tour." This is a time for you and your teachers to socialize without discussing or dealing with school issues. It is also an excellent time for teachers who do not know one another to meet and greet informally. These personal interactions help establish professional relationships that will benefit students and the school in the future.

Invite a Colleague to Lunch

Take a teacher, an administrator, or other staff member to lunch. This simple gesture may be the beginning of a valuable, long-term friendship. Breaking bread together is a traditional way of establishing beneficial alliances. Similar invitations to camaraderie might be bringing a box of candy for the faculty lounge, giving a plant to the secretary for the school office, or visiting a colleague who is in the hospital.

The preceding suggestions are a few of the countless ways that counselors relate visibly and personally to teachers and students. The main idea in all these suggestions is to allow people to *see* you and *know* you personally. This is the first step toward professional helping relationships. People can relate more comfortably with you professionally if they have come to know you on a personal level.

Being Invisible

Whereas visibility is important for people to know who you are, there are times when it may be more appropriate for your identity to remain unknown. Effective elementary and middle school counselors know when to promote themselves and when to remain silent and invisible in the background.

As noted above, a visible image helps people know you and what you do. However, when your visibility becomes too pronounced and overwhelming, some people may withdraw from relationships with you. Sometimes it is best to do your work, reach out to others, and seek assistance for students without fanfare and recognition. Artful counselors know the difference between being *visibly inappropriate* and *invisibly appropriate* in their personal and professional relationships. The stories that follow illustrate how invisible behaviors can accomplish intended goals.

In one elementary school, the teachers and staff were struggling to establish a warm working relationship. Teachers communicated very little except for the usual "student degrading" and "administrator bashing" that they exchanged in the faculty lounge. The principal and counselor had attempted to use warm-up activities and other strategies at meetings with the teachers, but these attempts failed to bear fruitful results. One day the counselor decided to put random gifts in teachers' mailboxes. The counselor did this secretly, without anyone's knowledge. The gifts were small, unpretentious presents. A typical gift was a card saying, "It is nice working with you!" or a candy bar with a note that read, "Enjoy! Share with a friend!"

Naturally, when the first few gifts appeared, the recipients wondered who sent them. When asked, the counselor pleaded ignorance (some fibs are justified!). Occasionally the secret gift giver put a surprise in the counselor's mailbox to throw off suspicion. As the weeks went by and more gifts were distributed, teachers became more deliberate in their efforts to discover the "phantom of the mailroom," but the identity went undetected. After a while, a strange and marvelous thing began to happen. Teachers started receiving cards and gifts that the phantom did not send! As a vaudeville comedian once said, "Everybody wants to get into the act!" What had begun as an invisible strategy to say and do simple, nice things for people had become a full-scale invitation to outsmart and outdo personal messages sent to each other. The result was that the staff had a common ground to talk, laugh, and enjoy one another's company, and school morale improved.

A middle school counselor demonstrated another example of invisible behaviors. The counselor learned that a particular student wanted to be a student council representative. Unfortunately, the student believed that no one would nominate her. The counselor quietly began asking students about the student council nominations and whom they were planning to select. During these informal conversations, the counselor would inquire about this particular student and ask, "What do you think about her as a student council representative?" By simply asking the question, the counselor placed the student's name before her peers for consideration. Eventually, another person nominated the student and she won election to the student council.

In every personal relationship, you determine the extent of your visibility. To make the most appropriate decisions, assess the value of your visibility regarding your identity in the school, and weigh that assessment against the value of your invisibility in regard to the recognition and development of others. The accuracy with which you make these decisions about your personal relationships strengthens your position from which to establish effective professional relationships.

RELATING PROFESSIONALLY

Successful school counselors capitalize on their ability to relate personally and use this ability to help them function at a high professional level. When perceived by their colleagues, parents, and students in more than personable and friendly ways, these counselors gain the reputation of being competent professionals who know how to help people and facilitate beneficial relationships.

Not all counselors who function satisfactorily at personal levels are able to make the transition to the professional level, however. Such counselors struggle to establish effective working relationships because they have difficulty communicating with staff about the counseling program, relating with parents, or following through on student progress.

To establish strong professional relationships in your school, you want to seek input from others; share appropriate information; facilitate professional interactions; provide staff development; follow up on referrals; and assist the school in developing an orderly, healthful environment for learning. Let us examine each of these processes.

Seeking Input

Chapter One emphasizes the importance of winning the support of your administration and faculty and sharing ownership of the school counseling program. In addition to using the formal interviews and questionnaires recommended in that chapter, you will also want to adopt informal systems of asking teachers, administrators, parents, and students for their opinions. This type of professional involvement can take many forms, including individual contacts, group discussions, input from your advisory committee, and written communications.

Individual Contacts

Visit teachers in their classrooms before and after school, and ask for their opinions about ideas you have for the counseling program, students you have observed, or concerns they have expressed at faculty meetings or on other occasions. Ask whether you can help them with anything. These interactions are excellent opportunities to inquire about guidance activities and topics that the teachers would like to integrate with their classroom instruction. The position to convey during these brief contacts is that you value teachers' opinions and want their suggestions for improving the school counseling program.

Group Discussions

Many opportunities exist for you to receive input from teachers. For example, in elementary and middle schools where team teaching is common, teachers meet regularly to plan and coordinate their instruction. If this is true in your school, find out the schedule for these meetings and ask teams whether you could sit in on these planning sessions. When the time is appropriate, ask teachers for input to help you plan services for the counseling program.

Faculty meetings are another place to seek group input. Ask your principal for a few minutes on the agenda of each faculty meeting. Use this time to listen to teachers' concerns, receive feedback about counseling activities, and generate ideas for improving the program. Accepting group input is risky at times, because teachers may tell you things you would rather not hear. Consider their ideas respectfully and carefully. The acceptance and implementation of teachers' suggestions strengthen your credibility and status with the faculty. When you give clear programmatic reasons for not accepting some suggestions, teachers will respect your decisions.

Committee Input

An advisory committee, advocated throughout this guide, is another vehicle for receiving input. The more your advisory committee reflects the cultural and ethnic makeup of the school, includes parents and students, enjoys administrative support, and is viewed by the staff as having an essential role in program development, the more valuable its input will be to the counseling program. By being representative of the school and community, your committee can better articulate the range of services included in the school counseling program. With accurate input from an advisory committee, you will define more clearly your role in the school, form working alliances with teachers, and enhance your professional relationships.

Your program's advisory committee can also facilitate cooperation between the business community and the school. Many counselors, on their own or with the assistance of committee members, establish strong relationships with local businesses that contribute products for the school to use in rewarding students and faculty for their efforts. Although the initial ideas for these types of relationships may come from you, their development and realization are frequently the result of effort by many teachers, students, parents, and community leaders.

Written Communications

At times, it may be inconvenient to meet face-to-face with individuals or groups at your school. Sending written notes or e-mail messages is one method of letting teachers know that you appreciate their support and seek their input. Because your time is valuable, it is tempting to design and print a standard form to use for these contacts, but this is probably not the most effective method. Instead, try a personal touch by sending a handwritten note. Form letters rarely receive the attention and regard that a brief handwritten message elicits.

Sharing Information

Similar in importance to seeking input is sharing appropriate information with students, parents, teachers, and administrators. By knowing what and when to share, you win the respect of people you serve. Chapter Twelve considers the legal and ethical issues involved; here I present practical methods and guidelines about sharing information.

Select Carefully

Whether you are counseling an individual, leading group meetings, or sending written communications, it is imperative to know what information to share. In making this decision, you determine whether the information in question is essential for the other person to have and how this person will use the information. Sometimes counselors share information freely because it is not confidential. Although some people might view this openness as cooperation, others might become concerned about your inclination to share so much. A more conservative posture is to share information only when it is imperative to do so for the welfare of the individual and group in question. There is a delicate balance between collegiality and professional integrity, which you have to judge on a case-by-case basis.

Know Your Audience

In order to share information carefully, you have to take time to get to know the professionals, volunteers, and others in your school and community. With this knowledge, you are better able to share different types and levels of information without fear that people might misconstrue or misinterpret what you are sharing.

Demonstrate Respect

When approached by teachers and others who seek information, always convey respect for their professional roles and their interest in student welfare. If you are unable to share details with them at a particular time, let them know that you appreciate their interest in students and willingness to be involved. Tell them that as time progresses, the situation may change. Promise to keep them as informed as possible and certainly to provide the information necessary for them to perform their functions effectively.

Following Up

Chapter Three discussed the importance of follow-up in coordinating school counseling services. The degree to which you successfully follow up on the cases referred to you by teachers, parents, and students determines to a large extent the success of your professional relationships. On the one hand, when you demonstrate results, ask about the progress observed by others, and share observations appropriately, you are likely to win respect for your professionalism. On the other hand, when you accept referrals but fail to respond with information about responsive services provided or progress observed, teachers, parents, and students eventually will stop seeking your assistance. Keep your professional relationships at a high level of functioning by staying in touch with your referral sources.

Facilitating Support Groups

Facilitating support groups among teachers and parents provides another avenue for developing strong, professional relationships. These groups are excellent vehicles for teachers and parents to help one another deal with the challenges of teaching and guiding children and adolescents. Your role is to advertise the groups, schedule a time and place to meet, and facilitate the discussions. This last responsibility relies on your knowledge and use of communication skills rather than on any expertise you might have about teaching or parenting. Let us consider two types of support groups for teachers and parents.

Teacher Support Groups

Teachers are the best experts to help other teachers. Even counselors who once were teachers themselves do not have the same level of credibility that a seasoned, effective teacher has. Support groups are one way of inviting teachers to share common concerns and give suggestions to one another about ways to resolve these concerns. Your role as group leader is to help members share ideas about a particular concern or issue, focus on the member who has raised the concern, and facilitate a decision about what suggestions to implement in alleviating the problem. All the skills you apply in group work with students are useful in leading these types of teacher groups. To help make teachers more receptive to the groups, consider asking a teaching colleague whom the faculty greatly respects to colead the group with you.

Parent Support Groups

Although these groups are similar to teacher groups, they focus on child development and relationships in the home. As with teachers, parents helping parents is a much more effective strategy than one-on-one consultation between parent and counselor. You can hold groups during the day for parents who do not work or who work evening shifts, or schedule groups in the evening for other parents. These support groups often produce beneficial by-products beyond the support for parents and the establishment of professional relationships. For example, they can serve as a mechanism to identify parents who could benefit from referrals to other community agencies, such as social services, local health departments, or family counseling agencies.

Leading Staff Development

Another way elementary and middle school counselors relate professionally with their teaching colleagues is through staff development plans and presentations. In Chapter Seven, I stressed the importance of seeking input from teachers about in-service they would like to have during the school year. In many cases, you are the best person to present these workshops. Other times, you will want to locate a suitable presenter. Either way, the workshops you present or coordinate will display your skills in a visible way to your school's faculty and administration. When planning and leading workshops for your teachers, establish a few guidelines to structure and organize successful presentations. Here are some helpful hints:

1. *Be prepared.* Know your subject well and have all the necessary materials ready. If you use handouts, PowerPoint presentations, SMART Board interactions, or other media, make them clear, professional, and accurate. Have a colleague or friend proofread your materials, because errors are distracting to participants and detract from the message of your presentation.

2. *Arrange the meeting room to facilitate discussion and participation.* In a school with a small faculty, arrange chairs in a circle for workshops. For larger groups, an auditorium or theater setup is best. Use tables only when essential. They tend to become barriers to communication and may inhibit interaction among group members.

3. *Start and end on time.* Begin the workshop on schedule. Usually a warm-up or icebreaker sets a positive, comfortable tone for staff development activities. Also, end the workshop at the designated time. By beginning and ending on time, you demonstrate respect for people's schedules and recognize that they have obligations and responsibilities to fulfill. Teachers will appreciate your punctuality and respect.

4. *Have refreshments and snacks ready for a break.* If you plan the workshop for more than an hour, schedule a break about midway through. Offer soft drinks, coffee, tea, and snacks so teachers can enjoy refreshments and conversation. Remind the group to help you keep on schedule.

5. *Try a little humor.* Show your personal side by telling a humorous story or two relating to the workshop topic. Usually the most successful stories are ones about you. Avoid telling jokes merely for a laugh, and never use humor that belittles, degrades, or offends other people. Profanity, even to emphasize a point, is off-limits in workshop presentations. Also ask other group members to share humorous experiences. These opportunities for self-disclosure can broaden perspectives and at the same time offer a "lighter" view of what normally might be serious topics.

6. *Allow opportunities for discussion.* Teachers have much to offer one another. Workshops will be more successful if you avoid a total lecture format. Use sharing activities and intersperse them with your presentation to alternate the flow and style of the staff development session. You demonstrate professionalism when you accept the views and contributions of others.

7. *Call on the expertise of others.* When you plan a workshop, see whether any other faculty member is interested in the topic and willing to copresent with you. With some topics, such as using guidance in the classroom, the credibility of the presentation is enhanced if a teacher leads the discussion.

8. *Avoid mandatory workshops.* Because you seek input from all teachers about their topics of interest, you know that not everyone is equally interested in every topic. Make attendance voluntary unless school policy requires everyone's participation. You treat people professionally when you defer to their judgment about whether a particular activity will be beneficial for them.

9. *Evaluate the workshop.* Design a brief evaluation form for participants to complete before they leave the session. Evaluation forms, such as that in Worksheet 10.1, are the easiest to use.

Promoting Positive Discipline

Student discipline continues to be a major issue in schools. Teachers want to be able to instruct their classes while devoting time to individual learning, and disruptive behaviors take that time away.

Counselors who view themselves as essential professionals in the school community understand the importance of discipline and accept a role in helping teachers, students, parents, and administrators face this issue. As an elementary or middle school counselor, you can take an active role by promoting positive approaches to school discipline.

To this end, countless models are available to help teachers and schools focus on student development, cooperation, and reinforcement rather than on punitive consequences of misbehavior. I listed some references to discipline models in Chapter Five; they included such concepts as assertive discipline (Canter & Canter, 1992), logical consequences (Dreikurs & Grey, 1993), the quality school (http://www.wglasscr.com), and invitational education (Purkey & Strahan, 2002).

The first step is to involve administrators, the advisory committee, and faculty in choosing an approach that is compatible with the school philosophy and community values. The next step is to plan and deliver in-service to educate the staff about the approach selected. In this staff development, teachers might also learn about a schoolwide behavior management plan, which provides a structure and philosophy for everyone to follow across the school. Exhibit 10.1 offers a few steps to serve as a sample framework for your schoolwide plan.

School discipline is a group concern. Therefore, everyone who works in the school—teachers, counselors, teaching assistants, custodians, cafeteria staff, bus drivers, volunteers, students, and administrators—want to cooperate in ensuring that the school is a safe and orderly place to work and learn. As the counselor, you can take a leadership role in this process. The only area of discipline that is unsuitable for a school counselor is the administration of punishment. Such a role is contrary to the ethical and professional beliefs upon which school counseling is founded. In elementary and middle schools, where a positive approach to student behavior is emphasized and applied, punishment is rarely a solution. For this reason, you will be of great service to your teaching colleagues and students if you assume a leadership role in designing procedures and strategies that promote positive discipline.

Workshop Evaluation Form

Please complete this evaluation of our workshop. Circle your responses and place the form on the table by the door. Thank you for your suggestions!

1.	This workshop was informative.	Yes	No	Unsure
2.	The presenter(s) stayed on task.	Yes	No	Unsure
3.	This is an important topic for me.	Yes	No	Unsure
4.	The presenter(s) answered my questions.	Yes	No	Unsure
5.	The setting was appropriate for this workshop.	Yes	No	Unsure
6.	I will be able to use this information to improve my teaching or my relationships with students.	Yes	No	Unsure
7.	The presenter(s) was (were) knowledgeable about the topic.	Yes	No	Unsure
8.	The presenter(s) listened to other views.	Yes	No	Unsure
9.	The presenter(s) was (were) well prepared.	Yes	No	Unsure
10.	I would like more in-service like this.	Yes	No	Unsure

Additional comments: _____

_____

_____

EXHIBIT 10.1

Behavior Management Plan

1. Guidelines for student behavior will be printed, distributed, and discussed with students at the beginning of the school year. Focus will be on the positive points of school discipline rather than on the penalties of misbehavior.
2. Each teacher will present and clarify guidelines for behavior in the classroom.
3. Initial instances of student misbehavior will be resolved between the teacher and student in accordance with school and classroom guidelines.
4. Continued instances of student misbehavior will result in one or more of the following actions:
   a. The teacher informs parents or guardians of the behavior and requests a conference.
   b. The teacher develops reinforcement procedures to recognize appropriate student behaviors.
   c. The teacher informs the principal of the behavior and steps taken thus far to resolve the problem.
   d. The teacher refers the student to the school counselor.
   e. The counselor assesses and determines what services, if any, are appropriate.
   f. The counselor provides follow-up with the teacher or administrator, or both.
   g. The teacher, parent or parents, student, and principal reach agreement on corrective measures.
   h. A referral to the exceptional children's program may be considered.

In addition to instigating a behavior management plan, you can assist your school with positive discipline by doing the following:

- Creating healthy, respectful environments in and around the school
- Developing procedures to improve student supervision during the school day
- Designing and delivering programs to help students with peaceful strategies for conflict resolution
- Advocating for alternative programs in your school and school system
- Examining policies and programs that discriminate against individuals or groups in the school
- Designing group activities for teachers to use in classes to focus on positive student behaviors
- Developing and coordinating bus safety instruction
- Implementing parent education programs

BEING WITH VERSUS DOING TO

When you foster positive, respectful personal and professional relationships with people, you establish cooperation across the entire school. All the activities and functions suggested in this chapter aim at helping you become an integral part of the school community and educational program. In this sense, a major goal is to form relationships demonstrating that you and the counseling program are essential to student development, effective teaching, and a healthy school environment. Simply put, you *belong* in the school.

To achieve a sense of belonging in your school, become actively involved in programs and services that go beyond basic counseling relationships with students. In sum, become a leader of program development, an initiator of policy changes, a facilitator of support groups, and a presenter of staff development activities to benefit the school and community. Most important, if you wish to *belong* in your school, nurture a spirit of togetherness and mutual benefit in all your relationships. This attitude conveys a spirit of *being with* and contrasts with the more clinical, separate, and distant posture of *doing to* others (Schmidt, 2002).

By fostering a *being with* stance, you demonstrate awareness that the most beneficial helping relationships are the ones in which respect and trust are central characteristics, manifested in carefully chosen and appropriately applied approaches and strategies. In *being with* relationships, you value mutually beneficial outcomes. Therefore, when you help students, the result is that you, the school, and students' families all move to more productive levels of functioning.

The notion of *being with* expresses a positive attitude toward egalitarian relationships that is respectful of the expertise of all participants. In contrast, *doing to* relationships place you above others as you "diagnose problems," "modify behaviors," "adjust contingencies," and perform other similarly detached functions. As an elementary or middle school counselor, you want to exhibit mutually beneficial *being with* attitudes, confidence about your professional abilities, and acceptance of the knowledge and expertise that teachers, parents, students, and others bring to a wide range of personal and professional relationships.

As a conclusion to this chapter, in which you have read about ways to establish yourself as a vital, contributing member of an elementary or middle school program, the following list provides suggestions to promote *belonging to* and *being with* your school and community. These starter ideas are for all the elementary and middle school counselors who have asked themselves, What can I do to become a visible, vital professional in the school program?

• *Give an apple (or other gift).* On the opening day of school (or any other day), carry a basket of apples around as you greet teachers and staff members, and give everyone you meet a shiny red apple. After all, apples are the traditional fruit of education!

• *Dial-a-home.* Every day, call one parent or guardian of a child in your school. Introduce yourself, let parents know who you are, and invite them to visit you at school. For working parents who have Internet access, you might consider a cheerful e-mail message.

- *Send birthday greetings.* Design and print birthday cards for faculty and staff, and send cards during the year. Ask the principal about broadcasting student birthdays each day during announcements on the intercom or on the school's Web site. You might also use one of the many free greeting card sites on the Internet.

- *Guard against insensitivity.* Help teachers avoid activities that discriminate against certain groups of students. For example, when you plan programs to honor parents or invite parents to school, help teachers prepare alternatives for students who are without parents.

- *Take a workshop on the road.* Plan a professional outing to a museum, university, laboratory, or other point of interest for teachers.

- *Offer advice reluctantly.* Because you are a professional counselor, people sometimes want easy answers to tough questions. Use your skills to help people explore and decide their own solutions to difficult situations.

- *Be available.* Post your schedule in visible places around the school and on the Web site and, barring emergencies, stick to it. Avoid using a "do not disturb" sign on the counseling office door when you are in conference. If you do, someone else will be disturbed. Try alternative messages, such as "Sorry, counselor is in conference. Please come back at . . ."

- *Confer regularly with your principal.* Let the administration know about the counseling program and observations you have made about students' and teachers' needs. Your principal is a key person to help you belong to the school.

- *Invite yourself to luncheon parties.* As your schedule permits, have lunch with groups of students. Listen to their observations about the school, their peers, teachers, the town, and other aspects of their lives. Through simple invitations, you will keep your "ear to the ground" and become more informed and aware of student concerns.

- *Serve refreshments.* Have a fruit bowl or a treat dish to offer a bit of refreshment to visitors in the counseling center when appropriate.

- *Send get-well wishes.* When students and teachers are ill for a while, send a note wishing them well, and ask whether you can do anything while they recuperate.

- *Show appreciation.* When a teacher or other staff member has assisted you in some way, let him or her know you appreciate it. Send a note or a simple gift saying, "Thank you!"

- *Accentuate the positive.* When meeting with teachers or having casual conversations, always focus on what people can do rather than what is impossible. Teachers try to meet all the educational needs of diverse students, and sometimes their job is difficult and frustrating. Hear their frustration, and avoid feeding the fires of discontent. Instead, support their efforts to find reasonable, workable solutions.

- *Listen completely.* Sometimes you may have a tendency to say "no" to a request before hearing it fully. When you feel you must decline a request, practice saying "no" slowly by listening to the entire plea, and consider it carefully before giving your response.

- *Advertise the program.* Use available media to promote yourself and the school counseling program. Write a column for the school newsletter, commandeer a bulletin board in the school hallway, send press releases to your local newspaper, set up a counselor's Web site, and let people know who you are and what you do.

- *Dismantle the bureaucracy.* School policies can sometimes be cumbersome to navigate. Help teachers and students find solutions by cutting through the red tape whenever possible, especially with local officials and agencies. A counselor who gets things done is a prized possession in any school.
- *Be inclusive.* Include all teachers in the school counseling program. In every school, one or two disgruntled teachers and staff members can make life unbearable for everyone else. The tendency is to exclude these negative types. Take the high road instead, and invite their participation. You may find, despite all their difficult behaviors, that they have some legitimate ideas and helpful suggestions.
- *Brighten up the center.* Your counseling center is a reflection of your professional posture and attitude. Hang some pictures and bring in living plants, rearrange the furniture, add fresh paint, and think of other ways to have your space emit a positive, optimistic, professional image.
- *Establish a resource library.* When you come upon beneficial materials and information, make copies available to teachers. Start a resource library in the school. Give teachers handouts of useful information you have discovered in your readings or at workshops. Encourage teachers to share in similar ways with one another.
- *Subdue paper monsters.* Schools are notorious for creating paper trails the length of forever. Sometimes counselors contribute to this unfortunate process. Use your advisory committee to examine ways of cutting down paperwork that you, teachers, and administrators have created. Streamline processes for reporting information, requesting permissions, and performing other functions.

Use these ideas as they fit your situation, and develop new ones for your counseling program. As you create new ideas, you will begin to identify countless ways that you can belong to the school and *be with* others in the process of helping. The next chapter explores ways that you can reach out to significant others—parents, grandparents, and guardians—and involve them in their children's development.

chapter 11

INVOLVING SIGNIFICANT OTHERS

Scenario 11.1: Parental Involvement

In your elementary or middle school, what challenges exist for getting parents and guardians more involved in children's education? (If your school has a high level of parental involvement, what issues does that pose for the school, and what ideas do you, as counselor, have to meet those challenges?) How does your school try to address these issues? If you are a new counselor, how could you find out what your school has done in the past? What ideas do you have that might get more parents constructively involved in the school? How would you begin to test these ideas? How would you measure your success?

Acomprehensive school counseling program includes many people in its development and implementation. Your willingness to invite participation; share information; and include students, parents, teachers, and others relates to your ability to survive and thrive as an elementary or middle school counselor. This chapter gives particular attention to the role of students' families or guardians in supporting and participating in the counseling, consulting, and coordinating components of your program.

You want to include all persons in the home who have an impact on the child's development. Parents, grandparents, guardians, and others can be included and informed about the child's concerns, needs, and progress in school. For a number of different cultures, significant family members often include participants beyond the mother and father. Latino families, for example, place importance on the role of the father and other male figures in making family decisions—an uncle, for example, may take more of a leadership role in some matters than a mother does. Without knowledge and understanding of these and other cultural differences, you are at a disadvantage in using family support wisely and effectively to benefit each student. A first step in winning parental and family support is to achieve a high level of knowledge about and understanding of the families and communities served by your school.

KNOWLEDGE OF FAMILY AND COMMUNITY

Gaining knowledge about the families and communities of students is a gradual process of coming to understand how people's customs and values interact with the mission of the school. You achieve such knowledge by meeting people, joining civic groups, interviewing students, reading cumulative records, and observing events in the surrounding community. Without this knowledge, you, administrators, and teachers would establish helping and teaching relationships in a vacuum, distanced from the varied influences on each child's development. When this happens, schools (and counseling programs) become isolated from the community. Consequently, they become detached, suspicious institutions, failing to win cooperation and support from families.

In many cases, families that make up today's communities are a potpourri of relationships, unions, and cultural groups, making it difficult to define exactly what society means by "home" and "family." When you embrace your school's communities, you learn about the varying cultures within, and invite families—parents and guardians—to become an integral part of their children's education. This puts you in a stronger position to make a significant difference in the lives of these students. When you reach out to parents and significant adults in positive ways, you create a respectful stance toward the family and community. Proactive strategies that enable you and your colleagues to learn about families and the community include interviewing students, using cumulative records, orienting parents, visiting homes of students, and assessing the needs of parents.

Interview Students

One way to learn about families is through their children. If you are new to your school, plan a brief classroom guidance activity, "Me and My Family," for each class you visit during the early part of the school year or in small groups in the counseling center. Talk about how families are different across the country, in the state, and in the town where students live. Show pictures to illustrate some of these differences. As part of the presentation, ask students to share information about their families or have them draw a picture of the people in their families.

Variations of the preceding activities are limitless. As you learn from children about the many different types of family structures, you will also discover more of the cultural differences existing in your school. In some instances, you might identify children to meet with individually and learn about their homes and cultures. Exhibit 11.1 contains some sample questions to use in this type of activity.

EXHIBIT 11.1

My Family and Me

1. How many people live in your home? Who are the people that live with you?
2. Do any animals live in your home? What kinds of animals? What are the animals' names? Who takes care of these animals? Do the animals live in the house, outside, in a barnyard?
3. What does your home look like? How many doors and windows are on the outside of your home? What color is your home on the outside?
4. Where do you sleep in your home? Do you sleep alone?
5. Where do you go after school?
6. If you go home after school, who is at home when you get there?
7. What is the first thing you do when you get home from school?
8. Do you have chores or jobs to do at home? How do you help the family by doing these chores or jobs?
9. What do you do for fun and play at home? Tell me about the people you play with.
10. Have you lived in other homes? What other homes have you lived in?

Review Cumulative Records

Sometimes counselors are hesitant to review student records because they do not want to bias their opinions about children and adolescents in their school. Although this may be an appropriate practice, there is information in student records that can help you learn about family backgrounds and conditions that influence student achievement and development. To attempt helping relationships without this information may be an inefficient use of your time.

To use student records appropriately and efficiently, focus on the facts. Ignore opinions, anecdotes, and other superfluous material that are unsubstantiated by your observations and documentation from other sources. Until you have assessed the situation completely, delay making judgments or forming opinions about information. You might design a simple summary sheet, such as that in Worksheet 11.1, to use when reviewing student records. Keep these summaries in your counselor's file to refer to as you establish counseling relationships with students. This may be particularly helpful if you serve a large student population.

Cumulative Record Survey

Student: _____ Home phone: _____

Address: _____

Family members: _____

_____

_____

_____

Physical or medical notes: _____

_____

_____

_____

Education notes: _____

_____

_____

_____

Previous schools: _____

_____

_____

_____

Other information: _____

_____

_____

_____

Orient Parents

Schedule times for parents and guardians to visit the school and plan activities to help them learn about programs and events coming up during the year. Hold these orientations at different times during the day and evening, and repeat them for parents who are unable to attend at the originally scheduled time. There are parameters and policies within which your school must operate regarding these types of programs and meeting times, but do what you can to determine whether the school can be flexible in its planning.

When sharing information at orientation meetings, consider having parents who have been involved with the school assist you with the presentation. Parents who are new to schools and anxious for their children will be more at ease listening to other parents who are pleased with the school program. In schools with culturally diverse populations, have discussions in small groups led by volunteer parents who understand the language and cultural differences of the new parents. Plan strategies and organize your meetings to accommodate the needs and interests of those attending. Keep in mind that these orientations not only help parents become familiar and comfortable with the school but also increase faculty awareness about the needs of parents and the challenges facing neighborhoods.

Visit Homes

In some cases, the best way to learn about a student's situation is for teachers and counselors to visit the family at home. At one time, this practice was a common tradition for teachers and principals. Today, schools face many economic challenges and expectations with regard to the amount of time to be spent on instructional goals, which make these face-to-face meetings more difficult and less frequent. On occasion, however, a home visit might be the only way to truly understand the family's perspective.

Survey teachers in your school to see whether they are receptive to home visits. Start with your principal to ascertain whether the administration supports this idea and if local regulations and contracts allow it. Informally canvass the faculty to get initial reactions. If a social worker and nurse serve your school, recruit their assistance. Let teachers know that you are available to make home visits with them if they would feel more comfortable having someone accompany them.

Encourage your teachers to make home visits for giving parents positive feedback as well as for addressing concerns about student behavior and progress. Part of teachers' resistance to making home visits may be that they usually bring bad news to the home. The school can lessen this resistance if the purpose of these visits is balanced between positive and negative reports.

Assess Parent Needs

Chapter Three discusses ways of surveying the needs of students, parents, and teachers in order to formulate program goals and objectives, plan a program of services, and coordinate your counseling activities. Similarly, a parent needs assessment helps you acquire knowledge about the home situation, which is beneficial when the school asks for assistance in handling student problems.

If teachers suspect that a family is having difficulties, you may need to assess the situation directly by calling or visiting the home. Stressful situations and tragedies in some families have a debilitating effect on student development and learning if they go unheeded. In these cases you should contact the family and offer to locate necessary assistance, which requires a working knowledge on your part of the community and its available resources.

COMMUNICATION AND INFORMATION

In some elementary and middle schools, good ideas and excellent programs go unnoticed and unsupported by parents because they need more information or have not received the communications. You can help your school by coordinating efforts to communicate clearly and accurately with parents. Some ways to do this include planning special schoolwide functions, organizing group conferences, and sending written communication home with students.

Special Events

Elementary and middle school parents and guardians care about their children's performance in school and enjoy seeing them show off their talents. You and the teachers can display student talent by planning special events and inviting parents to attend. These events can be schoolwide, such as a school bazaar to earn money for materials and equipment, or they can be limited to a single class, such as a kindergarten display of "new art forms."

When you arrange special events, use these opportunities to inform parents about other events and programs taking place in the school. For example, if your school holds a raffle to earn money, you could set up tables, staffed by students, parents, and teachers, to distribute information and answer questions about the counseling program. In the same way, if you want to attract parents for an open house to visit with teachers and learn about the instructional program, you could advertise door prizes for those who attend. Identify the main purpose of the event, plan ways to invite parents, make the invitation attractive by including incentives, and use every occasion to promote your school and the school counseling program.

Worksite Visits

Many parents work long hours and have obligations that often prevent them from coming to school to hear about their children's progress. One way your school can help these parents and guardians is to arrange with their local places of work for you to meet with them during work hours. One school system arranged with an area textile mill to have parents released for conferences with counselors in the mill itself. The conferences took place once per school semester so that working parents could receive regular updates on their children's progress. Most businesses and industries will view a half-hour release time for this type of consultation as time well spent. Talk with your principal and advisory committee to see whether this idea is worth pursuing.

Test Reports

As part of the federal legislation No Child Left Behind, elementary and middle schools across the country participate in testing programs to gather data on students' academic progress. In addition, many school systems supplement these assessments with their own testing to measure student aptitude and achievement. Standardized test results usually include home reports that explain results to parents. Sometimes schools do not send these test results home; or if they do, there is little explanation or discussion to help parents and guardians understand them. You as a counselor have a responsibility to see that the instructional staff use test results wisely and appropriately and parents receive and understand their home reports.

One way of disseminating test results is to send them home with children's report cards, in which case your school will want to include an explanation. This explanation needs to be clear and accurate, written in a layperson's language so parents are able to interpret the results. At the same time, you might extend an open invitation to parents who want individual conferences to receive further explanation and additional information about their children. In instances where written communications do not always make it home, you may need to call some parents directly to tell them the report is coming home and to invite them to meet with you at their convenience.

Holding group sessions, in which you inform several parents about how to interpret the information on their children's home reports, are another helpful and efficient method of sharing test results with parents. In these sessions, the information you share about test results is general; ask parents to see you individually if they have specific questions about their children's scores.

Parent Conferences

Face-to-face conferences, scheduled routinely throughout the year, are another means of communicating with parents and guardians. You can assist your school in the development of productive parent conferences in two ways. First, encourage the administration to schedule regular opportunities for teachers and parents to meet. Second, provide teachers with staff development activities to acquire the necessary communication and leadership skills to hold such conferences.

Regular conferences during the year, in which teachers establish working relationships with parents and guardians, may be preferable to calling on them only when problems surface. In addition, encourage teachers to communicate with the home throughout the year by calling when students have been absent with a long illness; sending congratulatory notes when family members are recognized for their achievements; inviting parents, grandparents, and guardians to have lunch with children at school; and planning other ways of promoting goodwill between home and school.

Providing in-service to teachers will help them strengthen the communication and problem-solving skills they will use with parents. Focus these sessions on active-listening skills, facilitative behaviors, conflict management, and decision-making strategies. In addition, help teachers learn about the importance of clarifying their roles, agreeing on a plan of action, and assigning responsibilities. To increase the likelihood of a workshop being successful, you might prepare an outline of specific stages of a parent-teacher conference. Here is a sample:

1. Establish rapport by helping parents feel welcomed, comfortable, and valuable as equal partners in this helping relationship.
2. State the purpose of the conference in a clear and precise manner. In most instances, a conference occurs for one of three reasons:

   Planning—to design a plan to handle an upcoming event, such as a student's transfer to a new school
   Sharing information—to report on data or other information about the student, such as testing results
   Problem solving—to address some issue of concern to the parent or teacher, such as the student's classroom behavior

3. Explore, discuss, and explain information and observations relative to the topic of the conference. Give parents specific information, and avoid generalizations that you cannot substantiate.
4. Listen to parent observations and opinions about the child and the school. This information can help you understand the child's perceptions better.
5. Generate ideas and recommendations from the parents and teachers to address issues raised in the meeting. These ideas can strengthen the plan of action you choose.
6. Narrow down alternatives and select those that are agreeable to all concerned. Assign responsibilities to the teachers, parents or guardians, the student, yourself, and other persons involved in the agreement and plan.
7. Close the conference with a summary of the agreement, a plan for follow-up, and a time for a second conference, if needed. Ask all participants whether they have other items to discuss before adjourning.
8. Adjourn the meeting by thanking everyone for their participation and genuine concern for the child's welfare.

In addition to the stages detailed above, use staff development opportunities to offer helpful hints and enhance teachers' leadership skills for working with parents and guardians of students. You can present suggestions in a handout during the workshop or by posting them around the room to use as catalysts for group discussion. Here are a few ideas for teachers to use when they confer with parents:

• *Invite parents to become equal partners.* Use the pronoun "we" as you discuss the issues and solutions explored. In this way, parents will feel that they have an important role and valuable information to contribute.

• *Acknowledge that parents are the experts on their children.* Listen carefully to their observations and respect their knowledge of the home situation.

• *Choose a comfortable setting for the meeting.* Sometimes parents are uncomfortable in schools. Do everything possible to ease tensions and relax the atmosphere.

• *Avoid placing barriers, such as tables and desks, between you and parents.* If you need a table for writing, sit at the corners, or as close to the parents as possible.

• *Be prepared.* If records, test data, and other information are needed for the conference, have all materials ready and at hand. Getting up to search for information in the middle of the meeting breaks the flow and continuity of the relationship.

• *Be truthful with parents.* Exaggerations and untruths destroy confidence and credibility. Parents will appreciate your openness and honesty. Avoid being brutally frank or telling parents what you think they need or want to hear in order to "gain an upper hand" or "weaken their resistance." You build healthy working relationships on trust and respect, neither of which is compatible with uncaring, thoughtless behaviors.

• *Invite the student.* In some conferences, particularly with middle school students, you may want to have the child sit in on part or all of the meeting. A decision about this should be made before the conference—discuss it with the parent or guardian when you schedule the meeting.

• *Summarize what went on.* When you end the conference and parents leave, write a brief summary of what was decided and who will accept what responsibilities. Keep a separate file of this information for all your conferences with parents and guardians.

Letters and Communiqués

Written messages provide another method of communicating information to the home. These might be letters that you mail to parents, e-mails, notes that students bring home, articles you write in school newsletters, announcements on the school's Web site, and reports that individual students receive from you and their teachers. Diverse forms of communication can help to let parents know about events at school, student progress, and other important information. Your goal of being a visible counselor should include issuing many types of communications.

In designing and implementing various strategies, remember that the messages and articles you write and distribute are reflections both of your professionalism and of the school counseling program. Here are some guidelines for achieving effective communication with the home:

1. *Proofread carefully.* Sometimes readers miss an entire message because they focus on one misspelled word or grammatical error. Be accurate and ask a colleague to read your work before sending it out.
2. *Look professional.* Give your correspondence the best possible image. Ask the school secretary and media coordinator for assistance in designing and producing a polished product. Use colorful paper for brochures, add graphics, put appropriate links on your Web site, and try other ways of making your messages visually attractive.
3. *Check your vocabulary.* Write for your audience, not for yourself. Choose a language that all parents understand and always avoid educational jargon.
4. *Use positive phrases.* Keep your letters, messages, and announcements upbeat. Even when letters must convey difficult news for parents to hear, choose optimistic words

and phrases to put forth the school's position of hope and promise. By gaining parental support, you more easily overcome barriers to successful relationships with students. The message in Exhibit 11.2 provides one example of positive wording.

EXHIBIT 11.2

Progress Letter to Parent

Dear Ms. Albright:

I am writing to give you an update on Natasha's progress with the behavior we discussed at our last meeting. We hope that you have been able to talk with her about the behavior. The teachers want and appreciate your support.

At this time, I cannot tell you that Natasha's behavior is better, but the teachers and I remain hopeful that she will begin to improve. Natasha is a smart girl, and with your help and the teachers' efforts, we believe that she will have a successful school year.

Call me at my office, 555-6677, if you want to talk about this. If I do not hear from you, I will be in touch with another progress report in two weeks.

Thanks again for your help with Natasha.

Robin Beach
School Counselor

Beyond designing and writing letters and other correspondence to homes, plan how you will distribute this information. Decisions about how to send notices home to parents are practical considerations influenced by the nature of your correspondence, the cost of mailing, the appropriateness of sending e-mails, and the dependability of students to deliver school notices to their homes. These considerations will have an impact on the success of your communication—you might write an excellent announcement inviting parents for conferences with teachers, only to have merely a handful of parents show up because the word never reached most homes.

When a letter is critically important, it is best to mail it—perhaps by registered mail if you want to be sure parents receive it—or deliver it in person. If you think students will deliver the message, try it. Students may want to know what the letter is about, particularly those in middle school. If so, tell them what the letters contain. If you cannot tell students what they are delivering, it is best to mail the information.

When you use students as delivery agents and want to be sure the information reaches its destination, offer incentives to students—a treat, decal, or other reward. For messages sent this way to parents, ask them to tear off a receipt you have attached to the bottom, sign it, and give it to the child, who will return the receipt to school.

Another way to both communicate your role to parents and inform them of guidance and counseling activities in the school is to send home student worksheets completed during a classroom guidance activity. Attach the worksheet to a memo explaining the nature of the activity and ask parents and guardians to talk with their children about the lesson. As noted in the previous paragraph, you could place a form at the end of your memo for the parents to sign and have students return the forms to you at school to receive an award, such as a sticker, a special treat, or a free pass to the counseling center. Exhibit 11.3 gives an example of a general memo to parents.

EXHIBIT 11.3

Memo to Parents

Dear (ask students to write the names of their parents or guardians):

Today in school, students learned about friendships and the ways that they can make friends. In our discussion, students talked about some of the friends they have and what they do to make and keep friends.

Please ask your child about this activity and about what he or she learned. After you talk about this activity, sign the form below, and your child will return it to me at school for a reward.

If you have any questions about this activity or other services of the counseling program, please call me at school (555-6677). Thank you for your support!

Sam Waters
School Counselor

_____

I have talked about the friendship lesson with my child and have learned about the activity that was presented at school.

_____

(Parent[s] or guardian[s])

_____

(Date)

PTA and PTO Presentations

Ask your principal about presenting at PTA or PTO meetings during the school year. These presentations can be short announcements about school counseling services and upcoming programs, they can spotlight a student project, or they can focus on information and skills for parenting.

A question-and-answer panel with the principal, counselor, and teachers is another way of sharing information with parents while soliciting their input concerning the school program. These exchanges illustrate a school's openness and willingness to share ideas and discuss concerns in a public forum. If your school plans this type of presentation, you will want to set parameters and topics for questions. Such structure will give the presentation a specific focus so that you can cover a few topics adequately rather than trying to address too many topics insufficiently. The success of one of these sessions will encourage your school to plan future panels and include additional topics for discussion.

When making presentations to PTA or community groups, use the guidelines suggested earlier in this chapter for communications between the school and the home. Because, as you have seen throughout this guide, the programs you present and speeches you make advertise who you are and what you do, you want to put your best foot forward. Here are some additional tips for planning and presenting successful programs to parents:

1. *Practice.* Before you present and as you are preparing your talk, try it out on yourself and others. Check the time frame and make adjustments as needed. If you are new at giving presentations, ask someone close to you, a spouse or colleague, to listen to the talk and give you helpful reactions and comments.

2. *Arrive early.* Give yourself sufficient time to survey the meeting place, set up materials, check out the microphone, and take care of other structural matters, such as the arrangement of chairs for the audience. Presentations sometimes fall short because of environmental factors that could have been adjusted if discovered early enough. If you finish the setup and have time while the audience is arriving, shake hands, introduce yourself, and greet people as they come into the meeting place. These simple gestures place you at an equal, receptive level with your audience.

3. *Be prepared.* Have all your materials ready and check any equipment you plan to use for the presentation. It is discomforting to a presenter and an audience to be ready for the "show" and have the projector light bulb burst or a computer malfunction.

4. *Dress appropriately.* Always look professional, even when the dress for an event is casual. Choose outfits that are attractive and appropriate, yet not flashy or overpowering. Your appearance should not overshadow what you have to say. The message is more important than the package it comes in.

5. *Keep a brisk pace.* Plan presentations that move smoothly and highlight the most important points as you speak. In most presentations of twenty to thirty minutes, you will have a couple of key points that you want the audience to hear. If most people leave remembering these main ideas, your presentations will have been successful.

6. *Move around.* Avoid standing in one spot or behind a podium. By walking around, you alter your proximity to members of the audience and allow yourself the opportunity to make eye contact with different people. This subtle change in distance and eye contact enables you to include people in your talk and illustrates the *being with* posture described in Chapter Ten. Moving around also encourages the audience to follow you with their eyes, which engages them in the presentation.

7. *Summarize.* At the end of your talk, highlight once more the main points and key ideas you have presented. You have something important to say; be sure to present it more than once.

8. *End on time.* It is a cardinal sin to keep audience members longer than they expected. When you are introduced, glance at the time and remember to stay within the schedule. If you go too long, no matter how good you are, some people will tune you out and miss your main points. Sometimes, when other items besides your talk are on the meeting agenda, the time allotted for your presentation will have to be cut. Be ready to adjust your program to meet the needs of the situation. In short, be flexible.

The previous paragraphs have presented a few suggestions to facilitate and enhance school-home communication. These suggestions invite parent and guardian participation and involvement in the school and give ownership of the school to the community.

Volunteers

As mentioned briefly in Chapter Three, parents, grandparents, guardians, and others can provide valuable time and support to school programs, including school counseling services. Administrators, teachers, and counselors who truly believe in the notion of a school community recognize the wealth of resources and assistance lying beyond the school's doors. Encourage your school to invite students' families and other outside individuals to contribute to the quality of the educational program. The possibilities are boundless, limited only by the imagination and willingness of the school to tap these resources. Here are some roles that volunteers can fill:

• *Tutors.* Diverse needs of students and the related challenges teachers face highlight the reality that there will never be enough support services for all children. Volunteer tutors help individual students and relieve some of this demand on teachers' time. In schools that recruit many tutors, a volunteer coordinator may be necessary to keep track of schedules, notify tutors of changes at school, plan training sessions, and communicate between the school and volunteers as appropriate.

• *Media assistants.* Keeping up with all the materials in a comprehensive media program is a major challenge. Volunteers in elementary and middle schools can help media specialists catalog materials and service equipment, as well as assist students in the media center.

• *Guidance assistants and presenters.* Parents and other volunteers can help teachers and counselors deliver guidance activities with small groups and in classes. Sometimes volunteers might share personal or professional expertise that relates to a guidance lesson. For example, a visiting grandparent could tell stories to primary children about friendships formed over her lifetime, or a mother who is also a police officer could talk about her career in law enforcement.

• *Supervisors.* As noted earlier, student safety and supervision are major concerns in all schools, regardless of their size. Having volunteers in the school increases the number of eyes and ears available to ensure a safe environment for children. The school administration will want to participate in the orientation of volunteers to discuss school policies and procedures and the role of paraprofessionals in the school. Be sure to invite your administrators to help plan all orientation functions. Parents and others can also assist teachers with supervision during peak times, when student traffic is high and monitoring is essential. These times include bus arrival and dismissal, lunchtime, and recess.

• *Clerical assistants.* Your school can use volunteers for clerical functions, such as typing, copying, making bulletin boards, or creating instructional materials. The school secretary is well positioned to coordinate these services and train volunteers.

There are many other ways that volunteers can help teachers meet the needs of students. Use your advisory committee as a resource to plan volunteer programs in the school, remembering always to involve your principal in decisions about volunteer participation. Worksheet 11.2 presents a volunteer application form, which you or a parent can hand out at the first PTA or PTO meeting or send home with students at the beginning of the year.

PARENT EDUCATION PROGRAMS

With involvement and support from parents and guardians, elementary and middle schools can more effectively help children through developmental stages and learning processes. Because children today face increasingly difficult challenges and pressures, parenting has become a complex adventure. Programs to assist and support parents in this process are an essential part of school counseling services. In addition to presenting at PTA or PTO meetings and sending communications home, you can take an active role in assisting parents by offering parent education opportunities.

The structure of parent education programs will depend on the nature of the group, the training and expertise of the group leader, and the leader's style and preference for leading particular types of discussion and educational groups. When you organize and present parent education programs, there are typically two formats from which to choose: discussion groups or instructional programs.

Discussion Groups

Counselors who have received preparation in facilitating group procedures are often comfortable leading parent groups in discussions about topics of mutual interest or concern. Group members can suggest topics or the counselor can preselect them. Topics for discussion with elementary school parents might be

- Parent-child communication
- Mealtimes
- Family responsibilities
- Allowances
- Bedtime
- Getting ready for school in the morning
- Sibling rivalry
- Television, cell phones, computer games, and the Internet
- School anxieties
- Parent-teacher communication

Volunteer Application Form

Check the appropriate responses and fill in the requested information. Thank you for volunteering in our school!

_____Yes, I would like to help in school as a volunteer.

Name: _____

Home phone: _____

Work phone: _____

_____I am available to volunteer during school hours.

_____I am available to volunteer in the evening or on weekends.

My volunteer interests are

_____ Tutoring students	_____ Doing clerical tasks
_____ Assisting in the media center	_____ Driving on field trips
_____ Presenting career information	_____ Helping teachers with classroom guidance
_____ Reading to students	
_____ Repairing the building	_____ Organizing fundraisers
_____ Supervising students (on buses, in the cafeteria, and so on)	_____ Sprucing up the school yard
_____ Providing technology support	_____ Contacting businesses for donations (for prizes, rewards, and so on)

The following topics may be of interest to middle school parents:

- Parent-adolescent communication
- Friendships
- Homework
- Physical changes
- Beginning at a new school
- Extracurricular activities
- Adolescence and independence
- Alcohol and drug awareness

Discussion groups are successful when group members feel comfortable with one another, and the leader's skills are sufficient for the task. When parents do not know other group members, or you do not have the necessary knowledge to present on certain topics for your parent education programs, you might consider programs available commercially.

Commercial Programs

Many parent education programs are commercially available to purchase for your counseling program, or you can design your own. Examples of a few commercial programs to use for parenting education are

- Systematic Training for Effective Parenting, by Don Dinkmeyer Jr. and Gary McKay, www.steppublishers.com
- Assertive Discipline for Parents, by Lee Canter, Canter and Associates, http://maxweber.hunter.cuny.edu/pub/eres/EDSPC715_MCINTYRE/Assertive Discipline.html
- Active Parenting, by Michael Popkin, www.activeparenting.com
- Parent Effectiveness Training, by Thomas Gordon, www.GordonTraining.com

In addition to these programs, books, and materials on logical consequences, behavioral and other approaches are available for teaching parenting skills. Many of these are included in the Resources at the end of this book.

Choose an instructional program according to the structure of the group you plan to facilitate, learning goals and objectives you have selected, and specific activities you will incorporate into the learning process. If you are not familiar with a specific approach to parent education, investigate what approaches other counselors in your school system have used successfully. Locate a training program to attend, or join a group that is learning about the approach and currently meeting in your school system or community. After you have reviewed different programs, received appropriate training, and determined which methods are best for you and your school, you will be in a better position to plan and implement successful parent education sessions.

Program Planning

When you have researched and determined which of the various approaches to parent education are best suited for your counseling program, plan a strategy for introducing the approach, recruiting participants, and evaluating your success. Consider the following procedures:

1. *Secure commitment from the principal and teachers.* The time you allot to run these groups has to come from somewhere in a very busy schedule. Talk about the program with your advisory committee and ask for assistance to guide you toward a schedule that is acceptable to your administration and faculty. In some schools, counselors run both daytime and evening groups to accommodate the work schedules of parents. Counselors also sometimes arrange evening groups at parents' homes and rotate the meeting place for each session.

In some communities, parents may have difficulty arranging transportation to a school or other location to attend sessions. If possible, bring the program to a convenient meeting place. One elementary counselor, for example, led groups in the recreation room of a housing project for parents who lived there. Whatever arrangements you make for your program, clear them with the school principal or other supervisor.

2. *Through surveys and informal conversations, ask parents about the types of programs and groups they would attend.* There is little point in taking the time and effort to design and implement a program to which few people will respond. Do your homework and gauge your audience.

3. *Advertise the program through school newsletters, local radio shows, PTA or PTO meetings, and other avenues to make sure word gets out.* The first few groups you lead may be sparsely attended. However, when you are successful, word will spread and future programs will become better attended.

4. *Use the same leadership skills you apply in group counseling and guidance to your parent discussion and education groups.* Facilitate discussion and place every parent in the role of an expert. De-emphasize your own expertise and rely on the suggestions and collective wisdom of the group.

5. *Limit the number of participants for each group to maximize discussion.* You can give presentations at PTA or PTO meetings on specific parenting topics to large audiences, but ongoing parent discussion groups should be limited to fifteen to twenty members.

6. *Set a schedule for every meeting date and time at the beginning of the program.* Having a schedule in advance helps parents plan their calendars and ensures good attendance at the sessions. Start each session promptly and end on time.

7. *Encourage everyone's participation.* Use your group skills to keep discussions going and prevent individuals from dominating the meeting. Create a spirit of belonging by giving everyone an opportunity to contribute.

8. *Summarize each session and ask parents for feedback before ending the meeting.* Similarly, begin each new session with a brief review of the previous meeting.

9. *Ask parents to complete an evaluation of the program during the last session.* Summarize these evaluations and present a report to the principal and faculty. Sharing the results of these evaluations with your colleagues will help win their support for future programs. Worksheet 11.3 is a sample evaluation form for a parent education program.

This chapter has considered a variety of ways to develop healthy working relationships with parents and guardians. Sometimes, because of the confidential nature of relationships counselors form with elementary and middle school children, communication with parents becomes delicate. Developing positive communication with parents throughout the school year will assist you during these sensitive, difficult times. In these instances, your knowledge of legal and ethical guidelines is of paramount importance. Chapter Twelve reviews legal and ethical issues related to counseling in schools. Before beginning the next chapter, however, return to Scenario 11.1 at the beginning of this chapter and brainstorm some basic starting points to enhance communication with parents and guardians in your elementary or middle school.

Parent Education Evaluation

Please complete this questionnaire to help me evaluate the parenting group and plan future programs. Thank you!

1.	Did you enjoy this program?	Yes	No	Unsure
2.	Were you comfortable in this group?	Yes	No	Unsure
3.	Was the information helpful to you?	Yes	No	Unsure
4.	Was enough time allotted for discussions?	Yes	No	Unsure
5.	Did the counselor respect your views?	Yes	No	Unsure
6.	Were you encouraged to help other participants?	Yes	No	Unsure
7.	Were your questions answered?	Yes	No	Unsure
8.	Have you successfully used any information learned in this group?	Yes	No	Unsure
9.	Would you join another group in the future?	Yes	No	Unsure
10.	Would you recommend this program to other parents?	Yes	No	Unsure

Additional comments: _____

_____

_____

_____

chapter 12

PLAYING ACCORDING *to the* RULES

Scenario 12.1: Therapeutic Counseling

A middle school counselor has ten years of experience as a mental health counselor specializing in self-injury among adolescent girls. She now works in a rural school without ready access to local mental health services. Teachers have referred a few female students to her because they have observed self-injurious behaviors. The counselor feels competent in working with these students and has parental permission in each case. A central office curriculum supervisor, however, wants each school counselor to follow the ASCA National Model, which states that counseling services delivered in a clinical and therapeutic mode by school counselors are inappropriate (Reiner, Colbert, & Pérusse, 2009). What is your position on this issue? What are the ethical and legal implications? If you were her principal, what would you advise this counselor to do?

In today's schools, administrators, teachers, counselors, and other professionals face increasingly difficult and complex legal and ethical issues. For you as a practicing school counselor, the responsibility of making the most appropriate decisions is dependent on a clear knowledge and understanding of legal and ethical guidelines. Such understanding begins with knowing the difference between ethical and legal issues.

You establish working relationships with students and other clients in accordance with legal parameters and ethical standards developed by professional associations and certification or licensing boards. Although legal and ethical guidelines are frequently in agreement, there are times when they appear to be in conflict with each other. At these times, your own professional knowledge and judgment will be the most important guide.

In daily practice, you interpret each legal and ethical situation within the context of school policies and your responsibilities for serving students, parents, and the local administrative unit. To place yourself in a knowledgeable position and to make appropriate decisions about legal and ethical issues, learn about state and national laws as well as local policies that relate to the practice of counseling in your school setting. At the same time, you want to have a clear understanding and working knowledge of professional ethics for school counselors. The ethical guidelines commonly followed by school counselors are the ethical standards of the American Counseling Association (2005) and the American School Counselor Association (2004). In addition, counselors who are certified by the National Board of Certified Counselors or other licensing boards follow their respective ethical codes.

This chapter examines legal and ethical considerations you might encounter as an elementary or middle school counselor. If you are not already knowledgeable and well versed in these issues, you may want to obtain up-to-date resources, attend conferences, participate in pertinent workshops, and read professional journals. Strengthening your knowledge base protects you, your clients, and the school from unwanted legal entanglements.

A first step in becoming informed is to learn about local, state, and national laws and policies that govern schools. As a professional school counselor you provide services according to regulations set by your administration, policies enacted by the local school board, state laws and procedures, and federal laws. All these come under the heading of *legal considerations* when you face decisions involving a law, policy, or other regulation.

LEGAL CONSIDERATIONS AND RESOURCES

Many resources are available to help you explore the breadth and complexity of legal issues faced by today's counselors. Your school principal, your counseling supervisor, the local school board, and professional associations can help you gain knowledge about local, state, and federal laws and policies.

School Principal

Ask your principal to locate manuals and guides for you to learn school regulations and local policies. These materials might include a copy of the student handbook, a faculty manual, school board policies, and a school principal's guide to state law. Such documents present the policies and regulations by which your administration manages the school. As a professional hired by the school system, you want to adhere to these policies and regulations; in particular, you want to be aware of potential conflict between these regulations and your ethical standards. If you have questions in this regard, ask your principal to discuss these issues with you. In these discussions, listen carefully to the principal's point of view, even if you do not always agree. In practice, balance your adherence to school policies with concern for student welfare and development. Sometimes it may be appropriate to illustrate for the principal how local regulations are inhibiting rather than facilitating student well-being and educational progress.

Overcoming differences of opinion about how regulations affect student development will be less difficult and stressful if you and your principal begin with a good working relationship. For this reason, it benefits you and the students to communicate consistently and openly with your principal about the school counseling program, the issues it addresses, and the services it provides. By maintaining open communications with your principal, you improve the likelihood of negotiating changes in school procedures and policies when they are detrimental to student welfare. Candid communication also places you in a stronger position to win the support of your principal when local policies raise ethical dilemmas regarding counseling services. The responsibilities you have to students, parents, and the school may not always be in harmony with one another, and having the support of your principal to help you satisfy each of these responsibilities is essential.

Counseling Supervisor

If your school system has a supervisor or director of school counseling services, ask this person for published state manuals related to the practice of school counseling. Determine which local school board regulations and state policies are applicable to the school counseling program.

Your supervisor may also be able to obtain information about actions related to school counseling handed down by state and federal courts. Because of the different levels and jurisdictions of courts, it is important to know which rulings apply to what situations. One avenue for learning this information is through a workshop on current legal rulings that pertain to school counseling. Your local school board attorney, a judge, or a district attorney can be an excellent resource to help plan and deliver this staff development. You also might ask the counseling supervisor to plan workshops that would help you and other counselors learn about the counselor's role and responsibilities when being subpoenaed. When counselors become involved in counseling children about family separations, abusive situations, sexual development, and other sensitive issues, they sometimes receive subpoenas to testify in legal hearings and procedures. Workshops and seminars presented by expert counsel can help you learn about your rights, legal proceedings, and appropriate ways of responding as a court witness.

Some states have passed privileged communication statutes to protect certain student-counselor relationships. Find out whether such protection exists in your school system and what exceptions or conditions, if any, are in place in your state. Privileged communication means that counselors cannot be forced to testify in court about information students have revealed in counseling sessions. Thus privileged communication relates to the ethical practice of maintaining confidentiality. When a state law grants privileged communication, the client is protected, not the counselor. Students protected by privileged communication in counseling relationships can waive this privilege if they so desire, and in some states parents are involved in this process for minor children. Be sure to learn all you can about privileged communication, the pertinent statutes in your state, and how these affect the practice of counseling in your school.

School Board

In school systems governed by local boards of education, regularly meeting board members review and act on policies to govern and regulate school practices. Attend your local board meetings if you are allowed to do so. Check the agenda of each meeting when it is released and see whether it contains any items pertaining to the school counseling program. Sometimes school systems post the agendas in the central office before meetings or announce them in the local newspaper.

By staying informed, you are able to design and implement counseling services that conform to local policies and procedures. At the same time, you learn about local regulations under consideration by the board, which may hinder or help the delivery of comprehensive guidance and counseling services. By keeping in touch with local regulations, you take a strong position to advise decision makers, such as local board of education members, about school counseling services and the legal and ethical responsibilities of counselors.

You may find that the school board attorney is a vital support person when legal matters interact with your helping relationships. As mentioned above, the school board attorney is an excellent resource to inform you about your role and responsibilities when testifying in court as a witness. Attorneys also can provide information about an array of subjects that influence or interfere with counseling services in schools. Competent attorneys can address matters related to exceptional children's rights, parent custody and access to children at school, privileged communications between students and counselors, due process, counselor malpractice, use of e-mail or other electronic forms in delivering counseling services, and limitless other topics.

The situations you face are not always simple to handle in legal or practical terms. For example, conflicts may occur between a principal and a counselor because of how each person perceives his or her role, authority, and responsibilities. Imagine that a teacher suspects that one student is being physically abused. This teacher has brought the evidence to you, the school counselor. In your school system, it is proper procedure to bring such cases to the school principal immediately, and you do so. The principal listens and says, "I know this family. This is not abuse; it is simply firm discipline." The principal makes it clear: "This will not be reported to the child protective services agency." Both you and the teacher feel otherwise. What would you do?

According to the law, all professionals are required to report a situation when they have sufficient reason to believe a parent or caretaker has abused a child. All states have laws that require school officials to report *suspected* child abuse. Knowing this, however, may not be sufficient in helping you and the teacher make a decision to act against your principal's orders. What you need is guidance from a local policy that clearly shows the legal responsibilities of all school personnel, in accordance with state and federal laws regarding child abuse. You may also need to consult your supervisor or the personnel director in the school system. In cases of suspected child abuse, the report is usually required within a specific time frame. Therefore, you may not have time to research the legal position of the school system on this matter. For this reason, it is all the more important that you have a working knowledge of local school regulations and the authority of the school principal and other administrators as well as your own. As noted in Chapter Nine, suspicion of child abuse requires a report to an investigative agency.

Most school officials—administrators and board members—want counselors to provide services that meet the expectations of local policies, state mandates, and federal laws. Hence, school systems generally are willing to provide staff development and make available legal experts who can educate counselors, teachers, and other professionals about appropriate regulations. In addition to the training that the school system provides, you could seek further information and education from professional counseling associations both nationally and in your state.

Professional Associations

You can acquire resources concerning legal issues and professional responsibilities from state, regional, and national counseling and educational organizations. The American Counseling Association, the American School Counselor Association, and their state divisions provide opportunities for counselors to learn about the legal and ethical standards and practices of professional organizations. This information will help you compare local school policies with the positions of various counseling associations, which will, for example, help you prepare a case to convince your principal and school system to adjust policies that are seemingly in conflict with the legal views or ethical standards of the counseling profession.

By attending state conferences, national conventions, and local workshops, you can learn from colleagues who are counseling in other elementary and middle schools and facing issues similar to those you confront in your school. Take advantage of these opportunities to increase your knowledge, and place yourself in a position of being able to prevent legal and ethical entanglements.

Although you may want to attain a general working knowledge of the law and how it relates to the practice of school counseling, your best resource in times of conflict will be the specific law or policy in question and an expert in the practice of law. Ethical considerations, however, are less precise than legal mandates (although many of these are also imprecise) and are guided by your knowledge, understanding, and acceptance of professional codes and standards.

ETHICAL CONSIDERATIONS

ASCA has presented its own code of conduct to foster and maintain standards of practice for school counselors. In these ethical standards, ASCA defines seven broad areas of counselor responsibility—to students, parents or guardians, colleagues and professional associates, the school and community, one's self, the profession, and maintenance of standards. You want to obtain and review a complete copy of this ethical code, which you can download from the ASCA Web site (www.schoolcounselor.org). The following sections offer a brief summary of counselor responsibilities as outlined in the ASCA ethical standards.

Responsibilities to Students

School counselors are primarily concerned with the total development of students, including their educational, vocational, personal, and social growth. You accept responsibility for informing students about procedures and techniques used in counseling relationships and encourage students to explore their own values and beliefs in making decisions and plans about life goals.

As a counselor, you are responsible for knowing about the laws and regulations regarding student welfare as you seek to protect the rights of all children. To protect the confidentiality of information received in your helping relationships, release information according to existing laws and policies and always use student records and data in an accurate and appropriate manner. In addition, balance the student's right to privileged communication with parents' rights to be involved in guiding their child's development.

As noted earlier in this chapter, confidentiality is an important ethical issue. Research indicates that school counselors have not reached a consensus about when to break confidentiality and what risk-taking behaviors by students might influence such decisions (Moyer & Sullivan, 2008). Because elementary and middle school students are minors according to law, when you should break confidentiality is a delicate and sometimes complex issue (Lazovsky, 2008). This is all the more reason for you to know your position in this matter. In brief, you inform parents or guardians and appropriate authorities when you believe situations present clear and imminent danger to students. Use careful consideration in doing so, and consult other professionals whenever possible. Furthermore, you will want to make necessary referrals when your assistance is no longer showing adequate progress with students who are receiving counseling. Your ability to make such referrals is contingent on your knowledge of existing resources in the school system and community.

According to the ASCA code, you want to avoid relationships with students or other persons that compromise your objectivity or increase the risk of harm to the student. Such relationships are referred to as "dual relationships," and sometimes they are unavoidable. For example, a dual relationship might exist if you were the only counselor in the school, and a student who is also the son of your best friend needs immediate assistance. When these types of relationships are unavoidable, you have the responsibility to minimize the risks to the student and thereby reduce the potential for harm.

Other responsibilities to students include appropriate selection and use of tests and other assessment procedures, evaluation of the effectiveness of the counseling program, adherence to professional procedures when facilitating group work, maintenance of student records used in rendering responsive services, and appropriate use and promotion of technology in delivering services.

Responsibilities to Parents

Although counselors in elementary and middle schools have the ethical obligation to protect the rights of children and confidential relationships established with students, they also have a responsibility to involve parents and keep them informed of services that are available to their children. According to the ASCA code, counselors recognize the rights and responsibilities of parents, and establish cooperative relationships with parents to ensure the progress and development of students. However, these rights and responsibilities are not always clearly defined, and today's challenging social issues, such as child neglect and abuse, coupled with continuously shifting family structures place you and your school in precarious ethical and legal positions. For this reason, be knowledgeable about your school's views on parental involvement in all services for children and about your role as counselor. In general, your role should include the following responsibilities:

- *Know local policies and state laws* that pertain to counseling with minors and to guidance and counseling services in schools.
- *Communicate frequently with your principal* about your program of services and about the nature of concerns that students bring to you. Although information about particular children is confidential, you generally inform your principal of the types of concerns that students are having in school.
- *Inform parents about the school counseling program* by making presentations at PTA or PTO meetings, distributing brochures, writing a column for the school newspaper, and inviting local media to cover special events in the school. When parents know you and are aware of their children's progress in school, they are more likely to accept confidential relationships between you and their children to some degree.
- *Seek permission from children to involve their parents* in the helping process. With young children in elementary and middle schools, the support and involvement of parents are critical in determining the success of a counseling relationship. Young people do not have sufficient control of their lives to make all the decisions necessary for moving the helping process forward, and parental input is essential in most cases. When appropriate, you should encourage children to inform their parents about their concerns and permit you to communicate with and involve their parents in helping relationships. As noted previously, when a student is in danger, you take the necessary steps to inform and involve parents and guardians. An exception is when the parents or guardians themselves are responsible for the imminent danger, such as in cases of child abuse. At these times, you follow local and state regulations for reporting to the proper authorities.
- *Provide accurate and objective information to parents*. When it is appropriate to share information with parents, you should give an accurate, complete, and unbiased account of the situation. Interpreting test data, discussing school policies, and sharing other information reliably and accurately build parent confidence in you and the school. One cardinal rule is that when you are unsure of the accuracy of data (for example, test results) or other sources, say so, and assume responsibility for following up and obtaining the most current and correct information.

Responsibilities to Colleagues and Professional Associates

The degree to which you form successful partnerships with professionals in your school and community is a measure of the regard and respect you will earn as a counselor. Your relationship with other professionals, beginning with your teaching colleagues, must be facilitative and genuine, because an effective counseling program cannot exist without sufficient collaboration among all professionals in the school.

Be respectful toward teachers, staff members, and administrators in your school. Let them know that you hold them in high regard as professionals and admire them for accepting the challenge of educating all children. Inform teachers and administrators about your role in the school and the ethical guidelines by which you practice. Be open, trustful, accurate, and objective when communicating and consulting with school staff.

Rely on the knowledge and expertise of teachers and other professionals to make appropriate decisions in your role as counselor. Teachers, media specialists, psychologists, social workers, and nurses offer a wide range of expertise and knowledge. By seeking assistance from these professionals, you avoid overextending yourself and running the risk of providing services and information beyond your competency level.

It is your responsibility to be informed about the roles and capabilities of professionals with whom you work. Learn about the other specialists who serve your school and find out about their professional preparation and skills. Also acquire such knowledge about professionals outside the school to whom you will refer children and families. You have an ethical responsibility to know your referral sources and to seek professionals and agencies that are highly competent, appropriate, and effective with their respective client populations.

Gathering this type of information may take time. One way to begin is to follow up regularly with the referrals you make. Ask students and parents whom you have referred to other professionals and agencies about the services they have received. Call referral agencies and, if appropriate, ask for progress reports. Base future decisions of whether to continue using various community resources on the follow-up you receive about past referrals.

In your relationships with community agencies and professionals, always consider the welfare of the students, parents, and teachers with whom you work in the school. It is improper to place your own personal and professional interests before those of the clients you serve, particularly when working with referral agencies and professionals in the school and community. The primary consideration should be: What is best for the student, parent, or teacher?

Responsibilities to the School and Community

As an employee of a school system, you have certain legal and ethical responsibilities regarding your role as an elementary or middle school counselor. As noted earlier, a working knowledge of the rules and policies governing the school and your counseling program is essential to function appropriately. It is imperative for you as a representative of the school system to follow these regulations in your practice as a school counselor.

Ethically, you have a responsibility to students first and the school second. At times, you may experience conflict between your ethical responsibilities and the regulations mandated by the school. When this happens, mention this concern to the school administration. By showing your principal, for example, how a strict school policy on attendance is limiting or jeopardizing your effectiveness and ability to assist a school-phobic child gradually return to school, you may be able to get the regulation changed for more flexibility. This could have a positive effect on many students. The potential for this type of conflict is another reason to have an open, cooperative relationship with your school administration from the outset.

On rare occasion, a school policy that contradicts your ethical standards cannot or will not change, and you will face a difficult professional and career decision. It comes down to two basic questions: Can I ethically continue in this counseling position, or should I resign? and, If I remain in this position, do I behave against policy to do what I believe to be best for students?

Ethical codes and legal regulations do not always provide clear answers. Each case is unique, and policies and laws are subject to interpretation. Sometimes you might decide that the best and most appropriate action to take is to behave against policy. If so, you risk losing your job. Only you can decide whether such a risk is worth taking. As a professional counselor, you encourage students and other clients to take risks in their lives and develop to their fullest potential. Sometimes you want take risks, too, and heed your own advice.

Responsibilities to Yourself

The ASCA ethical code states that school counselors should function within the boundaries of their professional competence and accept responsibility for the consequences and outcomes of their decisions and actions. Behaving in any other way places you, your clients, and the institution in physical, emotional, and legal jeopardy. In addition to practicing within your professional limitations, you also want to choose approaches and techniques that have the probability of generating positive outcomes with minimal risk to clients and yourself. You are committed to choosing the most beneficial services that will enhance rather than hinder the development of others.

By consistently behaving in a competent manner and demonstrating your commitment to ongoing professional development, you demonstrate a high level of self-responsibility. Keeping abreast of issues in school counseling, attending conferences and workshops, returning to school, and reading professional literature are a few ways to remain current and improve your counseling, consulting, and technological skills. Chapter Thirteen explores in detail some additional approaches to caring for yourself as a person and as a professional.

Another way that you demonstrate self-responsibility is by recognizing the diversity of students and communities your school serves. This includes an awareness of your own perspectives, attitudes, and beliefs about cultural values and differences, which, as noted in Chapter Six, are important aspects of your development and performance as a professional counselor.

Responsibilities to the Profession

As a member of the counseling profession, you join thousands of counselors who serve in a variety of settings and institutions. Although these various settings may differ in the populations they serve, their primary mission and the nature of services offered enable their clientele to reach common goals for human development and learning. For this reason, counselors from every area of practice—schools, universities, mental health centers, prisons, hospitals, and other settings—collectively establish a stance by which the general public views the entire counseling profession. All practicing counselors, regardless of the institutions in which they function, have an obligation to behave in the most responsible and ethical manner possible.

Behaviors you choose and the ways you function in an elementary or middle school will add to or detract from the credibility and worth of the school counseling profession. Everything you do and say will make a positive or negative difference in the ways people view you as a counselor and in their perceptions of your profession. Furthermore, each personal and professional action, interaction, and decision you make has the potential for either a negative or positive impact on some person or group. Realizing this responsibility and accepting the challenge of behaving in a dependably ethical and knowledgeable manner are the hallmarks of professionalism.

You also demonstrate professional responsibility through the accountability processes you use to assess your school counseling program. In this guide, you have learned the importance of measuring what you do and how well you do it. When undertaking program evaluation, conduct yourself ethically by collecting data in appropriate ways and reporting results accurately, completely, objectively, and in accordance with acceptable research practices. Counselors who exaggerate outcomes or omit data attempt to paint an untrue picture of their programs or themselves and behave irresponsibly and unethically.

Related to an accurate reporting of program evaluation results is the practice of presenting yourself to your clientele and the public in a clear, truthful manner. This means giving accurate information about your training and credentials as well as understanding your level of competence and skills in delivering appropriate services. Misrepresentations about your background and training are improper, and you should immediately correct any information that you or others have mistakenly conveyed. For example, if you are introduced to the PTA as a "certified family counselor" when you hold no such credential, it is your responsibility to correct this information for the audience before beginning your presentation.

Identifying your level of skill and practicing within the boundaries of your competencies are not always as simple as correcting misinformation about your background. For example, in a critical situation you might be the only professional available to help. Due to the immediate circumstances, you must take action quickly. In such cases, you intervene to the best of your ability and seek assistance from more qualified professionals as soon as possible. Behaving in accordance with your level of training and making appropriate referrals are ways of demonstrating responsibility to yourself as a professional and adhering to standards of practice.

Responsibilities to Maintain Ethical Standards

The last section of the ASCA ethical code encourages counselors to observe ethical practices and be aware of the responsibility and procedures for reporting instances of suspected unethical practice by other professional counselors. Such procedures begin with a confidential consultation with a colleague to confirm the suspicion of unethical practice, followed by a face-to-face conference, when feasible, with the counselor whose behavior is questionable.

This section also mentions state association ethics reviews and the ASCA Ethics Committee. You want to know the procedures, outlined by ASCA and other organizations that publish ethical standards of practice for counselors, for bringing suspected violations up for review.

Thus far, this chapter has reviewed legal and ethical issues to consider when establishing and implementing a school counseling program of services. These considerations are important in establishing a framework for professional practice, but they will not provide clear, precise answers for every situation. Although ethical standards do not supersede the law, legal knowledge is not always sufficient to guide decisions about the most appropriate course of action to take. Because each case is different and the welfare of the student or other client is paramount, your judgment always plays a pivotal role in legal and ethical issues.

GENERAL GUIDELINES FOR ETHICAL PRACTICE

This concluding section offers general guidelines to aid in establishing your own professional framework for making ethical decisions and demonstrating sound judgment. By establishing professional and personal guidelines, you become more consistent and dependable in the decisions you make and the actions you choose. These qualities lend credibility to your performance as a professional school counselor, and students, parents, teachers, and others come to rely on your judgment.

Over the years, businesses, industries, and other organizations have sought to define appropriate and pragmatic ethical standards. Many have adopted the Four-Way Test of the International Rotarian Society for establishing ethical relationships. The test was first published in the early 1930s and continues to be a template for many businesses. You can adapt the four key questions of this test, shown in Exhibit 12.1, to create a framework for ethical practice in professional counseling.

EXHIBIT 12.1

Four Key Questions

Ask yourself the following questions in your helping relationships:

1. *Am I being truthful?* Providing accurate information is essential to ethical practice in professional counseling. Counselors who function at the highest level behave genuinely and honestly at all times. They handle information appropriately and respect confidentiality in accordance with ethical guidelines. At times you may need to withhold information for the protection and welfare of a student or other person, but you choose to omit or withhold information only with the utmost care and respect for the individual.
2. *Am I being fair to everyone involved?* Fairness is frequently a matter of perception. It is also a condition to assess in examining your behavior. One way to ensure a high degree of fairness is to seek input from everyone involved. By including all parties, you increase the likelihood that people will agree with the decisions made.
3. *Will my actions result in cooperative relationships?* The goal of every helping relationship is to enable people to work jointly toward a common, beneficial goal. When counseling or consulting with others, you have an obligation to establish cooperative

(Continued)

---

relationships with all who are involved in the process. If you avoid seeking input from others or diminish their contribution to the helping process, you threaten the success of these relationships and damage your credibility.

4. *Are my actions beneficial to all parties?* You want every action to produce results that enhance human development. Therefore, behaviors that demean, degrade, and dehumanize in any way, shape, or form cannot be ethical, responsible actions. When you function at the highest level of ethical practice, you take every precaution to ensure that your behaviors lead to beneficial outcomes for every party involved, including the school.

In addition to the four key questions of the Four-Way Test of ethical behavior, there are other ethical considerations to include in your personal guidelines for professional functioning. These considerations include advertising your services clearly and accurately, knowing when to refer cases, understanding the voluntary nature of counseling, following through on cases, understanding your own values, informing parents, seeking appropriate assistance, and caring for yourself personally and professionally. Consider each of these components of ethical practice as you develop your program.

Advertising Your Services

This guide has encouraged you to be visible as a counselor in your elementary or middle school and to advertise who you are and what you do. As you prepare materials for distribution to students, parents, teachers, and other groups, check their accuracy. Counselors who announce their functions and services through appropriate channels and according to ethical standards are careful to describe their roles and functions clearly and correctly. Brochures you create, news releases you send out, Web sites you develop, and interviews you give are carefully prepared and presented so your audience has little doubt about the services of the school counseling program and your role as the school counselor.

It is also professional behavior to accurately describe your level and area of training when requested to give this information. In such a description, you want to offer a general summary of your preparation to become a counselor. Typically, school counselors who are properly trained during their graduate work have studied a range of human development theories, such as multicultural theories, numerous helping skills and processes, and measurement and evaluation theories and techniques. ASCA (2008) developed and published its School Counselor Competencies to help counselors establish comprehensive programs of services for all students. Competencies are those behaviors that professional school counselors are capable of performing and include in the comprehensive program of services. Exhibit 12.2 gives a brief outline of the areas of competency proposed by ASCA. To have a full understanding of the ASCA School Counselor Competencies, however, you will want a full copy for your professional library. You will find the competencies published in the July-August 2008 issue of *ASCA School Counselor* magazine, which is listed in the Resources at the end of this guide.

EXHIBIT 12.2

ASCA School Counselor Competencies

Area I

School Counseling Programs

I-A: *Knowledge.* These competencies pertain to knowledge of American educational structures and systems, the ASCA National Model, leadership principles, counseling processes and guidance programs, career development, collaboration processes, legal and ethical issues, developmental learning, social justice, multicultural counseling and career theories, and preventive and interventional mental health strategies.

I-B: *Abilities and skills.* The competencies in this section focus on all aspects of planning, designing, implementing, and evaluating a comprehensive school counseling program. They include a counselor's historical knowledge of the profession, use of technology, multicultural awareness, leadership, use of the ASCA National Model, student advocacy, and collaboration with stakeholders, and skills related to being a systems change agent.

I-C: *Attitudes.* Competencies pertaining to counselors' attitudes involve counselors' beliefs about student learning and success, opportunity for learning, employment and postsecondary education, access to a program of counseling services, the effectiveness of collaboration, the leadership role of counselors, and use of data in measuring program effectiveness.

Area II

Foundations

II-A: *Knowledge.* Effective counselors are competent in aligning their school counseling programs with current local, state, and national issues in education. They have knowledge of various theories of human development and learning and the three domains of student academic achievement, career planning, and personal and social development.

II-B: *Abilities and skills.* The competencies in this section encompass a broad spectrum of behaviors. They include the ability to align your program with current initiatives in school improvement and student success, understanding of the school's philosophy and mission and its integration into your professional philosophy, and the ability to write a school counseling mission statement and communicate that mission

(Continued)

to stakeholders. In addition, these competencies expect you to use student standards in developing your program and to align those standards with school goals. Lastly, this section includes competencies with which you demonstrate your ability to understand and apply ethical standards and legal guidelines in all aspects of a comprehensive school counseling program.

II-C: *Attitudes*. This section emphasizes that school counseling programs are organized for all students and are an integral part of the school mission. The counseling program operates within the policies and regulations of the local school system and the state.

Area III

Delivery

III-A: *Knowledge*. These competencies survey a range of topics that include the guidance curriculum, counseling theories and techniques appropriate for school settings, individual student planning, group counseling, classroom guidance activities, classroom management, and career planning. They also emphasize principles of working with diverse student populations and the importance of knowledge about crisis counseling for various issues.

III-B: *Abilities and skills*. This section includes an array of behaviors that demonstrate your ability to use a guidance curriculum, deliver individual and group services for students, provide appropriate responsive services as needed, and understand the role of counseling in schools. These behaviors also address the importance of support systems and the counselor's role, as well as the counselor's ability to provide supervision for school counseling interns.

III-C: *Attitudes*. By practicing within the framework of these competencies, you demonstrate that school counseling is one part of a continuum of care for all students. You coordinate and expedite counseling and other responsive services to ensure that all students in the school have appropriate care. The counseling services you provide are primarily developmental and short term. In general, you refer students to other professional helpers if they require long-term care or diagnosis of specific disorders.

Area IV

Management

IV-A: *Knowledge*. In this section you will find leadership, organizational theory, time management, decision making, and technological information as expected areas of knowledge.

IV-B: *Abilities and skills.* Management behaviors and evaluation of your school counseling program encompass many of the competencies in this section. These include the ability to gather, analyze, and synthesize data to understand student outcomes and make appropriate intervention decisions, create plans of action, and suggest changes in policy and practice.

IV-C: *Attitudes.* As you might imagine, the attitudes conveyed in this section relate to your beliefs about managing the program and your counseling department or office and your beliefs about collaborating in this effort with your school administration.

Area V

Accountability

V-A: *Knowledge.* To design and carry out useful evaluation plans, you want to have knowledge of accountability issues in the profession, basic research, statistical concepts, methods of using data in evaluation plans, and how to present findings in reports.

V-B: *Abilities and skills.* The competencies you need for program evaluation and other accountability plans involve abilities and skills related to how you collect both formal and informal data, how you conduct research for program evaluation, and how you use findings to make program changes. In addition, this section addresses self-assessment strategies and the use of appropriate performance appraisal instruments by your supervisors.

V-C: *Attitudes.* This last section focuses on your beliefs regarding results-based program accountability, the use of quantitative and qualitative data, and how you analyze and present findings of your program evaluation.

In using the ASCA School Counselor Competencies, you may find that some of the proposed competencies do not fit your preparation or belief system as an elementary or middle school counselor. For example, the ASCA National Model is fundamental to these competencies. If you use another model in designing, implementing, and evaluating your school counseling program, some of the competencies may seem irrelevant. In this case, you could adjust some of the competencies to fit your situation. If there are some competencies that you believe are important but are not prepared to deliver, you will want to acquire those competencies. You might do this by pursuing additional graduate work, attending conferences or workshops, and undertaking self-education through reading and forming collegial relationships.

Knowing When You've Gone Far Enough

As a practitioner you borrow methods and strategies from several disciplines, including human development and learning, sociology, psychology, group dynamics, and educational research. With this broad background of study, you are able to provide many beneficial services in your school. Yet your expertise and level of competency have limitations, and you should practice within these boundaries. In sum, know when you have gone far enough.

How long do you continue seeing any student for individual counseling? I once heard a consultant respond to this question by commenting that a counselor should refer a student if the counseling relationship lasts more than five or six sessions. It is important to set parameters for the duration of your counseling relationships, but such simple quantitative responses are troubling. You may find many factors to consider when deciding how long a counseling relationship should continue and when it is appropriate to refer. You want to develop guidelines for making these important and sometimes difficult decisions. Here are a few questions to ask yourself during this process:

1. Do I have the knowledge and skills to help this person explore the problem, examine alternatives, make decisions, and act accordingly?
2. Is there another professional who is better able to help than I am, and who is available and accessible to the person needing services?
3. Do I want to involve parents or guardians in this helping relationship?
4. By seeing this person on a regular basis, am I denying other people services or neglecting other vital functions in my role as a school counselor?
5. Am I making progress with this person, and can I show evidence of this progress?

Students in elementary and middle schools often need someone to listen to them on a regular basis and guide them toward appropriate decisions. Not all children and adolescents require intensive therapy; some simply need a caring person to be their confidant, ally, and friend. How much time to give to regular clients is a question only you can answer. The essential factor should be whether the services you provide make a positive difference in the life of a student, in classroom relationships, in educational development, and in the overall functioning of the school.

Developing guidelines for addressing these questions will help you be consistent in the services you provide. Ask members of your advisory committee for their opinions and suggestions about how to determine the length and duration of your counseling relationships with students. Of course, students also have something to say about this issue, based on their level of commitment and their voluntary participation in the helping process.

Understanding Volunteerism in Counseling

The issue of voluntary counseling is of particular importance in institutions in which clients make up a captive audience. Schools are among these institutions because students are required to attend and, in some cases, are required to receive counseling services. Classroom guidance, orientation services, and annual registration are a few activities that include all students. Individual and group counseling relationships occasionally are expected for some students who have behavior problems, learning difficulties, or other concerns that inhibit their progress. How you handle these expectations and at the same time respect the rights of students is a measure of your ethical and professional practice.

When students are referred involuntarily for services, the initial steps you take in developing helping relationships are critical. It is essential that all students view your assistance as genuine and potentially beneficial for them. In this regard, find out what each student would like to see changed in his or her life or in school. As you and the student explore these wishes, you are better able to determine what goals are possible within the scope of the helping relationship. When students are particularly resistant to your help, it may be necessary to establish a personal relationship before expecting them to accept your professional assistance. If after a reasonable time you are unsuccessful in winning acceptance, it is appropriate to seek assistance from other professionals.

On rare occasion, students will refuse help, even from the most competent and caring counselors. You do not want to coerce or pressure a student who does not wish to be involved in a helping relationship, or who absolutely refuses to participate in any form of a relationship. Referral to another professional is an option to consider, but elementary or middle school children may not respond any better to other professionals than they do to you. A second option is to provide indirect services by assisting the parents, teachers, and other students in the class. Such services as parent education programs, teacher consultation, and classroom guidance may help others discover new, appropriate behaviors to try when relating to the child in question. When others connected with the child make changes, the student in question may begin to make adjustments in his or her own views and behaviors. Whatever route you choose, it is important to follow through on all referrals, even when the student resists or rejects your assistance.

Following Through

You probably receive many referrals from students, teachers, and parents. By following through on all these referrals, you behave in an ethical manner and you function at an effective level of professional practice. To accomplish this, you need a workable referral system and a process for following up on the cases you receive.

The referrals you receive as a counselor may often be spontaneous comments from teachers. You could be walking down the hall, having lunch, or getting your mail in the front office when a teacher says, "I have a student who needs counseling." Because you have many responsibilities and provide services throughout the school, these spontaneous referrals are sometimes difficult to remember. Help yourself and your teachers by keeping a small notebook handy during the day. By writing these messages down, you accept responsibility for receiving the referral, which is more efficient than handing teachers a referral form and saying, "I would love to help. Please fill this out." It is also a better way to facilitate professional relationships. Although referral forms have their place, they are not always practical; a notepad will demonstrate to teachers that what they have shared with you is important and that you value their input and time.

Understanding Your Values

Another aspect of counseling in schools that relates to ethical practice is having a clear understanding and appreciation of your own values and their effects on various helping relationships. The ASCA ethical code states that counselors should refrain from forcing opinions and values on students and others whom they counsel. Yet it is impossible not to have one's beliefs color and influence personal and professional relationships. At the same time, you also want to follow the policies and guidelines established by your school, which have their own sets of values.

A few suggestions may help you in handling this value-laden issue. First, know where you stand. A clear understanding of your belief system helps you assess how others view you and how they perceive the assistance you offer them. Second, withhold your values and beliefs unless sharing them facilitates the client's progress toward a beneficial goal. When you share your beliefs, do so openly and honestly, and allow others to disagree. Third, provide several options from which clients can choose. Encourage students to list as many alternatives as possible, and refrain from judging these options solely on what you believe.

When working with students, some values that enter the relationship invariably will be those of their parents. With young children, these family values raise another issue related to ethical practice—the involvement of parents.

Informing Parents

Legal precedent may supersede ethical standards when considering the involvement of parents in counseling relationships with children. As we noted earlier in this chapter, you have an obligation to know your state laws and local policies regarding parent permission. Sometimes there is a delicate balance between your duty to protect the rights of the child and the ethical and legal obligations to honor the rights and responsibilities of parents. In counseling elementary and middle school students, it is good practice to involve the parents or guardians as soon as possible in the helping relationship.

With the exception of instances in which imminent danger is apparent and therefore immediate notification of authorities and parents is imperative, counseling relationships with school children should eventually include parent or guardian participation at some level. Students in elementary and middle schools do not control their lives to the extent that adolescents and adults do. For this reason, progress in helping relationships with young children can be greatly enhanced by the involvement and support of parents. In most cases, students will give you permission to include their parents in the helping process. If possible, involve students in planning how to inform their parents and what to tell their parents. By combining forces, counselors and parents can offer children stronger and more consistent support in resolving conflicts and addressing concerns. Parent input is also essential when deciding to refer a child to other services.

Seeking Assistance from Others

As discussed throughout this guide, you sometimes will be unable to provide optimal services, and will refer students for additional services within or outside the school. To make referrals ethically and professionally, in addition to learning about the agencies and practitioners that you are recommending you also want to give parents the opportunity to select a referral resource if possible.

Avoid giving only one option simply because you think it is the "best" choice. When offering suggestions to parents, give as many options as possible, be open about your impressions of these agencies and professionals, and share results that other families have reported. Then ask parents to choose one they think will meet their needs. At this point, you might ask parents whether they would like assistance in setting up the initial appointment, arranging transportation, or seeking financial aid.

All of the issues and processes presented here will help you make appropriate and ethical decisions as an elementary or middle school counselor. Worksheet 12.1 provides a checklist to follow when you face the most challenging situations and decisions.

Caring for Yourself

A further thought on ethical and professional practice relates to your own health and well-being. Ethical counselors who practice at the highest level of professional functioning do so because they take care of themselves. They maintain physical, mental, and emotional health, which allows them to behave at a highly skilled and principled level. This is extremely important in the counseling profession—to take care of yourself so that you can offer appropriate care to others. The final chapter of this *Survival Guide* explores this notion of self-care more fully.

Ethical Decision-Making Checklist

_____ Identify the issue or problem.

_____ Gather essential information.

_____ Consider your value system and beliefs.

_____ Understand your responsibilities and obligations.

_____ Inform the appropriate people (for example, administrators, teachers, parents).

_____ Review ethical guideline(s).

_____ Seek consultation.

_____ Consider the options and corresponding consequences.

_____ Determine the best course of action.

_____ Take action.

_____ Evaluate the outcome.

chapter 13

HELPING YOURSELF *to* HELP OTHERS

Scenario 13.1: Self-Health and Performance

Throughout this Survival Guide, *you have explored many ideas and suggestions related to taking care of yourself professionally. This chapter offers suggestions to help you personally. In this final scenario, identify the most important aspects of your physical, emotional, social, and intellectual self that contribute to or detract from your ability to perform as an elementary or middle school counselor. After you have identified these aspects, focus on one or two that you can control, improve, or otherwise change to make yourself a stronger and more effective counselor. What are the aspects? How much control do you have over them? What plan will you set in motion to help yourself?*

A variety of services and activities constitute a comprehensive school program, and most require a high level of training and skill. Equally important, these functions require counselors to be fit physically, mentally, emotionally, and socially. When you are in optimal physical shape, think highly of yourself and others, behave in a rational manner, and welcome interactions with people, you are well equipped to meet the challenges of your profession. You are most able to help students, parents, and teachers effectively when you enhance your own personal well-being and professional development.

Throughout this *Survival Guide* you have explored countless ways to organize, plan, and deliver counseling services in schools. These ideas and suggestions have the potential to help you design appropriate services and establish effective helping relationships. This potential is optimally realized when you, as a person and professional, function at the most hopeful, beneficial, and productive level in your own life. To achieve this level of functioning, you begin by helping yourself.

To survive as an elementary or middle school counselor, you first must endure the challenges of your own life. You will win the confidence of those you seek to help when they perceive you as capable of helping yourself. By caring for yourself, you become capable of authentically reaching out and caring for others. This ability to relate with others in thoughtful, understanding, and considerate ways is a hallmark of effective counselors and is more important than any single skill or area of knowledge you possess. Noted author and pioneer in the counseling profession Wrenn (1973) summarized the value of this ability when he wrote, "To me the most striking personal discovery of the past decade has been that people respond to my degree of caring more than to my degree of knowing" (p. 249).

A first step in developing your personal and professional self is to assess where you are at present. As emphasized throughout this guide, effective counseling requires an accurate assessment of people and situations. Similarly, the ability to care for yourself correlates with your knowledge of where you are and where you want to go in life. To assist students, parents, and teachers with the challenges of education and career development, you want an accurate accounting of your own purpose and direction in life, including your personal relationships and professional goals.

SELF-ASSESSMENT

There are numerous formal and informal methods for evaluating and assessing where you are in your own personal and professional development. No single method is any better than another. For this reason, a key to accurate self-assessment is establishing methods with which to continually evaluate where you are and where you are going in life. Here are a few ideas to get started:

1. *Create self-questionnaires to focus on particular aspects of your development.* Use self-help checklists from magazines and newspapers and adapt them to develop your own assessment sheets. One caveat to note is that most questionnaires and self-assessments found in popular magazines are unscientific instruments. Their validity and reliability as assessment tools are, at best, questionable. For this reason, do not rely on their scoring procedures—the individual questions on these surveys are what help in developing an individual assessment process. Therefore, scoring these questionnaires is not as important as your overall reactions and responses to specific questions. For example, an item that asks, "Do you smoke?" may assign a maximum score for poor health for a "yes" answer, but the score itself is not as important as your acknowledgment that smoking is a personally destructive and inappropriate habit.

2. *Set goals and choose behaviors to improve in areas that will benefit you personally and professionally.* As you set personal and professional goals and continually assess these aims, you are in a stronger position to assist other people in reaching their objectives. In contrast, if you are misdirected and disorganized in your life, you are unlikely to achieve credibility and instill confidence in students and others who seek your assistance. Counselors who set and assess their life goals are more inclined to be goal directed in their professional helping relationships. They are likely to act at a greater level of intentionality, choosing from several alternative behaviors, approaching situations from different points of view, and selecting helping skills to suit the individual needs of clients (Schmidt, 2002).

3. *Check the ingredients you put into your plans for success.* Setting goals and making plans are essential steps to achieving personal and professional objectives, but these steps are incomplete unless complemented by beneficial beliefs and values. You reveal these beneficial ingredients when you express genuine concern for the welfare of others; accept responsibility for your actions; respect individuals, groups, and institutions; and extend your trust toward others. Without these beneficial ingredients, plans of action have the potential to become paths of destruction rather than leading to the helping relationships you intended. When you function without high regard for the welfare and well-being of others, you choose behaviors that may degrade, demean, and defraud your counselees, yourself, and the counseling profession. To guard against this, always practice in the most ethical manner and consistently monitor your purpose and direction in all your relationships.

4. *Ask for input from people whom you trust.* You enhance the accuracy of self-assessment when you include the perceptions of those who know you best. As you evaluate your behaviors and goals, ask colleagues and friends to offer their impressions of your performance and the characteristics they see that help or hinder relationships. Naturally, a single response from one friend or colleague may not tell you much, but if several people offer similar observations, their views are worth considering. Accept these observations, compare them with your perceptions, and make decisions and changes you believe will be worthwhile in your personal and professional development.

From your study of human perception and development, you understand that human vision is often narrow in scope and distorted in focus. Counselors and other professional helpers know this better than do most people. For this reason, you want to seek out the perceptions of others, compare these views with your own, and make decisions based on sufficient sources and observations. This process of seeking and accepting input from friends and colleagues contains an element of risk because you may not always like what you hear. In most cases, however, the collective observations you compile from others will validate your beliefs about yourself and enable you to select characteristics and traits you want to change.

5. *Begin small and update your plan for personal and professional development regularly.* Choose a few behaviors or traits to strive for in your plan of action. In addition, select objectives that you can accomplish in a reasonable time. For example, if you want to learn a new skill, set a goal of reading a few articles or books about the technique before you

invest time and money to enroll in school or attend a national seminar. Take preliminary steps toward reaching your grandest goals. By doing so, you set up a gradual process of working toward goals in increments and increase the likelihood that you will succeed.

Write your plan down and review it regularly. By documenting your goals, you make a personal commitment to yourself. It is much like having a personal contract or agreement. Goals that you do not write down you might easily forget and will not review with consistency. In contrast, you can erase and alter written plans as needed. They exist as reminders of the purpose and direction you have chosen in your personal and professional lives. Worksheet 13.1 suggests a contract for your personal and professional goals.

Although caring for yourself personally and professionally go hand in hand, your personal development should be considered first. It is through your personal success that you accept professional goals with the confidence that you can accomplish them. Let us now examine more closely this area of personal caring. The few starter steps you select in Worksheet 13.1 will help you establish a routine for assessing your self-development and taking charge of caring for yourself. Each step entails decisions about personal and professional development. Both areas of your development are important. When you take care of your personal development and focus on your professional needs, you are in a better position to be a beneficial presence in the lives of others.

Sometimes counselors spend so much energy focusing on their professional responsibilities that they neglect their personal welfare. They forget that equal attention to both areas of development is essential. When you neglect your personal well-being, regardless of your level of attention to professional development, you risk losing the physical, emotional, and mental stamina to keep up with the rigorous pace of all your helping relationships. Similarly, when you look after your own personal welfare but neglect professional knowledge and skills, you cannot expect to function effectively in your counseling practice.

The next two sections focus on the responsibility you have both to care for yourself personally and to ensure optimal professional development as an elementary or middle school counselor. A key to helping yourself develop to optimal personal and professional levels is the belief that you can encourage others to do only what you are willing and able to do yourself. Helping students, parents, and teachers accept change and confront challenges means that you, as a professional helper, are willing and able to do likewise. If not, you may need to let others provide the help instead, and spend your energy on your own well-being.

PERSONAL CARING

To a large degree, effective helping relationships are dependent on personal interactions between counselors and their clients. If you are healthy, physically capable, emotionally stable, and responsible in your social interactions, you are more able to establish and follow through with services than counselors who are frequently in ill health, socially uncomfortable, and emotionally strung out. This is not to say that you do not have any limitations or disabilities, but rather that you understand your limitations and have placed

Personal and Professional Goals

During the next _____ days (or months), I will accomplish the following goals:

Personal Goals

1. Physical well-being: _____

_____

2. Social well-being: _____

_____

3. Emotional well-being: _____

_____

4. Other goals: _____

_____

Professional Goals

1. Intellectual growth: _____

_____

2. Skill development: _____

_____

3. Collaboration with others: _____

_____

4. Other goals: _____

_____

yourself in a position to put your physical, emotional, and other strengths to the best use. By being physically fit, for example, you will have the stamina to withstand the demands of being an elementary or middle school counselor. As an illustration, a counselor in a wheelchair who consistently works to keep herself in optimal physical condition may be more able to help clients than a fully mobile counselor who neglects his physical health. Caring for your physical self is an appropriate place to start, because bodily health affects emotional and social well-being.

Physical Well-Being

How healthy are you? If you have health problems, can you do anything about them? If so, are you doing anything about them? As noted earlier in this chapter, an effective counselor is one who takes care of the physical self and establishes a plan and routine to live a healthy life. Counselors who take control of their physical conditions and assume responsibility for their health demonstrate self-worth and dependability. Consequently, they are likely to be respected and trusted for the professional guidance they offer others. In contrast, counselors who do not take charge of their physical well-being may be in a less favorable position to win the trust and confidence of the students, parents, and teachers they aim to help.

There are numerous reports informing us how to live in healthier ways. We read them in periodicals, hear them on the radio, see them on television, and learn about them through the Internet. Despite the abundance of information, however, many people continue to follow paths of self-destruction with the foods they eat, the beverages they drink, and the drugs and other substances they allow into their bodies. If you eat poorly, drink too much, smoke cigarettes, and take unnecessary medications, you join the legions of people who diminish the value and importance of maintaining a high level of physical health.

To take charge of your physical health, start by doing a quick self-assessment, evaluating your attitudes and behaviors about your physical well-being. Assess where you are and where you are going, and determine whether there are ways to improve your direction and goals in this area of your personal life. The following are questions to ask yourself to assess your current state of physical health:

1. *Do you take time for exercise or recreation?* Most of what we read today indicates that moderate exercise is beneficial to physical well-being. Walking a few times a week or exercising a few minutes each day helps us stay in shape. In addition, physical activities, such as dancing, playing tennis, doing yoga, or riding bicycles, enhance stamina and tone muscles.

Counseling is a demanding profession that often stretches your patience and endurance to the limit. By being in top physical condition, you are likely to maintain optimal levels of functioning on the job. In elementary and middle schools, this is very important because young children and preadolescents have high energy levels, which require durability on the part of teachers, counselors, and administrators.

2. *Do you eat well?* Most Americans love food, and usually the food we adore most is high in fat, sugar, salt, and other unkind ingredients. Counselors who eat an unhealthy diet and are overweight, underweight, or undernourished place themselves in jeopardy. This

type of behavior cannot continue if they expect to be effective helpers, encouraging students and others to take charge of their lives by behaving in responsible and healthy ways.

Balance and moderation are the keys to eating well and enjoying what you eat. By planning and eating nutritiously balanced meals, you can still allow yourself occasional opportunities to deviate and enjoy snacks or desserts in moderation. If you have purpose and direction in your life, you are able to take command of your eating habits with the same intentionality you employ in your counseling program and services. If you find it too challenging to follow a nutritious regimen on your own, search for family, friends, colleagues, or other support networks willing to help you reach common goals.

3. *Do you use unnecessary or illegal drugs?* Do you smoke or drink alcohol excessively? Habitual, self-destructive behaviors contradict the beneficial action needed to maintain physical health. Counselors who take drugs, smoke, and drink to excess are choosing personally and professionally irresponsible behaviors. These destructive behaviors not only take a physical toll on the body but also demonstrate little regard for socially acceptable and responsible actions. When counselors and other helpers behave in such a destructive manner, they jeopardize their standing in the community and reflect poorly on the counseling profession.

4. *Do you follow your physician's instructions?* Most people occasionally need medical assistance to care for their physical well-being. When you are under a physician's care, do you follow instructions accordingly? By taking the appropriate medication, watching your diet, and getting sufficient rest, for example, you demonstrate commitment to good health and a willingness to take charge of your life.

Visiting dentists, physicians, and other health care providers to assess your physical development and well-being should be part of an overall plan for healthy living. These visits do not, however, relieve you of your own responsibility to have an appropriate plan of self-care. For example, making regular appointments at a health clinic does not mean you do not have to eat well, exercise, stay active, and treat your physical self with care and respect.

Caring for your physical self responsibly enables you to elevate your emotional self to an optimal level of functioning. In many ways, your emotional self relates closely to your physical well-being, and it is impossible to determine whether either is more important, or which one should receive your attention first. Some people ignore their physical health when they are emotionally distraught, and consequently have little regard for their own physical welfare. Others sometimes ignore their physical selves because they are so emotionally committed and devote an inordinate amount of energy to enabling others to reach their optimal potential that the helpers forget about themselves. For this reason, emotional well-being is another area to consider as you assess your degree of personal caring and development.

Emotional Well-Being

Being emotionally and psychologically healthy means relating with others in beneficial and constructive ways. By maintaining your emotional health, you demonstrate a high regard for yourself and others, show respect for your capabilities and limitations, and take responsibility for your own behavior.

Self-responsibility is crucial to your emotional health, especially in your role as a professional counselor. In school, where there are many demands on you to perform and resolve problems, daily pressures can be tremendous. Understanding your role, knowing your strengths, and accepting your limitations enable you to handle these job pressures. I recommend that, in addition to achieving this level of self-knowledge and maintaining your physical health, you focus on a few key behaviors for developing and caring for your emotional well-being, to which we now turn.

Avoiding Blame

With so much happening in elementary and middle schools, and so many people concerned about the welfare of children, mistakes will sometimes be made. At these times, when emotions run high and situations are critical, some people will try to place blame elsewhere. Counselors who are emotionally healthy avoid the issue of blame and instead seek to find alternative solutions and new directions that enable people and programs to move forward. In this way, they are more concerned about correcting a situation than punishing those who are to blame.

At the same time, emotionally healthy counselors accept responsibility for their own actions and encourage others to do likewise. They do not accept blame or responsibility for actions over which they have no control. When they do assume responsibility, they monitor their own physical and emotional stress to make appropriate decisions.

Handling Stress

Sometimes life is hectic and stressful, but you can plan measures and take action to handle stress in appropriate ways. Identifying stressful factors, learning relaxation techniques and other stress-reducing approaches, and seeking assistance from others are a few ways to take responsibility for your emotional well-being in stress-related situations. A first step is to identify negative factors in your life and measure how they are contributing to stress. In evaluating stress factors in your life and on the job, the following indicators and questions may be helpful:

• *Have you have been experiencing unusual and disturbing physical symptoms lately?* These might include muscle tension and pain, dizziness, nervousness, skin rashes, headaches, stomach problems, fatigue, excessive sweating, chest pains, loss of appetite or excessive eating, high blood pressure, back pain, frequent illnesses, feeling sick generally, or sexual problems.

• *Have some of your behaviors changed recently?* Do you have difficulty falling asleep at night, get confused easily, lack concentration at work, delay making decisions, forget things frequently, grow angry over minor inconveniences, become impatient with yourself or others, find yourself preoccupied, have frequent accidents, smoke or drink heavily, experience frequent nightmares, or have regular arguments at work or home?

• *Have you wondered about your state of mind lately?* Are you overly concerned with what people think about you or your performance as a counselor? Do you feel "hyper" much of the time, show your frustration easily, become depressed frequently, act impulsively, avoid being with other people, feel overwhelmed with responsibility, cry for no apparent reason, get irritated often, worry about things, or have wide mood swings?

All people experience some of these behaviors and feelings on occasion. When such conditions become major forces in people's lives, however, they inhibit individuals from developing in healthy ways and performing their duties effectively. Occasionally, situations become so intense that some may not understand the stress they are experiencing. If this happens to you, and you feel you are losing control, it is time to seek assistance from others.

Seeking Support

You have learned in this guide that competent counselors have a clear understanding of their knowledge and skills and at the same time recognize their limitations. You demonstrate your own competence by achieving this level of self-knowledge and understanding and knowing when to seek assistance for yourself. Because you are highly trained in human development and helping processes, you may sometimes forget that you also need assistance on occasion. Counselors are not immune to the tragedies and traumas of life. Understanding this and willingly asking for help when you are suffering, experiencing a crisis, or simply standing still in your personal or professional development are hallmarks of survival.

Identifying trustworthy colleagues in whom you can confide is an initial step. Teachers, administrators, and others whose judgment you respect are excellent sources of comfort and guidance. Seeking their assistance also may be the first step in your search for professional counseling when you face critical concerns in your life.

Taking Time Alone

It helps to spend time alone occasionally in moments of self-reflection, meditation, and rest. Being an active counselor, reaching out to others continuously, and implementing a rigorous schedule of program activities can be exhausting. Planning time to be alone allows you to recharge your batteries, examine personal and professional goals, make decisions about new directions, and adjust your plans accordingly. A solitary walk, a good book, peaceful music, a massage, and countless other opportunities exist to help you evaluate who you are and where you are going.

During a typical school day, filled with scheduled services and critical situations, intentionally set aside a few brief moments to be alone and gather your thoughts—a time to assess the day's progress and prepare for remaining events. These times of reflection enable you to check your perceptions and make adjustments to meet the professional challenges that lie ahead. You also, in these moments of reflection, strengthen your commitment to forming beneficial relationships with others. This brings us to a third area of healthful living—your social well-being.

Social Well-Being

People are not meant to be alone all the time. They need the company of others. Sharing experiences and celebrating life events are vital elements in the process of caring for your personal self. As a counselor you have a particular obligation to nurture and care for your social well-being, because through this process of social acceptance of others you develop and strengthen trusting relationships. If you are aloof and distant, you may discourage people from approaching you openly and honestly. At the same time, you might thwart your own development by limiting social interactions and thereby narrowing the scope of your perceptions. A narrow field of vision reduces the available opportunities for taking positive action as a helping professional.

When you limit social interactions you are also in danger of lowering your tolerance of human diversity and uniqueness. It is difficult to relate to people who are culturally different, who live with physical disabilities, or who are behaviorally eccentric when you have had little exposure to or contact with the variation within human existence. Elementary and middle school counselors who care for their social well-being gladly form beneficial relationships with a wide audience of students, parents, and teachers, which in turn raises their levels of professional functioning.

Chapter Ten explored ways to build social and professional relationships with teachers and others in the school. The following suggestions review and expand on the ideas presented in Chapter Ten, with a focus on your social well-being:

• *Volunteer in the community.* Civic organizations provide valuable assistance to children, families, and schools. By joining these groups, you increase your visibility as a school counselor and enhance opportunities for social interaction.

• *Identify social groups that pursue hobbies and activities of interest to you.* If you enjoy playing cards, making crafts, knitting, boating, or another activity, locate a group in the community that shares your interest. If no group exists, start one and invite other people to join you!

• *Initiate contact with students and teachers who are new to your school.* Learn about the backgrounds of new students and teachers. Invite them to lunch and socialize with them in other ways to demonstrate your availability and interest in their lives.

• *Plan special events.* Ask a group of students, parents, and teachers to organize special celebrations during the year. These can coincide with national celebrations, such as Thanksgiving, or can be unique to your school, such as an annual talent show or a "Founder's Day" to remember the historical beginnings of the school.

• *Search and deliver.* In every school, there are people who are alone and lonely. See what you can do to identify staff members, faculty, and students who would benefit from a kind invitation, and deliver one to them! Purkey and Novak (1996) presented a variety of ideas for sending positive messages in their book *Inviting School Success,* and Purkey and Stanley (1997), in *The Inviting School Treasury,* presented a wealth of inviting ideas to use in schools. Use these and similar resources to learn about sending kind messages and invitations to individuals in your school.

Caring for your personal self is the first step toward professional development. By focusing on your physical, emotional, and social health, you place yourself in a strong position to elevate your professional functioning, the ultimate goal of all counselors. To achieve this ultimate goal, you also want to care for yourself as a professional.

PROFESSIONAL CARING

The purpose of this *Survival Guide* is to offer practical ideas and strategies to assist you in becoming an effective elementary or middle school counselor, ideally moving beyond survival and toward a higher level of functioning as a professional. To do this you rely on your willingness and ability to plan comprehensive programs and deliver appropriate services, which in turn requires a proficient level of professional knowledge and competence. In other words, you care for your professional development with the same intent and commitment that you care for your personal well-being. This level of caring begins with your attention to an increased knowledge of counseling theory and related areas of human development.

Intellectual Development

Counseling in schools presents a continuing challenge influenced by changing educational, social, and cultural factors. Meeting these challenges requires a high level of training and a commitment to continuing your education throughout your career. The preparation you received in graduate study laid a foundation upon which to build an expanding knowledge for future practice.

School counselors who believe that their formal graduate studies, at the master's and doctoral levels, are sufficient to meet the daily concerns raised by students, parents, teachers, and other personnel in schools today are mistaken. Changing family structures, evolving sexual attitudes, debilitating substance and alcohol abuse, and advancing technologies and scientific discoveries, among other changes, require up-to-date knowledge and information on the part of all professionals. An expanding knowledge base allows you to make intelligent choices about appropriate approaches, techniques, and strategies to support student development, encourage parent involvement, and enhance teacher performance in your school.

As noted in Chapter Twelve, a first step in determining where to focus your quest for more knowledge is to assess what you know and how well prepared you are. By assessing your knowledge and skills, you commit to pursuing learning and enriching your professional development. Some activities to include in your continuing quest for intellectual and professional development are returning to school, attending workshops, and reading.

Returning to School

Contact universities and colleges in your region and see whether they have counselor education programs or other areas of study to continue your education. Courses in psychology, family relations, child development, counseling, and a host of other disciplines will keep you informed about the latest research and developments in the profession.

Attending Workshops

Watch for announcements about upcoming workshops and seminars that present information for developing your counseling program and improving your knowledge or skill. Sometimes community workshops sponsored by health agencies, churches, and other groups offer valuable information for counselors and teachers. Professional organizations, such as your state school counselor association, also are excellent resources for gaining these types of experiences. By joining state and local organizations, you are included on mailing lists and therefore eligible to receive current announcements about educational opportunities.

Reading

Counseling is a profession that embraces a number of disciplines and knowledge bases, and the literature for school counseling is expansive. To stay current, you will want to read from a wide range of sources, including counseling journals, books on professional helping and self-development, and scientific resources on discoveries about human development and learning. You may also want to subscribe to educational journals and magazines to keep up with trends in the teaching profession.

In addition to professional readings mentioned above, you will benefit from learning about trends in child behavior, cultural changes in society, and scientific advancement through magazines, newspapers, recordings, and other media. You might want to subscribe to one or more of the popular magazines read by children and preteens. By reading their literature, you stay in tune with fashion, music, television, and other trends that influence juvenile behavior, and therefore enhance your ability to communicate with these students.

Returning to school, enrolling in online or distance education courses, attending workshops, and reading widely are a few ways to care for your professional self. By keeping abreast of professional, social, and cultural trends, you strengthen relationships with students, parents, and teachers and raise your level of professional competence.

Counselor Competence

Because counseling is an emerging profession with a primary focus on assisting people with their development, the essential competencies inherent in the profession are continuously under examination. In Chapter Twelve, you read about the School Counselor Competencies presented by the American School Counselor Association (2008). Such competencies are constantly reviewed and updated by the profession. You want to use published competencies and standards of practice to keep yourself professionally up-to-date.

The suggestions offered in this chapter will help you monitor levels of professional competence and expand your knowledge base. In addition, two areas of competent practice echoed throughout this guide will enable you to care for yourself professionally—scheduling time and being accountable.

Scheduling Time

In this chapter you have been encouraged to take time to enhance and enrich your personal and professional development. When reading the suggestions, you may have wondered,

"Where do I get all this extra time?" If you ask yourself this question, you may want to consider that there is no such thing as *extra time* because everyone has the same amount. Like most people, you probably would like to have more time, but you are not going to get any more than twenty-four hours a day. Successful counselors understand this reality, yet they are able to balance their personal and professional lives by using their allotted time efficiently.

No single element is more important to a successful counseling program than the appropriate use of time. This is particularly true when you serve large student populations; more than one school; or communities damaged by poor economic development, crime, drug use, and other debilitating social factors. To be used in conjunction with the suggestions given in Chapter Two for balancing time in your school counseling program, here are ten *time controllers* to increase your efficiency:

1. *Make the call.* Counselors, like court justices and emergency medical personnel, frequently face tough decisions. Time is often critical. When confronting decisions, list the most viable options and the pros and cons of each choice. Examine your list, focus on major points, and choose one of the alternatives. Do not put off your decision.

2. *Strive for imperfection.* A common obstacle to success is the desire to excel. You may think that if you cannot do something perfectly it would be best not to do it at all. Avoid this pitfall by planning your tasks in phases. Set short-term goals and time limits to accomplish major projects. Aim for completion rather than perfection. A perfect project never started can never be completed. In contrast, an imperfect, completed project can always be improved.

3. *Remain underwhelmed.* Because you serve so many audiences and have such broad responsibilities, it is easy to try to become a hero to everyone and become overwhelmed. In contrast, I suggest you strive to remain underwhelmed. Keep control of your time, and use resourceful faculty, students, and parent volunteers to assist with services. Practice saying, "No, thank you." When your plate is full, let people know you can take on nothing more until you have finished what you have started.

4. *Reinforce yourself.* Tackle tasks that you enjoy the least and stay with them for a predetermined amount of time. You may surprise yourself by completing these jobs before time is up. Give yourself a reward when you finish. A two-minute walk around the school grounds, a brief encounter with a jump rope on the playground, a cup of tea with teachers in the lounge, and other rewards are simple ways of congratulating yourself on a job well done.

5. *Arrange your space.* Neatness may count, but it is not as important as organization, which means you have a method to your neatness. Keep materials you use most often in an accessible location so you do not waste time searching for these essential, frequently used items.

6. *Pad your memory.* Keep a small notepad or electronic device on your desk or in your pocket and write down tasks that you think of during the day. By having this list, you avoid spending time trying to remember, "What was that important thing I was going to do today?"

7. *Cluster tasks.* Group your jobs during the day so you can complete similar tasks at the same time. For example, if you need to make follow-up phone calls to parents and

agencies, make all your calls in one block of time. Set aside ten minutes, a half hour, or whatever you need, and make the calls during that one sitting.

8. *Write down goals.* Without writing down your major goals, you are less likely to accomplish them. Spend a few minutes at the end of each day writing down your mission for tomorrow. Rank these activities in order of importance and schedule time to accomplish each one. When you run out of time and jobs remain, carry them over to the next day.

9. *Access technology.* Use computers and other technology to assist in delivering services efficiently. Word processing, computer-assisted learning, the Internet, text messaging, videotaped instruction, and a host of other programs can broaden services in the school.

10. *Keep accurate accounts.* Maintain a calendar of your appointments and daily plans. A good calendar not only helps you use time efficiently but also is an excellent resource for being accountable.

Being Accountable

Chapter Three emphasized the importance of evaluating your program of services, why accountability is essential to future program development, and how it elevates your credibility with school staff. You exemplify professional accountability through the consistency and dependability of your behavior. How you spend your time, the effectiveness of your services, the attitudes and behaviors you exhibit in the school and community, and the regard you hold for yourself and others are a few of the countless ways accountability is measured. Here are some additional ideas for strengthening your professional accountability:

1. *Watch your image.* Your reputation precedes you. All that you do on behalf of others in the school and community creates the image that people have of you as a professional and of the school counseling profession in general.

2. *Give accurate information.* When in doubt, say so, and research the question thoroughly before responding. People will respect your honesty and admire your conscientious effort.

3. *Keep promises.* Follow through on commitments you make to students, parents, and teachers. If you know there will be a problem in keeping a commitment, let people know immediately. Excuses may help you save face, but when relied on too frequently they paint a picture of undependability.

4. *Follow up.* Stay in touch with people who seek your assistance. Check on students who saw you in the beginning of the year, send notes to teachers and ask them about concerns they shared with you earlier, and call parents to look in on the home front. In addition, make occasional contact with professionals in the community who have provided effective services to students and families. They will appreciate hearing from you.

5. *Take the high road.* Courtesy and civility are two essential hallmarks of professional counselors. Treat everyone with respect, regardless of their statuses or their attitudes toward you. A true professional never stoops to the level of the malcontent. Counselors who reach the peak of professional performance and accountability always maintain a position of optimism, trust, respect, and intentionality (Schmidt, 2002).

CONCLUSION

School counselors employ a variety of skills and a broad range of knowledge to establish beneficial helping relationships with students, parents, and teachers. Elementary and middle school counselors, in particular, are in an ideal position to enable students to achieve solid beginnings in their educational, personal, and social development. As a member of this profession, you have accepted this challenge.

This guide has sought to help you survive as well as flourish in the exciting profession of school counseling. It has offered ideas for establishing comprehensive school counseling programs; organizing efficient services; reaching out to special populations; handling crisis situations; using new technology; relating to students, parents, and teachers; and caring for yourself as a person and counselor. Although not all the ideas in this book may suit your needs or fit your setting, they might help you discover or create more appropriate and practical ideas for yourself and your program. If so, the purpose of this *Survival Guide* has been realized.

You have chosen a most rewarding profession as an elementary or middle school counselor. The success you experience and the rewards you receive, however, will largely depend on your ability to help yourself help others. By taking time to read and use this book as well as other resources, you have demonstrated a willingness to help yourself. I commend you for this effort and for your positive regard for the counseling profession.

Thank you for accepting my invitation to explore *survival* as an elementary or middle school counselor. I wish you all the best as you move toward *flourishing* in your career.

Resources

BIBLIOGRAPHY

Akos, P., Cockman, C. R., & Strickland, C. A. (2007). Differentiating classroom guidance. *Professional School Counseling*, *10*, 455–463.

Amatea, E. S., & West-Olatunji, C. A. (2007). Joining the conversation about educating our poorest children: Emerging leadership roles for school counselors in high-poverty schools. *Professional School Counseling*, *11*, 81–89.

American Counseling Association. (2005). *ACA Code of Ethics*. Alexandria, VA: Author.

American School Counselor Association. (2004). *Ethical standards for school counselors*. Alexandria, VA: Author.

American School Counselor Association. (2005). *A national model: A framework for school counseling programs*. Alexandria, VA: Author.

American School Counselor Association (2008, July-August). School counselor competencies. *ASCA School Counselor*, *45*(6), 64–73.

Association for Supervision and Curriculum Development. (1955). *Guidance in the curriculum*. Washington, DC: Author.

Astramovich, R. L., Hoskins, W. J., & Markos, P. A. (2007, December). Advancing school mental health counseling. *Counseling Today*, *17*(6), 27.

Baker, S. B., & Gerler, E. R. (2008). *School counseling for the twenty-first century* (5th ed.). Upper Saddle River, NJ: Merrill.

Bhat, C. S., & Probasco, B. (2008, September-October). The technology twist. *ASCA School Counselor*, *46*(1), 27–30.

Bloom, J. W., & Walz, G. R. (Eds.). (2004). *Cybercounseling and cyberlearning: An encore*. Austin, TX: Pro-Ed.

Bodenhorn, N., Moore, C., Obenshain, M., & Knott, D. (2008, May-June). Virginia Tech: Aftermath of a tragedy. *ASCA School Counselor*, *45*(5), 15–20.

Bonnington, S. B. (1993). Solution-focused brief therapy: Helpful interventions for school counselors. *The School Counselor*, *41*, 126–128.

Bowman, R. P. (1986). The magic counselor: Using magic tricks as tools to teach children guidance lessons. *Elementary School Guidance and Counseling, 21,* 128–138.

Bowman, R. P. (2004). *Test buster pep rally.* Minneapolis, MN: Educational Media Corporation.

Bradshaw, C. P., O'Brennan, L. M., & Sawyer, A. L. (2008). Examining variation in attitudes toward aggressive retaliation and perceptions of safety among bullies, victims, and bully/victims. *Professional School Counseling, 12,* 10–21.

Bruce, M. A., & Hooper, G. C. (1997). Brief counseling versus traditional counseling: A comparison of effectiveness. *The School Counselor, 44,* 171–184.

Canter, L., & Canter, M. (1992). *Assertive discipline: Positive behavior management for today's classroom.* Santa Monica, CA: Canter and Associates.

Carlson, L. A., Portman, T.A.A., Bartlett, J. R. (2006). Professional school counselors' approaches to technology. *Professional School Counseling, 9,* 252–256.

Carney, J. V. (2008). Perceptions of bullying and associated trauma during adolescence. *Professional School Counseling, 11,* 179–187.

Chibbaro, J. S. (2007). School counselors and the cyberbully: Interventions and implications. *Professional School Counseling, 11,* 65–68.

Clemente, R., & Collison, B. B. (2000). The relationships among counselors, ESL teachers, and students. *Professional School Counseling, 3,* 339–348.

Cole, C. G. (1992). *Nurturing a teacher advisory program.* Columbus, OH: National Middle School Association.

Cole, J.C.M., Cornell, D. G., & Sheras, P. (2006). Identification of school bullies by survey methods. *Professional School Counseling, 9,* 305–313.

Davis, T. E., & Osborn, C. J. (2000). *The solution-focused school counselor: Shaping professional practice.* Philadelphia: Accelerated Development.

Dougherty, A. M. (2009). *Psychological consultation and collaboration in school and community settings.* Pacific Grove, CA: Brooks/Cole.

Dreikurs, R., & Grey, L. (1993). *A new approach to discipline: Logical consequences.* East Rutherford, NJ: Plume.

Eder, K. C., & Whiston, S. C. (2006). Does psychotherapy help some students? An overview of psychotherapy outcome research. *Professional School Counseling, 9,* 337–343.

Falls, L., & Muro, J. (2009, May-June). Building bridges. *ASCA School Counselor, 46*(5), 34–39.

Galassi, J., & Akos, P. (2007). *Strengths-based school counseling: Promoting student development and achievement.* Mahwah, NJ: Lawrence Erlbaum Associates.

Geltner, J. A., & Clark, M. A. (2005). Engaging students in classroom guidance: Management strategies for middle school counselors. *Professional School Counseling, 9,* 164–170.

Glasser, W. (1998). *The quality school.* New York: HarperCollins.

Good, T. L., & Brophy, J. E. (2008). *Looking in classrooms* (10th ed.). Boston: Allyn & Bacon.

Gordon, T. (2000). *Parent effectiveness training*. New York: Three Rivers Press.

Greenberg, K. R. (2003). *Group counseling in K–12 schools: A handbook for school counselors.* Boston: Allyn & Bacon.

Gysbers, N., & Henderson, P. (2000). *Developing and managing your school guidance program* (3rd ed.). Alexandria, VA: American Counseling Association.

Hall, K. R. (2006). Using problem-based learning with victims of bullying behavior. *Professional School Counseling*, *9*, 231–237.

Hebert, B. B., & Ballard, M. B. (2007). Children and trauma: A post-Katrina and Rita response. *Professional School Counseling*, *11*, 140–144.

Horne, A. M., Bartolomucci, C. L., & Newman-Carlson, D. (2003). *Bully busters: A teacher's manual for helping bullies, victims, and bystanders.* Champaign, IL: Research Press.

Jacobsen, K. E., & Bauman, S. (2007). Bullying in schools: School counselors' responses to three types of bullying incidents. *Professional School Counseling*, *11*, 1–9.

Kennedy, A. (2008a, August). Plugged in, turned on and wired up. *Counseling Today*, *51*(2), 34–38.

Kennedy, A. (2008b, August). The calm after the storm. *Counseling Today*, *51*(2), 46–48.

Kohn, A. (2006, September). Abusing research: The study of homework and other examples. *Phi Delta Kappan*, *88*(1), 9–22.

Kress, V. E., Drouhard, N., & Costin, A. (2006). Students who self-injure: School counselor ethical and legal considerations. *Professional School Counseling*, *10*, 203–209.

Lazovsky, R. (2008). Maintaining confidentiality with minors: Dilemmas of school counselors. *Professional School Counseling*, *11*, 335–345.

Lumsden, L. (2002). *Preventing bullying*. ERIC Digest. Eugene, OR: ERIC Clearinghouse. (ED463563)

McAdams, C. R., & Schmidt, C. D. (2007). How to help a bully: Recommendations for counseling the proactive aggressor. *Professional School Counseling*, *11*, 120–128.

McLaughlin, L., Laux, J. M., & Pescara-Kovach, L. (2006). Using multimedia to reduce bullying and victimization in third-grade urban schools. *Professional School Counseling*, *10*, 153–160.

Maultsby, M. C. (1986). Teaching rational self-counseling to middle grades. *The School Counselor*, *33*, 207–219.

Moyer, M., Haberstroh, S., & Marbach, C. (2008). Self-injurious behaviors on the Net: A survey of resources for school counselors. *Professional School Counseling*, *11*, 277–284.

Moyer, M., & Nelson, K. W. (2007). Investigating and understanding self-mutilation: The student voice. *Professional School Counseling*, *11*, 42–48.

Moyer, M., & Sullivan, J. (2008). Student risk-taking behaviors: When do school counselors break confidentiality? *Professional School Counseling*, *11*, 236–245.

Murphy, J. (2008). *Solution-focused counseling in schools.* Alexandria, VA: American Counseling Association.

Nelson, J. (2006). *Positive discipline.* New York: Random House.

Parsons, R. D., & Kahn, W. J. (2005). *The school counselor as consultant: An integrated model for school-based consultation.* Belmont, CA: Thomson Brooks/Cole.

Paterson, J. (2009, June). Beyond an elementary approach. *Counseling Today, 51*(12), 34–37.

Pedersen, P. (2000). *A handbook for developing multicultural awareness* (3rd ed.). Alexandria, VA: American Counseling Association.

Pedersen, P. (2002). Ethics, competence, and other professional issues in culture-centered counseling. In P. Pedersen, J. G. Draguns, W. J. Lonner, & J. E. Trimble (Eds.), *Counseling across cultures* (5th ed., pp. 3–27). Thousand Oaks, CA: Sage.

Purkey, W. W. (1970). *Self-concept and school achievement.* Upper Saddle River, NJ: Prentice Hall.

Purkey, W. W., & Novak, J. M. (1996). *Inviting school success* (3rd ed.). Belmont, CA: Wadsworth.

Purkey, W. W., & Novak, J. M. (2008). *Fundamentals of invitational education.* Kennesaw, GA: International Alliance for Invitational Education.

Purkey, W. W., & Schmidt, J. J. (1996). *Invitational counseling: A self-concept approach to professional practice.* Pacific Grove, CA: Brooks/Cole.

Purkey, W. W., Schmidt, J. J., & Novak, J. M. (2010). *From conflict to conciliation: How to defuse difficult situations.* Thousand Oaks, CA: Corwin.

Purkey, W. W., & Stanley, P. H. (1997). *The inviting school treasury: 1001 ways to invite student success.* Greenville, NC: Brookcliff.

Purkey, W. W., & Strahan, D. B. (2002). *Inviting positive classroom discipline.* Westerville, OH: National Middle School Association.

Range, L. M., Campbell, C., Kovac, S. H., Marion-Jones, M., Aldridge, H., Kogos, S., & Crimp, Y. (2002). No-suicide contracts: An overview and recommendations. *Death Studies, 26*, 51–74.

Ratts, M. J., DeKruyf, L., & Chen-Hayes, S. F. (2007). The ACA advocacy competencies: A social justice advocacy framework for professional school counselors. *Professional School Counseling*, *11*, 90–97.

Reiner, S. M., Colbert, R. D., & Pérusse, R. (2009). Teacher perceptions of the professional school counselor role: A national study. *Professional School Counseling*, *12*, 324–332.

Roberts, W. B., & Morotti, A. A. (2000). The bully as victim: Understanding bully behaviors to increase the effectiveness of interventions in the bully-victim dyad. *Professional School Counseling*, *4*, 148–155.

Rogers, J. R., Lewis, M. M., & Subich, L. M. (2002). Validity of the Suicide Assessment Checklist in an emergency crisis center. *Journal of Counseling & Development, 80*, 493–502.

Romano, D. M., & Hermann, M. A. (2007, July-August). Advocates for all. *ASCA School Counselor, 44*(6), 86–89.

Schmidt, J. J. (1997). *Making and keeping friends: Ready-to-use lessons, stories, and activities for building relationships.* San Francisco: Jossey-Bass.

Schmidt, J. J. (2002). *Intentional helping: A philosophy for proficient caring relationships.* Upper Saddle River, NJ: Merrill/Prentice Hall.

Schmidt, J. J. (2006). *Social and cultural foundations of counseling and human services.* Boston: Allyn & Bacon.

Schmidt, J. J. (2008). *Counseling in schools: Comprehensive programs of responsive services for all students* (5th ed.). Boston: Allyn & Bacon.

Schmidt, J. J., & Medl, W. A. (1983). Six magic steps of consulting. *The School Counselor, 30*, 212–215.

Schneider, S. (2009). Learning about strength, identity, unity from ASCA. *Counseling Today, 52*(6), 56–57.

Sklare, G. B. (2005). *Brief counseling that works: A solution-focused approach for school counselors and administrators.* Thousand Oaks, CA: Corwin.

Stanard, R. P. (2000). Assessment and treatment of adolescent depression and suicidality. *Journal of Mental Health Counseling, 22*, 204–217.

Sue, D. (1978). Counseling across cultures. *Personnel and Guidance Journal, 56*, 451.

Thompson, C., Rudolph, L., & Henderson, D. (2004). *Counseling children* (6th ed.). Belmont, CA: Thompson Brooks/Cole.

Tindall, J. A. (2008). *Peer power, book two: Strategies for the professional leader: Applying peer helper skills* (3rd ed.). New York: Routledge.

Toporek, R. L., Lewis, J. A., & Crethar, H. C. (2009). Promoting systemic change through the ACA advocacy competencies. *Journal of Counseling & Development, 87*, 200–268.

Turner, S. L. (Ed.). (2007). Transitions [Special issue]. *Professional School Counseling, 10*, 224–336.

U.S. Department of Education. (2002). *No Child Left Behind Act: A desktop reference.* Washington, DC: Author.

Varenhorst, B. (2003). *An asset builder's guide to training peer helpers: Fifteen sessions on communication, assertiveness, and decision-making skills.* Minneapolis, MN: Search Institute Press.

VanZandt, Z., & Hayslip, J. B. (2000). *Developing your school counseling program.* Florence, KY: Cengage Learning.

Wallerstein, J. (1983). Children of divorce: The psychological tasks of the child. *American Journal of Orthopsychiatry, 53*, 230–243.

Wallerstein, J., & Kelly, J. B. (1996). *Surviving the breakup: How children and parents cope with divorce.* New York: Basic Books.

Wilczenski, F. L., & Coomey, S. M. (2006). Cyber-communication: Finding its place in school counseling practice, education, and professional development. *Professional School Counseling, 9,* 327–331.

Willard, N. (2006). *Cyberbullying and cyberthreats: Responding to the challenge of online social cruelty, threats, and distress.* Eugene, OR: Center for Safe and Responsible Internet Use.

Wittmer, J., & Clark, M. A. (Eds.). (2007). *Managing your school counseling program: K–12 developmental strategies* (3rd ed.). Minneapolis, MN: Educational Media Corporation.

Wrenn, C. G. (1973). *The world of the contemporary counselor.* Boston: Houghton Mifflin.

Young, A., Hardy, V., Hamilton, C., Biernesser, M. S., Sun, L., & Niebergail, S. (2009). Empowering students: Using data to transform a bullying prevention and intervention program. *Professional School Counseling, 12,* 413–419.

WEB SITES

The following list includes reputable Web sites that may be helpful to elementary and middle school counselors. Always use appropriate caution when ordering and purchasing materials from any Internet site. Neither the author nor publisher endorses any product or information presented on the sites listed here. There are seemingly limitless Web sites with helpful information, yet caution is necessary. Every school counselor who uses the Internet has the professional and ethical responsibility to ensure the accuracy and appropriateness of information found online when offering it as a resource to students, parents, and teachers.

Active Parenting, by Michael Popkin. www.activeparenting.com
Alateen. www.al-anon.alateen.org/
All Kids Grieve. www.allkidsgrieve.org
American Counseling Association. www.counseling.org
American School Counselor Association. www.schoolcounselor.org
ASCA National Model. www.ascanationalmodel.org/content.asp?contentid=28
Assertive discipline. http://maxweber.hunter.cuny.edu/pub/eres/EDSPC715
    _MCINTYRE/AssertiveDiscipline.html
Association for Assessment in Counseling. www.theaaceonline.com
Association for Multicultural Counseling and Development. www.amcdaca.org/amcd
Association for Specialists in Group Work. www.asgw.org
Center for the Prevention of School Violence. www.ncdjjdp.org/cpsv/
Center for Public Education. www.centerforpubliceducation.org
Council on Exceptional Children. www.cec.sped.org/
Education Law Center. www.edlawcenter.org
Guidance Channel. http://guidancechannel.com
IDEA and Section 504. www.ed.gov/about/offices/list/ocr/504faq.html
International Alliance for Invitational Education. www.invitationaleducation.net/

MiddleWeb. http://middleweb.com

>This site presents models and articles related to middle school issues.

National Association of Peer Program Professionals. www.peerprogramprofessionals
.org

National Association of State Boards of Education. www.nasbe.org

National Association of State Directors of Special Education. www.nasdse.org

National Board for Certified Counselors. http://nbcc.org

National Coalition for Parent Involvement in Education. www.ncpie.org

National Parents Information Network (NPIN). www.npin.org

Parent Effectiveness Training, by Thomas Gordon. www.GordonTraining.com

Peer Resources. www.peer.ca/peer.html

Positive Discipline Association. www.positive discipline.org

Puppeteers of America. www.puppeteers.org/index.html

Puppetry Home Page. www.sagecraft.com/puppetry/

Quality Schools, by William Glasser. www.wglasser.com

Renew Center for Personal Recovery. www.renew.net

>Focuses on issues dealing with crises, setting up crisis prevention plans, and response training.

School Psychology Resources Online. www.schoolpsychology.net

Suicide.org. www.suicide.org

>A nonprofit organization and Web site.

Systematic Training for Effective Parenting, by Don Dinkmeyer Jr. and Gary McKay.
www.steppublishers.com

Time 2 Act. http://time2act.org

>A site that focuses on a variety of youth concerns.

U.S. Department of Education's Office of English Language Acquisition (OELA).
www.ed.gov/about/offices/list/ocla/index.html

U.S. Department of Health and Human Services and SAMHSA's National Clearinghouse for Alcohol and Drug Information. www.ncadi.samhsa.gov/

United Way. www.unitedway.org

>You can enter your zip code and access available agencies, services, resources, and programs in the local area.

Index

Page references followed by *fig* indicate an illustrated figure; followed by *e* indicate an exhibit.